Letters from Abroad

Letters from Abroad

A.A. Ansari
M.A. (Aligarh)
B.A. Hons. (Oxon.)

Viva Books
New Delhi | Mumbai | Chennai | Kolkata
Bengaluru | Hyderabad | Kochi | Guwahati

Publisher's note

First Published 2013

Viva Books Private Limited

- 4737/23, Ansari Road, Daryaganj, New Delhi 110 002
  Tel. 011-42242200, 23258325, 23283121, Email: vivadelhi@vivagroupindia.net
- 76, Service Industries, Shirvane, Sector 1, Nerul, Navi Mumbai 400 706
  Tel. 022-27721273, 27721274, Email: vivamumbai@vivagroupindia.net
- Megh Tower, Old No. 307, New No. 165, Poonamallee High Road, Maduravoyal, Chennai 600 095
  Tel. 044-23780991, 23780992, Email: vivachennai@vivagroupindia.net
- B-103, Jindal Towers, 21/1A/3 Darga Road, Kolkata 700 017
  Tel. 033-22816713, Email: vivakolkata@vivagroupindia.net
- 7, GF, Sovereign Park Aptts., 56-58, K. R. Road, Basavanagudi, Bengaluru 560 004
  Tel. 080-26607409, Email: vivabangalore@vivagroupindia.net
- 101-102, Moghal Marc Apartments, 3-4-637 to 641, Narayanguda, Hyderabad 500 029
  Tel. 040-27564481, Email: vivahyderabad@vivagroupindia.net
- First Floor, Beevi Towers, SRM Road, Kaloor, Kochi 682 018
  Tel. 0484-2403055, 2403056, Email: vivakochi@vivagroupindia.net
- 232, GNB Road, Beside UCO Bank, Silpukhuri, Guwahati 781 003
  Tel. 0361-2666386, Email: vivaguwahati@vivagroupindia.net

www.vivagroupindia.com

ISBN: 978-81-309-2431-1

Published by Vinod Vasishtha for Viva Books Private Limited, 4737/23 Ansari Road, Daryaganj, New Delhi 110 002.

Printed and bound by Syndicate Binders, New Delhi.

L0000

Dedicated to

My Friends and Former Colleagues
Mr. Abdul Matin, Prof. K.M. Yusuf Amin
and
Prof. Abdur Raheem Kidwai

Contents

Introduction

The bunch of letters, collected in this volume, covers a fairly long time-span. They were written to me by the outstanding Western scholars and critics as a response to my writings pertaining to literary criticism. My book *Arrows of Intellect,* soon after its appearance in 1965, first in India and later in the UK, was hailed as a significant contribution to the study of Blake by eminent Western critics like F.R. Leavis, Northrop Frye (the initiator of Myth criticism in our day), F.W. Bateson, Wilson Knight, L.C. Knights, Kathleen Raine and others.

A few words on Blake will not be out of place here, because the poet is a "blind spot" for many critics as very modestly confessed by Douglas Bush in his letter. His significance lies in the fact that he succeeded in breaking the labyrinths of the materialistic and mechanistic framework of the 18th century as represented by Bacon, Newton and Locke. He succeeded in evolving a kind of holistic vision of life. Attracted by the abstract and the esoteric he was no less engrossed by the Kabala as brought out by me in the *Festschrift* presented to Foster Damon of Brown University, USA. The fact of his antipathy to the materialistic culture and breaking its constraints on his mind and soul was very convincingly brought out by David Erdman in his monumental book, *William Blake: Prophet Against Empire*, (USA, 1967). Blake was thus moving in the direction of the emancipation of the human soul and helping man carve out his destiny. While *Arrows of Intellect* deals with Blake's major Prophecies, my other book, *Blake's Minor Prophecies*, Foreword of which was written by Prof. Kathleen Raine, the University of Cambridge, is concerned with his minor Prophecies.

Later in my book on Shakespeare I tried to study Shakespeare's dramaturgy in terms of the modern philosophical approach, Existentialism. The book, *The Existential Dramaturgy of William Shakespeare,* was published by Edwin Mellen Press Ltd.

simultaneously in UK, USA and Canada in 2010. In another book, *Shakespearean and Other Essays,* I tried to apply my critical stance to some of Shakespeare's plays and to the masterpieces produced in the post-Shakespearean and modern literary world. Since articles on William Blake always kept on pouring in I compiled a volume of half a dozen articles including one by Mrs. P.N. Junglawala and the other by me in a single volume on Blake.

As mentioned earlier, the letters received during the sixties and early seventies were written mostly in appreciation of my books. Meanwhile I started *The Aligarh Journal of English Studies* in 1976 and ten years later *The Aligarh Critical Miscellany.* Eminent scholars from UK, USA and the Continent of Europe were kind enough to extend their co-operation to me. Their contributions came pouring in generously. Needless to say I received these letters in response to my requests for their contributions.

I wish to record, with a sense of pride and gratitude, the fact that I received the last piece of writing of F.R. Leavis entitled "Eliot's Permanent Place" and it was published in the 1977 issue. I feel rather flattered by the fact that this is the only article of his to be published outside his superb and celebrated quarterly journal, *Scrutiny* and that *The Aligarh Journal* was at that time in its infancy, i.e. only two years old. Later on, his wife, Q.D. Leavis, very graciously informed me that she showed the *Journal* and his article to him while he was lying on his death-bed and that he received it with a contented look on his face.

In the end the compiler of this volume is deeply grateful to the writers of these letters for their unusual generosity and open-mindedness for expressing their approval of his critical writings.

March 2013 **A.A. Ansari**
Aligarh

J.H. Adamson
125 South 13th East
Salt Lake City, Utah 84102

Dated: 05 October 1970

Dear Professor Ansari,

I spent the summer at Harvard and just recently returned home for the opening of the school year. In my accumulated mail, I found your letter of August 18. In answer to your principal enquiry, I need to explain that, at the last minute, Sarup Singh informed us that he could not come last March. He felt bad about it, and hoped that we could postpone the arrangement until this March.

When Sarup Singh was here in mid-September, he met with the Department Head and the Dean of the College. I think he has been given reasonable assurance that he will be invited in March of 1971. After he is here, there are two men whom he would like to invite. You are one and Professor Kantak of Baroda is the other.

I should also say that other universities in the area might very well be interested in your services if you were inclined to stay for more than one quarter. I would be glad to find out and certainly I will continue to press your candidacy here for the following year. There is always the problem of funds as I am sure you are aware from your own position at Aligarh.

Would it be too much trouble for you to send me a *curriculum vitae*, just a simple statement of education, experience and publication? With your permission, I should like to give it some distribution here. I should like to see you here for professional reasons, but my wife and I would also like to see you for personal ones, always the most compelling.

We have a little contingent of Delhi students here now as a result of my visit there. But if you came, met our staff and worked in our library you might feel that you would wish to recommend one of your students from time to time. I am eager to keep the exchange going.

I regret the delay in my answer but, as I say, I was away for the entire summer. I enjoyed my stay at Harvard very much and continued research on a new book. Mrs. Adamson and my son David were with me. My older son John is now a student there.

I hope you are well, having no student unrest and enjoying your academic duties. I regret the delay occasioned by Sarup Singh's change of plans but have good hopes for the following year. My wife sends her greetings and best wishes along with mine.

Sincerely,

J.H. Adamson

Michael Cook,
M.A. Arts
Reading Room Bedford Street
South, P.O. Box 147,
0 Liverpool L&93Bx,
Tel: 051-709-6022 Extn: 2315
Telex No. 627095
[In Reply Please Quote
Reference;
ARA/ADO/A.4/1 (1249)]

Dated: 23 January 1987

Dear Professor Ansari,

Thank you for your interesting letter of 14th January.

I'm afraid that the only letter of Sir Walter Raleigh which we hold is shortly to be published by Emeritus Professor Kenneth Muir, one of his successors in the Chair. Sir (as he later became) Walter held the King Alfred Chair of Modern Literature and English Language at University College Liverpool from 1890 until 1900, and there are passages on his work and career in Thomas Kelley, *For Advancement of Learning: The University of Liverpool 1881-1981* (Liverpool U.P. 1981), which also provides bibliographical references.

As it happens I have been trying to locate – so far unsuccessfully – the papers of Sir Walter. In the preface to an edition of a *selection* of his correspondence, edited by Lady Raleigh (2nd ed., 1928), it is implied that there was a large collection of letters. I have been in touch with the publishers, etc., but my correspondence with Dr. Michael Halls, Modern Archivist, King's College Library, Cambridge etc., has revealed that:

(a) K.C. Library holds 11 of his letters to Oscar Browning, 1884-1908, 9 letters to Sir John Sheppard 1905, 1911-20, and a letter to Provost Austen Leigh.

(b) Cambridge University Library holds 13 of his letters to M.R. James, 7 to Frances Jenkinson, 3 to the Marques of Crewe, and 1 to G.W. Prothero.

(c) The Location Register of 20th Century MSS., University of Reading Library Whiteknights, Reading, RG6 2AE has notes of quite a number of his letters in other people's collections, but again they are not aware of any major collection as such – which, if it survives, I think must be with the Raleigh family, whose descendants I am trying to locate.

Perhaps you would be good enough to keep me informed of the details of your proposed publications, please, so that our University Library might consider acquiring a copy?

Yours sincerely,

Adrian Allan
Assistant Archivist

Dated: 13 July 1987

Dear Professor Ansari,

Thank you very much for your kind letter of 30th June: it is very good of you to agree to send two copies each of *AJES* for 1986 and of your forthcoming publication on Sir Walter Raleigh – they will be much appreciated.

We ourselves have relatively little information on Sir Walter, our reference library collection being quite small but I enclose a photocopy of:

(a) the sections of a bibliography of the University's history which I maintain which refer to works about Sir Walter. I take it that you will have access to most of these works? I should be able to arrange the supply of a photocopy of the articles you are unable to obtain.

Allan, Adrian

(b) passages in several works which I suspect you may not be able to obtain access to – in Professor Thomas Kelly's *For Advancement of Learning: the University of Liverpool 1881-1981* (Liverpool U.P., 1981), R.W. Champman's essay, and *The Sphinx*, 13 Nov. 1922 and 20 Feb. 1895.

I hope this assists you.

With best wishes

Yours sincerely,

Adrian Allan
Assistant Archivist

---

706 West Stone Avenue,
Fairfield, Iowa-52556
USA

Dated: 01 March 1990

Dear Professor Ansari,

I wish to thank you for your kindness in sending me a copy of the special William Blake number of *The Aligarh Critical Miscellany*. Since I have spent many years studying Blake, it was a welcome surprise. And your name has been familiar to me for a long time because of your 1969 essay on "Blake and the Kabbalah", which gave me many useful ideas.

I am enclosing two copies of my article entitled "Quantum Physics and the Experience of Shakespeare," which I hope you will consider for publication in *The Aligarh Critical Miscellany*. My approach, as the title probably indicates, is somewhat unconventional, and it may be that the essay has little merit. Or may be it has – I simply do not know, and would be pleased to have an independent opinion. I could of course revise it if you thought that parts of it were promising.

I have not been able to locate the *MHRA Style Book*, so the essay may be incorrectly formatted for your journal, but I would be happy to put that in order if you decide to publish it. If you cannot use the essay, there is no need to return it to me. It is cheaper for me to print out another copy than to enclose the return postage.

I look forward to hearing from you in due course, and my thanks once more for sending me a copy of your journal.

Sincerely yours,

Bryan Aubrey

Date: 12 September 1990

Dear Professor Ansari,

I have just noticed a minor omission in my article "Quantum Physics and the Experience of Shakespeare," which you kindly accepted for publication in the November edition of *The Aligarh Critical Miscellany*. In footnote 8, I omitted to give the date of publication for Richard Levin's *New Readings Vs. Old Plays*. It was 1979.

I am also enclosing a check for $ 15.00. This is to cover a subscription to your journal, and also a copy of Vol. 1 no. 1, in which the review of my book appeared. If I have not sent the money in correct form, please let me know and I can send an international money order.

I hope to send more articles for your consideration in the future. However, I am no longer a full-time academic, so working on scholarly articles is a rather slow business, done in my spare time.

Sincerely yours,

Bryan Aubrey

The Queen's University of Belfast
Department of Italian
Language and Literature
Belfast BT7 INN
Northern Ireland

Dated: 11th July 1987

Dear Professor Ansari,

Many thanks for your letter and for the copy of A.J.E.S. I am delighted and honoured to know what you think of my article on "Wordsworth Today" and that you are going to publish it in your scholarly journal of whose repute I know a lot through Professor Singh. I also know about your own standing and reputation as a scholar which makes your approval of my article all the more flattering and significant. I look forward to collaborating with you in the future.

With best wishes,

Yours sincerely,

Gabriella Banfoot

Dated: 02 December 1987

Dear Professor Ansari,

Many thanks for your last letter. I am happy that the Wordsworth articles pleased you. I shall he delighted to contribute an article on "Dante's Influence on T.S. Eliot" for your Journal. As you will see from the enclosed *Curriculum Vitae* (which I send *English translation* of biblio- biographical data given the urgency for such) it has been a subject of interest to me. The photo which I include is the only one which I have at hand.

With best wishes,

Yours sincerely,

Gabriella Banfoot

The Uniiversity of Liverpool
Jonathan Bota

Dated: 21 November 1994

Dear Dr Ansari

I do indeed remember your fine review of my book for the *Miscellany*, and Kenneth Muir always speaks very warmly of both you and the journal. But as for the possible article on Keats, I'm afraid I shall have to decline, as I did with that on Marlowe: I have so many writing commitments at the moment that I can't take on any new ones. It is, however, always worth asking, in case I have an unpublished essay on a relevant topic in need of a home.

With best wishes

Jonathan Bate

F.W. Bateson
Corpus Christi College
Oxford: Brill, Aylesbury,
Bucks (Brill 255)

Dated: 08 December 1964

Dear Ansari,

Nice to hear from you. I will be glad to act as your supervisor if you come to Oxford and give you any help I can with your Blake Project. The English Board must be asked to accept you as 'Recognized Student' but I feel sure that will be all right. Harwood and I are both members of the English Board now.

Best Wishes,

Yours Sincerely,

F.W. Bateson

Dated: 25 July 1965

Dear Ansari,

The Oxford term is at last over and I have been reading your book and the article in the *Indian Journal of English Studies* with avidity. It is a splendidly ambitious effort. Perhaps in some ways too ambitious. The kind of vaulting ambition that overlaps itself. By going into so much detail about "The Infernal Trinity" you invite the criticism that you are not really an expert on Bacon, Newton and Lock – whereas you are an expert on Blake. It is true, of course, that you know a great deal about the trio than Blake did.

But the chapter is written and has clearly given you a great deal of trouble. What you must do is to placate the critics by getting the presentation as scholarly as possible. In discussing Bacon you quote the Novuum (sic) *Organum* as though he had written it in English. Whose translation of the Latin are you using?

It would be better to eliminate the popularization like Will Durant. You must get the Latin right (e.g. SCISNTIANUM in note 17). In note 19 and on page 45 it to accept Willey's *paraphrase* for the work famous of all Pascal's. Pen sees, generally speaking there is too much dependence on Willey, White Luad, Frye, James item and not enough use of the original sources.

The Chapters on Blake suffer from the obscurity of the subject-matter. For *Vala* it would probably be better to use the new text edited in facsimile by G.E. Bentley or failing Bentley edition is much better than Erdman has recently recovered many of the obliterated passages in 'Jerusalem' (see his article in the Bulletin of the N.T. Public Library). Rex where I *suppose the text* to use in that of Keynes.

I wish I would say "yes" to your invitation to write a preface to the book. Unfortunately I am terribly busy just now and (worse still) I think I really disagree with you fundamentally. The "Infernal" three are my heroes as the prophets of naturalism, whereas they are clearly your villains as they were Blake's. I see Blake as almost the last deluded supernaturalisms in a series of uneducated geniuses since Langland and Bunyan. But what is valuable in him as in them is surely the ethics and not the metaphysics.

To the question "And did those feet in ancient time its? To say "No" But to the ethical problems later in soup of experience and else where we say "yes".

I hope you won't think me just a Voltaire or Rousseau. As it happens I have never written

Best wishes

F.W. Bateson

Dated: 19 December 1965

Dear Ansari,

Arrows of Intellect has been sitting on my table for several weeks now. The arrow keeps pricking my conscience all the time. But the last term has been a very busy one and I have literally had no time at all for private reading. However the Xmas vacation has at last arrived and the final examiners' meeting (for L.C.C scholarships) took place on Thursday. For a brief interval I am more or less my own master.

I am delighted the book has been published and am honoured by your reference to me in the Preface. I found the later chapters particularly interesting. It was useful for example, to have "Ah, Sunflower" associated with Marvell's "On a Drop of Dew" And on the discussion of Coleridge in Chapter V seems to me first – rate.

I am enclosing a review I did in the autumn of the new *Erdman-Bloom* edition of Blake. Textually this shows a great improvement on Keyne's and in future you should certainly use it. Bloom's commentary is adequate but a bit "thin". W.H. Stevenson is doing a Blake for Longman's Annotated English Poets, a series of which I am the general editor. Stevenson's editions won't be out until 1967, but it is for me thoroughly annotated then any earlier edition. I will see that he makes use of your book for it.

It was disappointing that we were not able to come to England this year.

Best wishes

F.W. Bateson

Dated: 17 May 1970

I hope your October copy of *Essays in Criticism* eventually turned up. Apparently the closing of the *Suez Canal* has slowed up the post appallingly. I have now retired from Corpus and hope soon to read you on "Blake and Kabbalah."

All the best

Yours

F.W. Bateson

Dated: 14 January 1974

Dear Ansari,

Your able colleague M.H. Khan sent me a copy of the *Essays on Wordsworth*, some time ago, but I have been involved in so many other matters that it is only now that I have been able to explore it. Naturally it is with what you had written that I turned to first. In its own subtle and subjective way it is a performance- though more as you won't need to be told in John Jones's view than in mine. I suppose I was always a little suspicious of that Egotistical Sublime – too much ego and not enough. You write very well now. I can't help contrasting A.A.A's prose style today with that of the first essay you read me.

It was on Eliot's sense of time-or something equally abstract – and it took my breath away. But your English is more polished then it was. In fact, I consider your present English quite first – class. If only all Indian academics wrote as well!

Christopher Ricks told me a few years ago that he had met you on one of the British Councils' whirlwind tours. I was asked to do a three weeks' lecturing tour too just after I retired, but I had to decline. So if we are to re-meet it will have to be in England. Why not?

Until then

Your gratefully

F.W. Bateson

Dated: 13 July 1976

Dear Ansari,

I have been reading the first number of your journal with great interest. You are lucky to get Jeremy Bentley on the 'Book of Enoch' for it is a most interesting article. I also read your piece on *Twelfth Night* without leaving a word. It reminded me vividly of those tutorials we used to have in the distant past.

I continue to be active and as controversial as ever. I am also glad things are going well for you.

My very best wishes for your own and the Journal continued prosperity.

Yours as ever,

F.W. Bateson

Date: 11 May 1977

Delighted to get the last number of your *Aligarh Journal of English Studies.* Your are doing a very good job as editor and I particularly look forward to reading yours on *Macbeth.* I am deep in critical edition of the *Canterbury Tales* and (on the other hand!) *The School for Scandal.* I remember one Corpus Tutorial of language with great pleasure.

F.W. Bateson

Dated: 10 August 1978

Dear Ansari,

I am taking the opportunity offered at the sea-side to catch up with my letters etc. among others of want to thank you for that excellence Centenary No. of the *Aligarh Journal.* To have obtained that piece by Leavis, one of his best later things and one that particularly interested me, as I am committed to an obituary/appreciation of F.R.L for *Essays* in *Criticism.*

I suppose my Chaucer material did finally reach you. Of course, you need not use any of it for your Journal, but it was all I had by me at the time. If you are short of material the first four or five papers might be detached. But of course you are under no obligation to use a word of it.

I hope all is well with the department and yourself. It was a pleasant surprise to see you again.

Did you ever print that essay on T.S. Eliot which was the beginning of our acquaintance?

All the best

Freddy Bateson

Dated: 01 February 1979

Dear Professor Ansari,

Thank you very much for your kind letter of January 17th and I am glad that you have fond memories of my husband. I recall with pleasure your visit to us in July 1977 with Mr. Press and I am pleased that you and Fready had the chance to meet and talk again.

Yesterday my son came down from London to go through the many boxes of papers etc. left by my husband, but at present he has not found any copy of the article his father sent you. He will continue the search today and if it is discovered I shall mail it soon directly and also let you know by letter.

My son also telephoned to Longmans (The publishers who dealt with his Chaucer material)., and has asked them to look and see if the article intended for you was put among the papers sent to them. This could have happened in error, as very soon after Fready's death the Longman's representative collected several boxes of type-script or manuscript. I am very sorry that you did not receive the promised article.

Thank you again for your nice letter.

Yours Sincerely,

Jan Bateson

---

246 Macpherson Avenue
Toronto, Ontario M4V 1A2
Telephone: 416 922 5613

Dated: 5 April 2001

Dear Professor Ansari,

I have just received your letter, for which I thank you heartily. Please note that mail addressed as above will reach me most expeditiously; now that I am retired, I go down to the College only occasionally to collect mail sent there.

I thank you also for the copy of the *Aligarh Critical Miscellany*, which I read with particular interest because of the Blake essay there.

I enclose some issues of Blake: An Illustrated Quarterly which I hope may be of interest to you.

I write by this post to Candida Brazil, Yale University Press, 23 pond Street, London, NW3 2PN requesting that a review copy of The Stranger from Paradise, should be sent to you. If it does not arrive in the next few months, you might write to her directly. I have not yet seen a copy of the book and believe that the official publication date is late May.

You could do me a very substantial service if you would be so good as to assist me to obtain at my expense copies of the following works for which I have looked in vain on three continents:

Brooks, Harold F. Reintegration. "Aligarh Critical Miscellany, V, 1 ([India] 1992), 41-89.

Raine, Kathleen. "The Spiritual Fourfold London. "Aligarh Critical Miscellany. V (1992), 181-198

Jose, Fr. C.P. "William Blake's Interpretation of the Bible through his Poems and Paintings. University of Calicut {India} Ph. D. (1991)

Indeed, should you know of any other recent publications on Blake in India, I should much like to learn of them.

Yours sincerely

G.E. Bentley, Jr

Dutch Boys Landing
Mears, Michigan 49436
Telephone: (231) 873 7146

Dated: 14 June 2004

Dear Professor Ansari,

It was very kind of you to send me the issue of the *Aligarh Critical Miscellany* with the essay on Coleridge by Morton Paley and, of even more interest to me, the review of your book on William Blake's Minor Prophecies,

The review seems judicious and thoughtful, and I hope that it pleases you.

Thank you very much for your generosity.

Should you learn of other articles in Indian Journals or Indian books relating to Blake, I should be most grateful if you would let me know of them, for I fear that my coverage of them is a good deal less than comprehensive.

On 27 April 2000 I sent to you essays entitled "A Fifth Zoa" and "Blake in the Eighteenth Century Short Title Catalogue" and "Johnson in Prison". I wonder whether you have received them and, if so, whether you have reached a determination as to their publish ability

Yours sincerely

G.E. Bentley, Jr

English Department
Case Western Reserve University
Cleveland, Ohio 44106
U.S.A.

Dated: 8 August 1993

A.A. Ansari

Dear Sir:

My colleague Dr. Glen Bush encouraged me to submit to you my manuscript that explores Spenser's brief description of Rosalind within the context of the *Shepeard's*

Calendar. I mailed that to you on January 25 and have not heard. I also have a study on Donne's exploration of women ready should you want it. Thank you for your consideration—I await your reply and or editorial suggestions.

Sincerely,

Deborah Bice

Please address correspondence to my home:
2960 Lost Nation Road
Willoughby, Ohio 44094
U.S.A.

Harold Bloom
Linden St. Haven

Dated: 15 December 1977

Dear Professor Ansari

By various mischances, I am only now in receipt of your kind letter of 15 September.

My little book, *Kabbalah and Criticism*, is published by the Seabury Press, 815 Second Avenue, New York, N.Y. 10017, USA.

I admire your work, always.

With best wishes

Harold Bloom

Peterhouse
Cambridge CB2 IRD

Dated: 22 April 1994

Dear Professor Ansari,

It was a great pleasure to meet you again in Aligarh and to know that you are still flourishing. Unfortunately, I do not think I can send you anything at the moment, since I am at present straining to complete a book which I have been engaged on for the past twenty-five years, and I have told myself that I ought not to undertake any other writing until that is completed. Once that is out of the way in another year or two I hope that I may begin to think about other things again!

With all good wishes,

Yours sincerely,

John Boer

---

91 Chesterton Road,
Cambridge CB4 3AP

Dated: 31 January 1984

Dear Professor Ansari,

Many thanks for the interesting number of the *Aligarh Journal of English Studies* on Joyce and V. Woolf. It was very varied and of course I am particularly concerned with *To the Lighthouse* but one of my pupils who is the chief exponent of Mrs. Woolf in Japan, had translated *Mrs. Dalloway*, and will be very interested too when she comes to visit me in the summer.

I do not think I can agree that Mr. Ramsay's refusal to go to the lighthouse because the weather signs are likely to be bad is indefensible. Whether one is thinking of Cornwall or the Hebrides, one cannot set out on those coasts in bad weather except at great risk. Whole boatloads were drowned near my own childhood home last summer in a sudden squall. This last month men have been isolated on a Cornish lighthouse without supplies for a week because of bad weather. Forgive this passionate defence of Mr Ramsay! My father was a sailor and treated us with great firmness on these matters!

I hope the *King Lear* number is going well. Kenneth Muir told me he had written on two text theory which is the great subject of contention at the moment. I do not find the *Division of the Kingdoms* entirely convincing myself.

With renewed thanks

Yours sincerely,

M.C. Bradbrook

Dated: 11 October 1984

My Dear Professor Ansari,

Many thanks for the *Aligarh Journal of English Studies* – the special number of *King Lear* which arrived this week. Kenneth Muir had already given me a copy of his piece; the controversy rages on, and the Oxford editors are now expanding this method of approaching the plays to others. I think they are in danger of being over excited by the possibilities of a new line in editorial procedure.

Lee Salingar has done a very thorough survey of his two sources. He is one of my earliest pupils – it is dreadful when one's *pupils* enter upon retirement! This is happening to me every year now. I feel myself part of history – I have written a chapter for the collection Denys Thompson made for Cambridge University Press on *The Leavises*, which is to appear next week. Not quoted everything can yet be said about them – but a good deal is emerging.

With renewed thanks and kind regards,

Yours sincerely,

M.C. Bradbrook

Another of my pupils – Anne Barten-has just returned to Cambridge to a chair. Lionel Knights is undergoing great difficulties owing to his own illness and that of his wife, who had a stroke in August and needs much care from him.

Dated: November 1988

Christopher Ricks' *T.S. Eliot and Prejudice,* Faber and Faber, 1988. pp. 290. These 290 pages are a landmark, the most important since Leavis's *New Bearings*, of fifty six years ago. The style reminds me most of Empson, a friend of Ricks, in the ability to extract juices, the very veined vitality of a phrase. The extracting however of every use of a single word, however far, in Eliot's total text-poetry or prose is a feat of memory. It is like some trick game at cards, and very exciting. Sometimes it is fidgety, and I cannot follow this jumping jack for very long, it is too exhausting. But really enlightening; Eliot has attracted a critic as clever as himself.

The shaping of Eliot's development, however, is the most masterly effect; the sections on the emptiness of *The Hollow Men,* the different emptiness of *Ash Wednesday,* the absolute power of *Marina* and *Little Gidding* sound a deep level beyond the 'prejudice'. (Ricks does not mention Shakespeare and Herbert who are hovering, beating their luminous wings not entirely in vain). Ricks gives far more here than in the early chapters, which are the reviewers notice. They presumably do not read beyond the anti- Semitcism, the fashionable cry.

M.C. Bradbrook

Dated: 07 December 1988

My Dear Dr Ansari,

I am sorry I do not have anything prepared on T.S. Elict's plays and I am in the middle of proofs for my next and final volume of my Collected papers and so I cannot send anything on that subject.

Briefly I think Eliot's *poetry* ended with 'Little Gidding'; the only poetic drama he wrote and the only one that stays in action is *Murder in the Cathedral.* Eliot's later dramas are more or less autobiographical – *the Family Reunion* should be set in New England not in Northern England, and the mother is of course his own mother. *The Cocktail Party* is about the break-up of his marriage and the exit of Celia is his own (though not the end). *The Confidential Clark* uses the title he had in Lloyds *Bank,* and is again about his sublimation (Claude and Colby are *both* Eliot in different aspects) as in *The Elder Statesman* the father and the lover are *both* Eliot – he married Valerie Fletcher in the course of writing this play. I think, therefore, the dramas are of interest as *indirect* autobiography – for instance B. Kaghan is the husband that Lucasta – Vivienne *ought* to have married, and the father figure, Claude, is a kind of repentance about what he said about Jews in the years 1917-1922, whilst Eggerson is modelled on the kind older man who taught him his job at Lloyd's bank. Of course one must not make one – to – one equivalents between these figures in the dramas and figures in Eliot's life; the relation is oblique but I think it can be felt. Eliot is behind more than one figure in these later plays, whereas in *Murder in the Cathedral* the hero even has his name, Thomas; and represents a saintly guide rather than an identification; but there are ties here with the poems of this period, whereas later he moved away from poetry, or 'put it on a thin diet' as he said himself. The later plays have not survived, as stage production, indeed last is more an oratorio than a play, dedicated I think to Valerie; and one unkind critic remarked 'Poor Tom's aflame;' at the time. They were works of a man who has really dried up as a poet and as he said to his second wife 'I paid to high a price for poetry as I have said in this piece *The Dove Descending*.

If you wish to use these thoughts as a note you are welcome! See pp. 1-2 of *The Dove Descending*.

Yours very sincerely,

M.C. Bradbrook

Dated: 28 April 1989

My Dear Professor Ansari

Many thanks for the Eliot number of the *Aligarh Critical Miscellan*y with my piece on Eliot, which came yesterday. This was my 80th birthday, which gives most happiness to see myself in such good company.

I gave an address with this title in King's College Chapel by invitation of the Dean. It was the first time I imagine that a woman presented a sermon in King's College at Martin's!

I hope the plans for the *Critical Miscellany* are going well.

Yours sincerely

M.C. Bradbrook

We are very busy about the ---------- building Globe Theatre in Southwark ______.

Birthday at Stratford this year was celebrated by theatrical and academic celebrities as the theatre last year refused to join with the forum to reserve the ambassador of South Africa with the others and lots of the embassy's only start third secretaries ____ ____. There was a riot!

Dated: 16 December 1989

My Dear Dr. Ansari

Thank you very much for the *Aligarh Critical Miscellany* 2.1 with your article about "Time and History in Little Gidding". I think the strong hold of Little Gidding is relocation or displacement from St. ________ Gloucester Rd. for the scene is set in Kensington but the church where Eliot served for many years - it is a very dull and drab Victorian building – which __________ only the Church Eliot visited once, but which is now thanks to his poem the centre of small community "The Fellowship of Christ the Sower". The two time books cover in all 4 quartets – in Burnt Norton through meeting again after years his first love Emily Hals, suddenly by encounters, breaking with that past self in so far as it was a 'fantasy refuge'. We have seen on stage J V Foster Brookes *Mahabarata.*

We are concerned by the trouble in India, which to me seems very nearer of a solution. But at this time of the year we may rejoice at the wonderful new liberty in Eastern Europe – something scarcely hoped for coming so suddenly.

With the best wishes for the new year

M.C. Bradbrook

This air letter is designed to celebrate the restoration of Ely Cathedrals – which is mostly thirteenth Century, but with fragments of older buildings (it was founded in 673) and is called the Ship of the Fens, because it rides above the plant/fen land all around.

Yours sincerely,

M.C. Bradbrook

Arthur Bradley
English Department,
University College Chester,
Cheyney Road,
Chester,
CH1 4BJ
GREAT BRITAIN

Dated: 26th November 1997

Dear Professor Ansari,

I am writing to ask if you would kindly consider the enclosed paper for publication in the *Aligarh Critical Miscellany.* The paper explores the paradoxical and previously undetected influence of the Christian, anti-revolutionary philosopher Joseph de Maistre on the atheist, pro-revolutionary poet Percy Byshe Shelley.

I recently completed a Ph.D. thesis on Shelley's poetry at the University of Liverpool, and am currently employed as an English lecturer at University College Chester. The *Aligarh Critical Miscellany* was originally recommended to me by the examiners of my thesis- Professor Kelvin Everest and Mr. Bernard Beatty- and like them I have always found it a source of great scholarly interest. Professor Everest and Mr. Beatty suggested that I send the enclosed paper to you and I am only too happy to do so now.

Please accept my sincere thanks for agreeing to consider the paper for publication in the *Aligarh Critical Miscellany*, and my very best wishes for the future of the journal. I look forward to hearing from you when you have reached a decision.

Your sincerely,

Dr. Arthur Bradley

Dated: 4 May 1988

Dear Professor Ansari

Thank you very much for my copy of Essays on Sir Walter Raleigh. I am very much honoured in being associated with such a company of scholars. I think that it is most important that librarians should show from time to time that they have scholarly and bibliographical interests which complement their day-to-day activities, and I am most grateful to you for giving me the opportunity to share some of my own knowledge with others.

I must also thank you for your patience with the slowness in completing the chapter, and for the enthusiasm with which you received it when it reached you.

With kindest regards and all good wishes

Sincerely

Richard Brankley

Professor Harold F. Brooks
"Talbothays"
32 Conyngham Lane
Bridge Canterbury
Kent CT4 5JX

Dated: 07 March 1987

Dear Professor Ansari,

I was pleased to have your letter, and hoped to have answered it before, but – a situation I have no doubt is familiar to you – I have been extremely occupied with publications. My edition of the *Poems of John Oldham* came out on 5 February. I have completed revisions to ch 2 of my *Dryden the Satirist* (a book which is likely to be published by subscription of £10 a copy) and almost completed revision to another chapter. From what I have discarded from chapter 2 I have written a prolegomena to English Verse Satire 1640-1660, with a final section on continuities between Satire before and after the Restoration. I am awaiting proof of my contribution (on *Troilus and Cressida)* to the Harold Jenkins Festschrift.

The delay in replying has given Mrs Brooks time to reflect on your invitation to contribute an article on *Love's Labour's Lost.* On one condition, she would like to do this. The condition is that she can have till the end of the long vacation to write it: her College work leaves her little or no time for writing during term or in the short Christmas and Easter vacations. But she is pleased to be asked, and the experience of the production from which the photograph we sent was taken (we are glad you liked it) has furnished her with plenty to say. It is an excellent idea to use the photograph as an illustration to the article.

I haven't forgotten my hope of doing you an article on Blake and Jung, even though it is having to take its place in a queue – where it occupies a firm place. I am glad to hear of your commissioned volume on Raleigh (the 19/20 C. one) I knew he had taught in India but not that it was at Aligarh. I was just too late to hear him in Oxford. I went up in 1926, and he had died in 1922 (I believe it was). I have the two volumes of his collected letters, and used to hear about him from my tutor, Percy Simpson. In Shakespeare he advised me, in a very short reading list, to read Raleigh's short volume in the English Men of Letters series and told me that when Raleigh had done all his reading for it, he went away and wrote it without books. Simpson's summing up was: 'Raleigh was not a scholar: but he knew the value of scholarship': (I can hear Percy saying these words: Strong stress on value'). When he had to deal with something which required scholarship, he consulted those who possessed it. If you are writing, as I presume you are, an introduction to the Raleigh Volume, what Simpson said (as reported by me) might be worth quoting. I owed to Raleigh's book on Wordsworth a widened appreciation, and to his book on Johnson the start of an enthusiasm for that great writer outside *Boswell's Life.*

Yours sincerely,

Harold F. Brooks

Dated: 07 June 1987

Dear Dr. Ansari,

My wife will no doubt, once the pressure of examining is over, reply to your confirmation of the invitation to contribute to the *Journal,* on *Love's Labour's Lost.* I know she is very pleased about this.

You will be pleased to hear that next week I expect to complete an article on Blake and Jung – I have just the conclusion to write, and then it will be ready for the typist. The typescript shall then be sent off immediately to you. I have the material for a sequel. Which if live I will write (I have just passed my 80th birthday). The present one is about the similarity in the raw material of Blake's *Four Zoas* myth and Jung's picture of the psyche; in their respect for that material, and in their treatment of it. Numerous notes give references to prove or illustrate what I say, and are an essential part of the article. The second one would be on the resemblance between the two accounts of the personality's fall into division and its re-integration.

Piloo will be interested to see the article or articles. Please remember me to her. I am grateful for your kindness in continuing to send me the number of the *Journal,* in which I always find something of interest and value; particularly in what you write yourself.

Yours sincerely,

Harold F. Brooks

I have just sent the typescript of a big book, *Dryden the Satirist,* to publishers in Oldham, *The New Century Press,* who expect to publish it by subscription.

Dated: 29 July 1987

Dear Dr. Ansari,

Here is my essay on Blake and Jung, which has just arrived from my typist. I have proof read the typescript. I hope you will pardon the unsightly correction on the first page: I noticed a slip of my own in grammar, and a nasty jingle, and bungled my first attempt to put them right.

The present essay is a comparative study of the two authors' materials, their attitudes towards them, and their treatment of them. Though complete in itself, it ought to be followed up by comparison of how they actually portray the fall of Man, or the personality, into disintegration; and the reintegration. I have carried these comparisons far enough to know that the fall requires an article about the length of this one, and the re-integration on another. Might you accept these sequels – for publication when opportunity serves? For Blake and Jung II I have the typescript I produced in the late 1930s when I had got to that point with the book I projected. There is now more Jung to be drawn on, and the old version of the study must be revised. For the re-integration, 'Blake and Jung III', there was only a collection of quotations towards it. Since if I were to die or lose my faculties, it would not be impossible for someone else (Piloo?) to revise 'II', I decided 'III' was the more urgent task. I have completed and classified the evidence for it; and am about half way through the writing. (I enclose Xerox copies of opening paragraphs, in MS of 'Blake and Jung II and 'III').

Piloo has just written to let me know she and her husband are again visiting England. I am sending her a Xerox copy of the present article, pending its appearance in print; and hope to see them before they leave.

My personal news is unfortunately unpleasant, and in part very gratifying indeed. I am waiting to see surgeon: I have a hernia on the opposite side from the one he dealt with last September, and expect it will ensure another comparatively minor operation. My feet are troubling me, and I have been losing the edge of my hearing: but I am seeing a chiropodist and my admirable physician is going to syringe my ears; so no doubt both these disabilities will be lessened.

I think you know that, for my published work, Oxford-my University-on 29 November 1986 conferred on me its highest doctorate in my field, the D. Litt., and that on 5 February 1987 the Clarendon Press Published my edition (started 50 years ago) of John Oldham, chief literary worthy of St Edmond Hall, Oxford. A Week or two ago, the Principal and Governors of the Hall (where I am also a minor benefactor) elected me an Honorary Fellow. This has been for some time a private ambition of mine, but one I never believed would be realized.

I am keeping your contributor's name before the public. A short book on *T.S. Eliot as Literary Critic* will appear this summer. In May I had a note in the volume presented to Kenneth Muir on his 80th birthday. I have corrected proofs of a 'Note' in *R.E.S.* on Peacock and Byron, and c. Sept. shall have an essay on Shakespeare's *Troilus and Cressida* in the Harold Jinkins Festschrift (Methuen). The New Century Press in Oldhams are about to seek subscriptions for my big book *John Dryden the Satirist.* The new periodical (also based in Durham) *The Seventeenth Century,* has accepted a long article on 'English Verse Satire 1640-1660'; A Prolegomena'; and I am waiting for proofs from the *Durham University Journal* of the 'Principal Conflicts in the Restoration Comedy of Manners: The Battle of Sex, and Truewits V. Witwould and Lackwits'. I did a great deal of research while I was still teaching, but had no time to write it up. The longer I am spared to continue an active retirement, the more of that harvest I shall gather. But I am doing new research, too: 'Blake and Jung III' will be largely new.

Sincerely yours,

Harold F. Brooks

Dated: 08 June 1988

Dear Dr. Ansari,

Many thanks for the *Essays on Sir Walter Raleigh,* which I shall read with great pleasure. I notice among the contributors, besides your own, the exceptionally distinguished names of Kenneth Muir and Mary Lascells.

I like the subjects of the articles. I well remember reading, as an undergraduate his *Style,* his *Johnson* and *Wordsworth* which left me much more appreciative of two authors who until this, I had thought of, except for some of Wordsworth's lyrics, as not my 'cup of tea'; and his *Shakespeare* (the Vol. of *Shakespearean Criticisms,* ed. by Nichol Smith, came later), one of the only vols., on Shakespeare recommended to me by my tutor, Percy Sampson: the others were Bradley, A.C.Swinburne, 'that fine but too ecstatic critic,' said Percy, and Tranwills Barker's *Prefaces to Shakespeare:* I was proud of having, before Percy's recommendation, bought the two volumes then published.

I arrived as an Oxford freshman four years after Raleigh's death, but Percy Simpson, my tutor while I was residing for my second degree, had of course, known him well. He told me that in preparation for the English Men of letters vol. on Shakespeare, Raleigh read all he felt that he needed to, and then went away and wrote the book with nothing but a complete Shakespeare for a companion.

I am now at the last stage of chocking up on the Jung copyrights for the 'Blake and Jung' articles. Princeton U.P. who hold most of the copyrights, have sent me criteria according to which they should be covered by 'fair use'. I am consulting the society of Authors as a final precaution. Even in advance of their reply, I am confident you can safely go ahead with 'Blake and Jung.I'

Yours sincerely,

Harold F. Brooks

Dated: 28 July 1988

Dear Dr. Ansari,

You will be glad to know of the good progress being made with 'Blake and Jung II' and 'III'. I have now got copyright for all but the quotations from three volumes, worldwide, and for those three volumes everywhere but for U.S.A. and Canada.

The three volumes are *Modern Man in Search of a Soul,* the *Integration of the Personality,* and *The Secret of the Golden Flower*. Outside the U.S.A and Canada, the copyright in these is held by Routledge and Kegan Paul. They replied to my enquiry (which enclosed a word count) by agreeing that my quotation were 'fair use', and by giving me the address of the holders of the trans-Atlantic copyrights – to whom I am about to write.

Routledge and Kegan Paul stipulate acknowledgement of the author, titles, and Routledge and Kegan Paul. Author and titles are of course already acknowledged in the Footnotes; you will need to add (no doubt at the end of the article?) an acknowledgement to Routledge and Kegan Paul – as also to the Bollinger Series, University of Princeton. These had better go in 'Blake and Jung I' as well. In that volume they cannot be thanked for permission since I did not seek any, relying on fair use: one could say something like: Acknowledgement, are due to ... For the use of copyright quotations from C.G. Jung.' I shall let you know at once when Harcourt Brace Jovanovich have replied from America. So far no one has charged me any fee.

What typescripts of 'Blake and Jung II' and 'III' do you hold? I expect to see Piloo in mid August, and have an idea she has a typescript of one of them. I have copies of all three articles; but as mine are all in MS., I must have sent the typescripts either to you Piloo, or Kathleen Raine. I have shown or sent them to no one else.

Shall you be at Stratford for the international Shakespeare Conference, beginning of August? My wife and I plan to be there.

With every good wish,

Harold F. Brooks

Dated: 25 March 1989

Dear Professor Ansari,

Thanks for everything you have sent me, and especially for the publication of the First 'Blake and Jung' essay in the *Aligarh Journal of English Studies.*

I am glad to know that 'Blake and Jung II' and 'Blake and Jung III' will shortly be appearing. Your editing has made Aligarh a centre of Blake studies. As my typist was being rather slow, I gave a hand written MS of Blake and Jung II to Piloo, on her kind offers to type it, and let you have her typescript. My typist has now provided the typescript she was busy on, and I have proof - read it; naturally I have had no opportunity to check Piloo's.

I therefore enclose this corrected typescript, so that if the essay is not yet in print, you may substitute it for Piloo's typescript as the printer's copy; but if the essay is already set up, perhaps you will be so kind as to check the prints, as you proof - read it by what I now enclose.

I have been obtaining copyright permissions for my Jung quotations. One is still being negotiated: with Harcourt Brace Jovanovich Inc. Ohando, Florida 32887 U.S.A. for the copyright in America of quotations from *Modern Man in Search of a Soul* and *The Secret of the Golden Flower*. The copyrights outside America for these volumes and for all the other Jung volumes everywhere, are held by (1) Princeton University Press and (2) Routledge and Kegan Paul (London). They have given me permissions without fee, regarding the quotations as covered by the principle of 'fair use'. I think it likely that Harcourt Brace Jovanovich will do the same, but if they require a fee I shall pay it, so I do not think you need worry about them.

However, it is a condition of such permission that acknowledgment should be made; so I will be grateful if you will find a place for the three acknowledgements, I suggest.

'The author and publishers would like to thank Routledge and Kegan Paul ltd., the Princeton University Press, and Harcourt Brace Jovanovich, Inc. for permission to include the quotations from C.G. Jung.'

I must ask your pardon for troubling you at this late stage with these matters, and trust they will not result in too much inconvenience.

Cordially yours,

Harold F. Brooks

Dear Professor Ansari,

Those of my friends with whom I have corresponded frequently since last Exams are fairly up to date, with our news. For others, this year I can only manage 2-page bulletin. To save the flourishing drama options at her college and the part of a colleague indispensable to them, Jean has gone on Half pay: a money saving was the only acceptable inducement. But after long batting by her head and her departmental chiefs the brick wall has yielded and the colleague has a 3-year contract instead of renewal year by year. The options Jean pioneered should be safe till her age of retirement. I need not face her retirement to Yorks at the end of the session. Bridge may see me out. She has had two letters of sympathy on my death: a report as with Mark Twain's and L. Hoysman's, 'much exaggerated'. As Honorary Fellow, I much enjoyed the Hall's Gaudy and St Edmund's Feast. I am busily publishing and writing. To the Harold Hankins festschrift I contributed reminiscences and an essay on the unity and genre of *Troilus and Cressida*. My 'English Verse Satire 1640-1660, which also treats the Restoration inheritance from those years, appeared in *The Seventeenth Century*; and 'Principal Conflicts in the Restoration Comedy of Manners: The Battle of Sex; and TrueWis V. Witwoulds and Lackwits' in the *Durham University Journal*. I await the last installment of page proof of *Dryden the Satirist*: a big book *the New Century Press* is publishing by subscription. The first of three articles on 'Blake and Jung' has appeared in *The Aligarh Critical Miscellany*. These have required permissions from the owners of Jung copyrights; all granted as 'fair use'; for help in seeking them I have joined the Society of Authors. Two books combine old and newly written essays. *Four Masterpieces* (by Yeats, T. S. Eliot, Virginia Woolf, Bernard Shaw) needs only a last installment from my typist, completing a substantial introduction on the common features in the very disparate works. *Approaches to Criticism and Scholarship* consists of 'The Use and Abuse of Literary Criticism'; 'What is Dramatic': (unfinished): 'A Poetic Form and its Varieties: The Sonnet'; "Practical Criticism": of Passages Illustrating some different kinds of prose (Descriptive, Persuasive, Polemic, Expository, Kindling Imagination by Poetical Methods)'; 'On the Romantic Movements' (begun); "Two Principles in Source Study,' with 'Browning's "Fifine at the Fair" as a source for Conrad's *Lord Jim*': 'The Editor and the literary Text: Requirements and Opportunities.

The author designate of the final volume of a *History of the University of Oxford* having appealed for reminiscences of student life, 1914-50, I sent him three budgets on 1926-50. The minutes of the Labour Club have a gap from 1931: he tells me that my membership programmes, term by term, help to fill it, and may be valued by Bodley. I urged him to recognize the 'superiority complex' of radical Grammar

School men like me: I believed that we and the women were making the University more, at undergraduate level, a place of study, and less a finishing school for what we should now call the Establishment; one which did not know what the country needed – I and my socialist friends did (I still think so). I have been getting to let lots of protest into the *Guardian* and *Times Higher Education Supplement* during the threat to Birkbeck; and on making University staff dismissible without fault; and on the under funding of education, libraries, museums, public transport, the N.H.S., not forgetting the arts: Jean and I were among the supporters who helped to save the Kent Opera Company from closure by protesting against withdrawal of its grant. We are also friends of Sam Wanamaker and his Southwark Globe, now begun after year of his prodigious effort.

Ever since in 1945 I was appointed at Birkbeck I have urged the establishment of at least a University department on Birkbeck principles in every contribution. And now my mother and Aunt Lillie the physician's University, Durham, in the Country where my grandfather, George Johnson 'the little alderman' was chairman of the Education Committee, announces its project of founding a 'Birkbeck of the North'. I have just had an appreciative reply to the letter of congratulation I sent the Vice-Chancellor, to which I added a statement of the principles that make Birkbeck what it is. First and foremost, all the undergraduate are part time mature students, so that they do not, as elsewhere, have to fit in with arrangements made for the 18 + school level: all arrangements are made with their needs in mind. Besides the practical advantages, this brings a psychological one: at Brikbeck they feel themselves the normal student. Second, the part time student has the services of a full time staff: opportunities for contact hours may be more limited than with the full-time staff, but preparation, and correction of the student's work occupy no less time and energy. Third, admission often disregard A and O levels: over the years, the University through its special Entrance Board, has learned to trust Birkbecks judgement in this respect. A *sinequa non* is being in full-time gainful employment during the day, or else housewife with domestic responsibilities; ahead the nation Birkbeck regards that as a job. As things are now, the unemployed who in a proper state of society would be in employment ought to qualify for admission, too. Finally an answer is needed against anyone who says 'It was only a part-time degree after all'. We reply: 'a degree not of the college but of the University." Examined alongside Full-time students; tested by the same criteria and equalling the full-times in First II is and II ii achieved. And one might add, acquired by sacrifice and special dedication: my great Professor, Geottrey Fillotson, used to say: "every Birkbeck graduate should have a George Cross with his or her degree.'

I have been busy writing references, particularly in support of applications for the unusual crop of recent vacant Chairs and Fellowships. My candidates are a pleasure to back: lucky those who enlist their services.

I scarcely need add that my private correspondence is one of my keenest pleasure: whether it is academic or personal. I have made a new scholar friend a Professor at the Lund University in Sweden. I wrote to her about an excellent article on Rochester which appeared next to my contribution in the *Durham University Journal*. She turns out to be a specialist on T.S. Eliot as well as the Restoration, and sent me her two books on him. She responded warmly to my writing to a stranger and foreigner, enabling me to begin my next: 'No foreigners in the commonwealth of letters'. Above all, I am fortunate in a frequent correspondence with an inner circle of intimate friends.

With best wishes for Christmas and New Year

Harold & Jean

PS: Heath: minor ailments, top to toe: nothing disabling so far.

With best wishes for 1987 From Harold Brooks.

I do appreciate the number of *The Aligarh Journal* and have not forgotten that I hope to offer you an article on Blake and Jung.

Pillo (that eminent Blakean) and I had a happy reunion in London before she left.

The still is from my wife's production of *Love's Labour Lost,* 1986.

Harold F. Brooks

Dated: 15 January 1981

Dear Professor Ansari,

I appreciated your gift of *The Aligarh Journal of English Studies:* You have certainly attracted some good contributions and contributors. Among these last I was interested to see Piloo Nanavutty, whom I knew for a while long ago in Oxford. Could you favour me with her address?

With regard to your invitation to contribute, I can only say that should I find myself well something I want to place I shall remember that you would very likely be willing to publish it. I am afraid it would more probably be in the comparatively modern field – Shaw, Yeats, T.S. Eliot, Virginia Woolf for example, than on Shakespeare, but one never knows.

I cannot respond by sitting down to write something for your, because I have four books which in my 74th year I am trying to complete – 'Work while it is day. For the night cometh, when no man can work'. They have the chief claim on my hours for writing.

But I appreciate the invitation, and will bear the *Journal* and you in mind.

That was a pleasant contact me had in Stratford.

Cordially yours,

Harold F. Brooks

182, Mayfield Ed,
Edinburgh EH93AX
Scotland

Dated: 18 October 1977

Dear Professor Ansari,

For a considerable time I have been meaning to write and thank you for the *Aligarh Journal*, II. 1, which you kindly sent me, and I must apologize for my indolence!

It is an excellent number, well-balanced in scope and weight. You have got together an admirable set of papers and reviews – all on topics of importance on which the authors have something of value to say. It appeals to me especially because of my interest in methods of criticism, and in psychological study applied to poetry and drama.

I was very pleased to see my old friend Professor A. G. Stock still in the field with a notable study of Milton: yourself deeply engaged with *Macbeth,* and the two essays on Wordsworth, always one of my favourite poets; besides the perceptive exploration of Jane Austen's method.

I wish you every success in keeping the *Journal* going in these hard times.

Yours sincerely,

Geoffrey Bullough

Dated: 09 January 1979

Dear Professor Ansari,

Your kind request that I might write something for the *Aligarh Journal of English Studies* arrived a day or two ago, it proved very invigorating and distracting for I was working on an un-Shakespearean subject. Recalled by you to my proper function, I want to know what is the maximum number of words you want and when?

I think of an essay on the Country Side and Country People in Shakespeare's plays – whether all of them depends on your answer: Long query above. I have started with *Henry VI* & can select *ad lib* showing different approaches, from realistic to artificial pastoral. Nothing very now I fear.

I shall enjoy reading the latest issue of the *Journal,* as I usually do.

With best wishes for 1979.

Yours sincerely,

Geoffrey Bullough

Dated: 12 July 1979

Dear Professor Ansari,

Your letter reminding me of my offer came two weeks ago and has been on my conscience ever since. During this time I have written much of a short article (upto 6000 words) on *Shakespeare's Country Comedies*, in which I deal, first with two plays concerned with Country type humours – The sort of fun they got in tableaux (coarse jests about women & horseplay with seducers), & would no doubt enjoy in Stratford when Shakespeare was boy, as well as later when he got to London. The plays are, of course, *The Taming of a Shrew* and *The Merry Wives of Windsor.*

I proposed to compare this kind of fun with that of *As You Like It* where all is more sophisticated, and the courtier's view of the country and country folk is given. In addition I hope to include a brief note of *Love's Labours Lost* as a country play with country setting – or alternatively I might consider A *Midsummer Night's Dreams* and its 'rural supernatural' and its 'village workman.'

I hope to finish it this week but alas, nowadays my typing is very slow, so I may not send it off to you until towards the end of next week.

Is this too late for your needs?

Yours sincerely,

Geoffrey Bullough

Flat 1b
4, Gellsland Road
Edinburgh

Dated: 22 February 1984

Dear Professor Ansari,

Your letter and its enclosure about the proposed Commemorative Volume was forwarded to my new address this morning. My husband, Geoffrey Bullough, died suddenly 2 years ago. He had had a slight stroke from which he fully recovered and was working in libraries up to the last moment.

He would have been only too ready to agree to your request for an article on some aspect of Shakespearian Studies.

When the *Aligarh Journal of English Studies* came I should have let you know of Geoffrey's death but there has been so much to do closing our big house and removing to a small flat that I did not write although I very much enjoyed the *Aligarh Journal*. I send you my good wishes

Yours sincerely

Margaret Bullough

Allegheny College
Department of English
Meadville,
Pennsylvania 16335

Dated: 04 December 1984

Dear Professor Ansari,

Forgive me for having taken so long to reply to your letter of August 6. It reached here while I was abroad; and when I returned, it lay at the bottom of a stack of mail that had accumulated during the summer. Only when I heard from James Ogden a month ago that you were trying to get in touch with me did I go back to that stack of mail and find your letter. Thus, with apologies, and if it is not too late, I shall tell you what papers Professor Nosworthy left that may be publishable.

There is, alas, virtually nothing he wrote on Shakespeare that can readily be published. His best work on Shakespeare has already appeared in journals; the most recent, an essay on *Macbeth* that appeared posthumously in a book called *Mirror up to Shakespeare* (University of Toronto Press, 1984). His unpublished Shakespeare material is for the most part very old and not of such quality (he may well have abandoned it).

I have evidence, however, that he was planning and well along on a book on Tennyson. I have three or four essays (or chapters) on Tennyson's poetry that I would guess he wrote within the last ten or twelve years. He never mentioned this project to me, but the chapters are quite polished. They are now in the hands of one of my colleagues, a specialist in Romantic and Victorian poetry, who has promised to tell me whether, with some revision, any of the chapters might be publishable as individual essays. Would you be interested in looking at one for your journal? If so, please let me know, and I shall forward the best one – if my colleague deems any of them worthy enough to honor Professor Noswothy's memory – to you.

Yours sincerely,

James C. Bulman

Dated: 01 March 1985

Dear Professor Ansari,

Please forgive me for having taken so long to get back to you about Professor Nosworthy's essays on Tennyson. In fact, my colleague who is a Victorian specialist has just returned the essays to me, with the following assessment.

None of the essays is very recent (all of them are undated and without notes); and as none seems to take account of scholarship written in the 1970's (beginning with Christophre Ricks's book), it's probably safe to assume that Nosworthy wrote them in the 1960's. Of the four essays, one in particular is quite original and stands up well, even without consideration of recent scholarship. That essay concerns the possible influence that Mrs. Gaskell's story, *The Manchester Marriage,* had on Tennyson while he was composing *Enoch Arden*: Nosworthy makes a persuasive case and, as you know, his style is wittily readable. Nothing has been written about a connection between Gaskell and Tennyson.

Thus I offer this essay to you for your Journal. But it will need some revisions – some minor matters of style, and perhaps a more major cutting (in its present from, it is nearly thirty pages – too long, I suspect, for your purposes). I also would want to add some basic notes for reference. All this, I am afraid, will take me some time: but in the interests of giving you an essay that will do credit to Nosworthy, I feel that these revisions and notes must be done. If you would like me to revise the essay, please let me know and I shall get to it as soon as possible. Specify the approximate number of pages you would like as well. And if, in the mean time, you would like to look at a copy of the essay as it presently stands, I shall happily send one to you.

With best wishes and thanks for your patience, I am

Yours sincerely,

James C. Bulman

---

3 Clement Circle
Cambridge, Mass., 02138

Dated: 19 March 1968

Dear Mr. Ansari,

It was very kind and generous of you to send me a copy of your book. I am glad to congratulate you on the able accomplishment of a difficult task, difficult not only because Blake is what he is but because there is such a mountain of commentary. I have to confess that, among all the major English writers, Blake has always been – or at least the Prophetic Books have always been – my chief blind spot, so that I am not qualified to give anything like an adequate judgment of your exposition. So far as my limited knowledge and understanding go, it seems to me thorough, informed, and discerning, and it does much to place Blake firmly in his large context, both vertical and horizontal (if one may use such terms for his spiritual heritage and his doctrine in relation to that of his contemporaries). I am also prepared to accept your account of Blake because you have much to say that is good on authors whom I do know more or less well, Bacon, Milton, Wordsworth, and Coleridge. While I cannot go along with some particulars (such as your making Milton's God Calvinistic, whereas one main theme of *P.L.* is the repudiation of Calvinism), I think most of what you say about these writers is sound and valuable, and your commentary helps both to define their positions and to illuminate Blake's.

Again, my thanks and congratulations,

Sincerely yours,

Douglas Bush

Dated: 04 November 1976

Dear Professor Ansari,

I thank you very much for the copy of *Essays on John Milton*, which reached me a few days ago. Along with thank I must offer congratulations to you and your fellow essayists on the fact that so many men, mainly from one university, can write on various Miltonic works and themes with so much scholarly knowledge and intellectual, imaginative, and sympathetic understanding and insight. It is indeed remarkable – however much in this century India (and Japan) have contributed to English studies – that the essayists in this book are able to enter so fully into poetry not merely of another language and culture but of a remote period which presents difficulties to people of English inheritance.

With thanks again, and all good wishes,

Sincerely yours,

Douglas Bush

Dated: 03 July 1977

Dear Professor Ansari,

The arrival of another issue of the *Aligarh Journal of English Studies* is an embarrassing reminder that I was very remiss in not returning thanks for a previous issue. I will not try to catalogue the jobs and miscellaneous worries that for months have caused me to fall behind in various obligations. I do appreciate your sending me these copies of the *Journal* and I congratulate you and your many authors on the variety and the quality of the contributions. It is remarkable that so many scholar-critics have such a sophisticated command of not merely English literature but of a body of Western criticism, that they can enter so understandingly into an alien culture through an alien language. If the situation were reversed, and Western scholar – critics were to deal with Indian literature, the results would be minimal in quantity and probably painful in quality for Indian readers. One infers that you have large numbers of students who respond to English literature; I hope so. At present, in this country, many students seem to be turning away from the humanities to directly vocational training; we hope of course that is a temporary phenomenon induced by economic pressures.

Again, my thanks and congratulations,

Sincerely yours,

Douglas Bush

Dated: 13 January 1979

Dear Professor Ansari,

I did not receive your letter of December 15 until two or three days ago.

I appreciate your cordial invitation to contribute to the Marvell issue of your journal, and I heartily wish that I could accept. However, I am almost 83, and my mind works at a snail's pace, so that anything I try to write – chiefly in the way of book reviews – takes far longer than it used to and is not as good as it ought to be. There is also the constant pressure of jobs thrust upon me, such as reporting on book manuscripts for publishers. Altogether, I have to say that a piece on Marvell, to be done in the next few weeks, is quite beyond me, I am very sorry.

I thank you for sending me your valuable journal, but you really should not continue. At my age, to speak of that again, I am reducing subscriptions – and donation – rather than extending either. I trust you will understand such a submission to fate (to use a grandiloquent phrase).

With thanks again and all good wishes,

Sincerely,

Douglas Bush

University of Arkansas
Pine Bluff, Arkansas 71601
Dr. Glen Bush
Assistant Professor of English

Dated: 19 April 1988

Dear Professor Ansari,

Enclosed you will find a copy of my paper "Mrs. Ramsey as The Archetypal Guide in Virginia Woolf's *To The Lighthouse*." I would sincerely appreciate it if you could review this work as a possible selection for your journal. Please feel free to make suggestions or comments. Your opinion is valued and respected.

Sincerely,

Glen P. Bush

Dated: 14 July 1988

Dear Professor Ansari,

Thanks you for your kind letters. I am looking forward to receiving your journal. As for your T.S. Eliot issue, I am honored that you have invited me to participate in this wonderful event. *Ash Wednesday* is an excellent poem; I hope that my submission will do both your journal and the poem justice. I plan to have my manuscript in your hands by September 1, 1988. If you have any further wishes, please feel free to contact me.

Once again, thank you for your consideration.

Sincerely

Glen P. Bush

Dated: 24 August 1988

Dear Professor Ansari,

I hope this letter finds you in good health. It is my pleasure to enclose my manuscript on Eliot's poem *Ash-Wednesday*. If for some reason, such as form, length, or content, you feel that this manuscript needs editing, please do not hesitate to send it back for the needed changes. However, if you feel that you or your staff can make the needed changes, please do so. I consider this an honor; therefore,e I want to make sure that the manuscript is exactly what you need and desire.

Thank you for your consideration, and good luck with your journal. I will appreciate hearing from you whenever it is convenient for you.

Sincerely

Glen P. Bush

Dated: 08 December 1988

Dear Professor Ansari,

Please, immediately, allow me to apologize for the lapse in communication. I sincerely hope that you have not been inconvenienced by my oversight. I did, however, notify several of my colleagues about your need for an Eliot article. I was under the impression that they, or at least one of them, would have contacted you before your last letter. I apparently was wrong. Since your last letter I once again informed them of your desire to help them. One person, Professor Cynthia Ho, is sending you an article on the *Four Quartets*. Hopefully you will be able to use this manuscript. Others may follow from other faculty members; however, I do strongly suggest that if you have other articles, please do not await these from my colleagues. We all appreciate favors, but no one should be expected to continually await only a possibility.

As for my Blake article, I will be sending that shortly. I must confess that I thought with the Eliot project, you would be too busy to read another article until the Eliot issue had gone to press. Since our current semester is winding down and we are entering the Christmas season, I will devote my holidays to re-evaluating the Blake manuscript. There are a few updated ideas that I would like to include. You know how that is, when something sits on your desk, it begins to accumulate ideas and a life of its own. Well, Blake, Ginsberg, and Ferlinghetti are alive and well – on my desk.

Once again, please accept my apology. I am looking forward to reading your successful Eliot issue.

May God's love shine on you and your family during this holiday season.

Sincerely,

Glen P. Bush

Dated: 2 May 1989

Dear Professor Ansari

I hope this letter finds you in good health and high spirits. I sincerely want to thank you for publishing my articles. I must admit that I am quite proud to say that your journal has accepted my manuscripts. As you requested, I have informed my associates of your desire to read their work. Hopefully, they will send you some interesting material.

Today, however, I have another request of you. If this request is considered unappropriate, please accept my immediate apologies. The request considers the Fulbright Scholar Program. Because of my research in archetypal criticism, mythology, and post-modernist literary criticism, I feel that India offers a most unique opportunity. Therefore, I am preparing to apply for a fellowship from the Fulbright Scholar Program. In the material provided by the Fulbright Program, it is mentioned that a contact with a local university is often helpful. Thus, I now turn to you. Do you see any chance that you might act as either a reference or liaison for me with either your university or another Indian university? Quite honestly, I am not familiar with the Indian university system. Once again, if this is an unreasonable request, please accept my apologies.

Although my major field of study is neither British nor Indian literature, in fact, it is American literature, my work in literary criticism, especially the archetypal, structuralist, and post-structuralist theories, have led me to study some non-Western influences on Western literature and literary theory. Due to this research, I feel that the Indian culture along with other Asian cultures have greatly influenced Western thought. Consequently, an opportunity to work and study in India would be a great opportunity to explore the literary and philosophical connections that exist between our two worlds.

Thank you for your time. Please feel free to ask any questions or add any suggestions that you may feel appropriate.

Sincerely,

Glen P. Bush

Dated: 26 September 1988

Dear Professor Ansari,

I received the copy of your new journal. Thank you very much. It looks like a fine journal, and I can assure you that I am very proud to be included in the first volume. Also, thank you for your kind letter concerning the Eliot manuscript. I am looking forward to seeing the second edition of your journal.

I understand how difficult it must be to establish a new journal, even when it is a sequel. You have my best wishes and prayers with this great undertaking.

If at sometime in the future you need another article on William Blake, I have a comparative paper on Blake and two American poets, Allen Ginsberg and Lawerence Ferlinghetti. From your journal I noticed that you are not particularly interested in American authors; thus, I can understand how this may limit your desire for this manuscript. Once again, I only suggest this to you in case you would like something like this for next year. Of course, I realize that you have many people submitting articles to you, and I do not want you to think that I am trying to flood you with my works. Please accept this offer as one founded in friendship and goodwill.

Once again, thank you for your wonderful correspondence. Stay in good health.

Sincerely,

Glen P. Bush

Dated: 19 August 1993

Dear Professor Ansari,

Thank your for writing! I must apologize for my lack of correspondence to you. However, I have not forgotten you. There have been numerous times over the past few years that I have urged worthy American and African scholars to submit their manuscripts to you. Some, I understand, have been published.

I received you letter requesting a Marlowe manuscript just this past week. For the past two years I have been living and teaching in Nigeria as a Fulbright lecturer and researcher. Thus, much of my correspondence has been slow both reaching me and in my responding. Another unfortunate aside to my recent return is that I am currently overwhelmed with academic and personal obligations. I am very, very sorry. I simply do not have the time to write a Marlowe manuscript. However, I have taken the initiative and am requesting my colleagues to respond. Hopefully you find suitable manuscripts from those that submit to you.

As my schedule stands, I will not begin writing any new manuscripts until after the first of the year. Currently, my area of interest is African, colonial, post-colonial, and Third World literatures. Also, I am working on orality, oral traditions, and colonialism's effect on indigenous oral traditions. If any of these topics are of interest to you, I would be happy to submit something to you in several months.

In any case, I sincerely hope your Marlowe issue is successful. Please, keep up the fine work you are doing and stay in good health!

Sincerely,

Glen P. Bush

Natalya Cadle

Dated: 05 June 1994

Mr. Asloob Ansari,

Please find enclosed my analysis of Shakespeare's use of sources when creating his play *Othello*. With the female characters as the central component, this paper studies the cultural influences which may have affected Shakespeare's modification of the original sources, and Shakespeare's attempt to change society's attitudes concerning women in the Elizabethan society. You can reach me at the following address and phone number:

1810 Costley Mill Road
Conyers, GA 30208
(404) 483-2517

Thank you for your time and consideration.

Natalya Cadle

Prof. Wolfgang Clemen
8207, Endorf (Oberbayern)
Hohamer Weg 3

Dated: 2 January 1984

Dear Professor Ansari

I must apologize for the delay in answering your letter of 8.11.1983 asking me to contribute an article on *King Lear*. I am very sorry that I cannot accept your kind invitation because of several other obligations which keep me busy. May I express my admiration for the fine achievement shown by the *Aligarh Journal of English Studies*? I was very glad to receive the special *Hamlet* number.

With my best wishes for the New Year.

Your sincerely

Wolfgang Clemen

Dated: 20 May 1984

Dear Professor Ansari

I had been away for some time and when I came again to the Shakespeare Library of Munich I found the two volumes of your periodical which you kindly had sent to me. Thank you very much indeed for this gift which will be of great interest to me. At present I am again absent from Munich, having gone to a mountain resort in Italy for a period of recovery which I badly needed.

With all good wishes,

Your sincerely,

Wolfgang Clemen

Dated: 3 March 1984

Dear Professor Ansari

Thank you very much for your letter of 23 February. It is with great regret that I must explain to you that I shall be unable to contribute an article to the Commemorative Volume in your honour which I very much welcome. However, because of my age and my unstable health I have given up any further publication of articles and essays. I am sorry that my reply thus is bound to be negative. But I am certain that a sufficient number of scholars will be pleased to prepare a contribution, as your work and your high reputation is well known in Europe too.

With my best wishes,

Your sincerely,

Wolfgang Clemen

Dated: 12 October 1984

Dear Professor Ansari

I have just received Vol. 9, 1984 number 1 of *The Aligarh Journal*. Thank you very much indeed for sending me this interesting publication which again contains important essays and reviews concerning Shakespeare. I am looking forward to reading this number before long. It was kind of you to have remembered my name although I retired from the University ten years ago.

With all good wishes,

Yours sincerely,

Wolfgang Clemen

Dated: 11 November 1986

Dear Professor Ansari

Thank you very much indeed for sending me No. 7 vol. 10 of your *Aligarh Journal*, which arrived yesterday. I was pleased to find your stimulating and interesting essays on D.H. Lawrence's *Women in Love* in this volume.

With all good wishes and kindest regards

Yours sincerely,

Wolfgang Clemen

Dated: 26 November 1985

Dear Professor Ansari

It is with great pleasure that I received today *The Aligarh Journal of English Studies*. It contains again interesting and important contributions some of them by people known to me. I am looking forward to reading them and wish to thank you warmly for your kindness which I appreciate.

Yours sincerely

Wolfgang Clemen

The University of Liverpool
4 Park Road
West Kirby
Wirral L48 4DW

Dated: 2 July 1997

Dear Professor Ansari,

Many thanks for sending me the *Aligarh Critical Miscellany* that contains my review. I should say, by the way, that when I wrote the review, I was not clear as to which journal was to print it: hence my praise of your own (here reprinted) piece was entirely disinterested. It's good to have the magazine.

And not least because I was touched to see that the circumstances surrounding the publication of the review were the subject of Kenneth's last letter to you. Kenneth was very encouraging about my *Sudden Shakespeare* and I was moved to see my name in that letter of his for purely personal reasons.

Thank you for sending me the magazine,

With good wishes,

Dr. Philip Davis

Brown University
The Library
Providence
12, Rhode Island

Dated: 05 September 1966

John Hay Library

Dear Dr. Ansari

I have been reading your *ARROWS OF INTELLECT* with keen interest. I believe that you have established the philosophical and religious background of Blake's thought more clearly than any previous scholar. Blake no longer can be treated as a vague dreamer out of touch with reality.

Congratulations!

Sincerely yours,

S. Foster Demon

Dated: 12 December 1974

Dear Professor Ansari,

Thank you very much for sending me your impressive book on William Blake and the Imagination. It looks like a very considerable contribution to the subject, and I am sure my daughter will enjoy it very much as I hope to myself.

It was a great pleasure meeting you in Mussori.

With very kind regards and the hope that we may meet again.

Yours sincerely,

Richard Ellmann

Dated: 12 September 1982

Dear Professor Ansari,

Thank you for your letter of 30 August. I am grateful for your sending me copies of your Journal during the last several years.

It would not be possible for me to write an article on *Finnegan's Wake,* much as I should like to do so. But there may be something I could send you, on Joyce's religion and politics, for example, which might do. Let me know if you would like that.

All good wishes,

Richard Ellmann

The New Dark Public Library
Astor, Fenox and Tilden Foundation
Fifth Avenue and 42nd Street
New York

Dated:

Dear Sir,

Will you kindly send me a review copy of the book listed below? As chairman of the committee which edits the Selective and Critical Bibliography of the Romantic Movement, published annually in *English Language Notes* (September Supplement), I will see that it is forwarded to the appropriate critic – reviewer and that you are supplied with two copies of the review or notice when published. (N.B.: This Bibliography was published in *Philological Quarterly* through 1964.)

Your including this committee on your regular list for review of all books in English or Continental European and Latin American ROMANTICISM will be appreciated.

Arrows of Intellect: A Study in William Blake's Gospel of the Imagination, Asloob Ahmad Ansari.

Sincerely,

David V. Erdman

Dated: 16 July 1968

Dear Professor Ansari,

A copy of your *Arrows of Intellect* did finally reach me, just in time for a quick examination and very brief notice in the *Romantic Bibliography*, now in the press. I am sorry for this but felt it better not to wait another year. I look forward to a more leisurely reading, later.

It is too bad that transportation from India is so hazardous that the first copy you mailed failed to reach me. I would like to pay a share of this cost and enclose a check for your reimbursement.

Cordially yours,

David V. Erdman

Robert N. Essick
1379 2a Salona Drive
Attedena, Calif 91001

Dated: 15 February 1990

Dear Professor A.A. Ansari,

I would very much like to purchase one copy of the special William Blake issue of your journal, *Aligarh Critical Miscellany*, December 1989 (vol. 2, no. 2) Please send to my home address, given above, via air mail. I can pay with either a cheque in U.S. dollars or in British pounds payable at a London bank. Please indicate which you prefer, or if some other payment procedure would be better.

Thank you for your kind attention to my request.

Yours sincerely,

Robert N. Essick

R.A. Foakes
Department of English
University of California
Los Angeles, California

Dated: 6 February 1984

Dear Professor Ansari,

Your letter of 22 December has been forwarded on from England to me here, where I am now teaching. You have indeed been most kind in sending on to me copies of your journal, and I will try to contribute to it, but just now you catch me when I have a pile of exams to mark, and an essay to complete for a collection honouring the editors of the Revels plays (the general editors I mean), and this must be sent in March. You don't say when you aim to publish your issue on *Lear*, but I expect it is already too late for that. Can you tell me what your plans are for issues forthcoming over the next year or year and a half? – If I have enough notice, I should be able to do something.

With very best wishes,

Yours sincerely,

R.A. Foakes

Victoria College
Toronto 5

Dated: 18 August 1965

Dear Mr. Ansari,

Thank you very much for your book on Blake, which I have been reading with great interest. It seems to me a comprehensive and very central study of Blake's Myth. Such things as Blake's conception of imagination, the attack on Locke, the realization that Locke, Newton, and Bacon are "states" rather than individuals, the fact that Blake is both revolting against and attached to his own time, are all essential to the understanding of Blake, and all of them are dealt with here with great lucidity. I like the chapter on Wordsworth and Coleridge, which deals very well with the tricky problem of cultural analogy where there is no question of direct influence. You show a very unusual grasp of the three long poems, which most commentators on Blake skip over or avoid. Your book is a genuine contribution to the scholarship not merely of Blake but of the whole Romantic period.

With best wishes and renewed thanks.

Your sincerely,

Northrop Frye
Principal

Dated: 18 August 1968

A.A. Ansari
7 Zainul Abedin Road
Muslim University, Aligarh

Dear Mr. Ansari,

Thank your very much for your book on Blake, which I have been reading with great interest. It seems to me a comprehensive and very central study of Blake's Myth. Such things as Blake's conception of imagination, the attack on Locke, the realization that Locke, Newton, and Bacon are "states" rather than individuals, the fact that Blake is both revolting against and attached tohis won time, are all essential to the understanding of Blake, and all of them are dealt with here with great lucidity. I like the chapter on Wordsworth and Coleridge, which deals very well with the tricky problem of cultural analogy where there is no question of direct influence. You show a very unusual grasp of the three long poems, which most commentators on Blake skip over or avoid. Your book is a genuine contribution to the scholarship not merely of Blake but of the whole romantic period.

With best wishes and renewed thanks,

Yours sincerely,

Northrop Frye,
Principal

University of Toronto
Massey College
4 Devonshire Place
Toronto, Ontario
M5S 2E1

Dated: 16 August 1976

Dear Professor Ansari,

Thank you very much for the Journal which shows a great variety of interests and a quite unusual range of scope. There is a great deal that interested me particularly, such as the Blake articles and the one on symbolism.

I wish very much that I could contribute to the Journal, but my desk is piled so high with previous commitments that it does not look like a physical possibility.

With best wishes,

Yours sincerely,

Northrop Frye

Dated: 02 March 1984

Dear Professor Ansari,

Thank you very much for your letter and invitation. It would be a great honour to be included in the proposed Commemorative Volume in your honour, and I wish very much that I could contribute an article on some aspect of Shakespearian Studies. The trouble is that my writing schedule for the foreseeable future is already so full, that it is really physically impossible for me to take on anything further. I am very sorry about this, and would certainly be more cooperative if I could.

Yours sincerely,

Northrop Frye

University of Durham
School of English
Elvet Riverside,
New Elvet, Durham

Date: 02 November 1989

Dear Professor Ansari,

A colleague here, Dr. Derek Todd, has just passed on to me a copy of your *Aligarh Journal of English Studies*, Vol. 11 (1986), no. 1 to show me Piloo Nanavutty's piece on a previously unpublished Blake drawing for the *Divine Comedie*. The essay described the drawing as reproduced here for the first time-but, alas, in Dr. Todd's copy it is not produced. Were you able to reproduce it in fact, and if so do you have a copy containing this reproduction? If so I would be very grateful if you could send one. (Since I see that you write about Blake yourself I enclosed an advert for my next book, for information.)

Yours sincerely,

David Fuller

Dated: 04 January 1990

Dear Professor Ansari,

Thank you for your note about the *Aligarh Journal of English Studies*. I am sorry there was no illustration: I would like to see it. But I can follow up Piloo Nanavutty's reference. I am glad to hear of your new journal too: I look forward to the copy you mention. I am sorry that I can't ask Routledge (who have now taken over Croom Helm) to send you a copy of my *Blake's Heroic Argument*. Though the leaflet I sent you describes it as 'new' this was just the only information leaflet I had: actually it came out in December 1987, so they have closed the review list. But I am grateful for the offer.

Looking forward to your *Miscellany*.

With best wishes,

Yours sincerely,

David Fuller

University Degli Studi Director Trieste
Facolta Director Lettere E filsofia
Institute, Director Filologia GErmanica
34123 Trieste
Via Dell'Universita 7- Tel. 301010

Dated: ____________

Dear Professor Ansari

I do hope you are keeping well. It is a long time since I've heard from you. Please forgive the delay in sending the Spender article, but we have had problems in the university regarding contracts and my academic work has got behind. I hope to hear from you soon.

With best wishes,

Yours sincerely,

Gabinelle

St. Hilda's College
Oxford OX4 1DY
Switchboard

Dated: 08 June 1991

Dear A.A. Ansari,

Your package has just this minute arrived and I wanted to write at once to say how kind of you to send me a copy of *The Critical Miscellany* and also of the interesting Eliot issue of 1988. I liked the commitment to 'sensitivity of response' and 'responsibility of judgement' and look forward to reading the articles.

With all good wishes for future of the Journal.

Your sincerely,

Syndal Garden

Dated: 12 June 1991

Dear Mr. Ansari,

Thank you for the letter (which arrived this morning) with its very kind words about *Eliot's*. I have just done two articles on Eliot (Eliot and Women, for a new collection ed. By Ronald Bush, and 'The American Eliot' for a collection to be edited by Edward Lobb in Toronto) and do not feel at the moment, but I have anything fresh to say which does not mean there is my dearth of fresh admiration in reading Eliot-enough I teach the poetry nearly every term, there is always renewed interest (perhaps because the students here bring such a strong response to it).

If something does stir, I will remember your suggestion and thank you for asking me. At the moment I am doing a non-academic book: a memoir of three women from my South African past, who died young. It is called *SHARED LIVES* and will be published in England by Bloomsbury.

With all good wishes for the continued excellence of your Journal.

Your sincerely,

Syndal Garden

Mythe House
12 Mill Street
Eynaham, Oxford

Dated: 13 June 1977

Dear Professor Ansari,

I feel very guilty at not having acknowledged the two prior numbers you sent to me of *Aligarh Journal of English Studies*. I have been much occupied with proof of a book, two articles & with journeys abroad lecturing and I am afraid my desk became piled with books & journals put aside to read.

I have now spent a morning reading the two issues you sent me with pleasure and interest. I was particularly impressed by the reviews, which in some ways are more important in a journal than original articles. I was particularly impressed by Mr. Usmani's very cogent and discriminating review of David Wardi's book on Eliot, though I do not mean by singling this not to under-value his article on Dante and Eliot in the second volume. I was also pleased at the praise you gave to Murray Ruskin's book on Dante. I don't think myself its funeral thesis convincing – I am not happy by all purpose explanations of everything that happen in period, but I thought he said excellent & illuminating things on many of the poems.

With all best wishes for the success of your journal and apologies for delay in reading it.

Yours sincerely

Helen Gardener

Dated: 15 January 1979

Dear Professor Ansari

Thank you for your letter of 15 December which only arrived this weekend. I am sorry to be unable to send you an article on Marvell by the end of February. I am very busy at present. I really have nothing to say about Marvell who I feel is in need of wholesome reflection.

Yours,

With regards,

Helen Gardener

The British Library

Dated: 30 July 2004

Dear Ansari,

Thanks for the lovely, very interesting journal you sent, received just before I left New York for the U.K. I saw a fine whibit, the Silk Road, as the British Library. This image comes from that exhibit, which displayed manuscripts from the Hindu, Muslim, Nestorian, Manichean, Zoroastrian, Buddhist religions, all found in caves and graves on the Silk Road.

Hope this finds you well?

Affectionately,

(Gardiner)

---

5 Ferndale Rd.
Breuster

Dated: 25 June 2003

Dear Asloob,

I am very sorry indeed I did not reply sooner. I have been feeling very exhausted – perhaps it is my age, I'm turning 65 – and find it difficult to write. But I can assure you of this – that you have been in my thoughts and prayers. I have prayed heartily that you will not go blind, and I feel assured that my prayer will be answered. I prayed for you yesterday 24 June – a special novena to St. Joseph, foster-father of Jesus to intercede for you with God, that your eyes may be saved.

Yes, I have received your daughter's splendid and learned book. I am impressed with her range of scholarship. You are right to be very proud of such a daughter. Good children are one of the greatest blessings in life, after good parents. I married late and have no children by God's will, but I have adopted many people into my spiritual family and I pray for these each day. Asloob, be assured that you too will be remembered daily, even if I do not write often. Bon courage, have no fear. This terrible ordeal will, I trust, end in a safe harbor.

I'm leaving for England on July 7 – probably the last time I go there, one never knows. I'll send you a message from Oxford.

Affectionately

Anne Barbean Gardiner

PS: I am mailing you a journal that comes out as an annual volume. I have a little essay in it, but your daughters may find the other piece of interest.

University of Oxford
University Laboratory of Physiology
Oxford

Dated: 18 February 1987

Dear Professor Ansari

Thank you so much for your letter about Sir Walter Raleigh. He was my father's predecessor as Merton Professor of English literature here; and what has happened is that Merton College has forwarded your letter to me as my father's namesake. In fact my father ceased to hold the chair in 1928 when he became President of Magdalene, and sadly he died in 1942.

There are a number of references to Walter Raleigh in my father's published letters and in a memoir of my father written by my mother; but I am afraid there are scattered remarks which would not be useful to you; and I have no unpublished material of my father's on the subject of Raleigh, even though I imagine he must have written somewhere about him (in fact I see from the D.N.B. article written by Nichol Smith that my father wrote in his honour in the Times Literary Supplement of 8 June 1922 – I do not have a copy of this). If *The Times* was willing, I should naturally be very happy for this to be reproduced. I know my father had a very great admiration for Raleigh.

May I offer you my best wishes for the success of your Project?

Yours sincerely

George Gordon

Dawson College
Selby Campus
350 Selby St., Westmount
Quebec, Canada H3Z 1W7

Dated: 15 September 1977

Dear Mr. Ansari

Thank you very much for your journal and your letter I have just received. I am very sorry that I took so long in sending you the article on Shelley, but it took me longer than I expected to cut down a longer paper into 15 pages. Finally, when I triumphantly handed it over to the secretary for typing, she returned my manuscript of 14 ½ pages as a 20 page long script. Since I do not want to spend another week on having it retyped, I send it to you in this form, hoping I did not cause too much trouble or aggravation with the delay and the longer format. (Typed properly, it should be 15 pages).

I would be very glad to hear your comments, and to see your work. I have just made my enquiry about your book on Blake at McGill on the telephone.

Looking forward to your reply.

With best regards,

Erika Gottlieb

Dated: 18 January 1978

Dear Professor Ansari,

It was with great pleasure that I received the December issue of your literary journal.

In the meantime, I got hold of the collection of essays on Wordsworth published by your Department in 1972, and was very much impressed by your discussion on the spots of time, particularly on your emphasis on the unusually intimate relationship between a down-to-earth, natural, and a transcendental, quasi-religious, dimension in Wordsworth's moment of epiphany. In a short analysis of Wordsworth's Sonnet on Westminster Bridge, I came to a very similar conclusion. It seems to me that this imperceptible leap into the numinous, not beyond, but somehow within the very centre of the natural event or object is the very essence of Wordsworth's often elusive magic.

Most recently, I also managed to get your *Arrows of Intellect* from the McGill University Library. It seems to be very popular, judging from the borrower's slip. They also keep a special copy of the book in their Blake collection. Your focus on Blake's reaction against the mechanical, 'scientific' concept of the universe is very illuminating, and I found your summary of Blake's vision of human Imagination conceptually comprehensive, and yet far more accessible than a number of other analyses I have read so far on this very complicated question.

Are you working on any other writer at present, or do you find that teaching takes up too much of your time during the year? I have not been too active during this first term, although in September I received a Canada Council grant for the publishing of my book on Romantic tragedy ("*Darkness Deepening Darkness*": *The Romantic Poet as Tragedian* is the working title). Negotiations with publishers are also far more time-consuming than I expected.

Due to the rather unfortunate political situation in Quebec, our family is planning a move to Toronto-my husband has just been re-located, and I will follow with our two children at the end of this academic term. Professionally this may mean a considerable setback, because academic positions are rather scarce in general. On the other hand, I decided to become somewhat more adventurous, and work on certain topics in Comparative Literature. For example, I am very much interested in the undercurrent of significant unifying themes in England and on the Continent in the Romantic period, and in the closer connection between the Metaphysical poets, Donne in particular, and the Baroque on the Continent.

I hope you and your family are well, and we shall keep exchanging news and views about literary events. By the way, I have just received Richard Wordsworth's announcement about the Eighth Annual Summer Conference, with the speakers' list. Except for four or five, the speakers are all familiar from last year. Are you planning another trip in the near future? Many thanks again for the journal.

Looking forward to your letter,

With warmest regards,

Erika Gottlieb

Dated: 21st January 1978

Dear Professor Ansari,

I have barely mailed my last letter to you, when I received your very generous gift of the Donne and Milton Essays, and of the second number of the *Aligarh Journal* of *English Studies.* I find the range of your interests – Macbeth, Caliban, Donne's Secular and Divine Poems, Milton's *Paradise Lost*, not to mention your comprehensive analysis of Blake's works – really extraordinary. I shall also recommend to the Librarian of McGill to order these excellent anthologies, since they are not yet represented in their collection.

I am particularly interested in your Donne essay, since I concentrated on Donne for my Ph.D comprehensives, and analyzed his "Nocturnal" quite extensively for my Master's thesis on the metaphor of polar opposites. As a matter of fact, the title of my thesis was a Donne quote, "The long-short Progress". I am still fascinated by that characteristic imagery of the mystic which, I believe, can be recognized by the pattern of a mystical dialectic, or, in Donne's case, a pattern aimed at achieving a mystical resolution of contradictions (in his various poems, be they dealing with the themes of secular or divine love). Therefore, I very strongly agree with you that the traces of religious sensibility – I would say, the very characteristic image pattern of a mystical sensibility – are recognizable also in many of his secular poems.

There is another point in your Donne essay which strikes an extremely resonant chord: you point out the very interesting connection between the little world of the lover's rooms, the poet's own world, and the huge, and threateningly expansive outside world of the scientist and the explorer, the connection and contradiction between the micro and macrocosm. The first effect of this contrast is more obvious. The poet is frightened by the new, changing and yet uncategorized wider world, and would impulsively, and intensely, concentrate upon and withdraw into the subjective reality of the inner world. Yet, in addition to this, I feel that Donne's imagery often reveals something else besides such a psychological escape from the theological dimensions. Many of his poem (e.g the Anniversaries, & Nocturnall, Canonization, the Sun Rising, etc) use juxtaposition as a continuous device, to establish a series of contrasts, expansion reversed by contraction, contractions reversed by expansion again. The aim of this, I feel, is to reach a point in which the difference between the largest and the smallest horizons simply disappears, a point for the mystical coalescence of opposites. Whether or not this point is ever reached in Donne's poems, I feel that his tendency for the repeated juxtaposition between minuscule and majuscule reflects the pattern normally leading to, here, as it were the desire for, a final coalescence of opposites, for the coalescence between container and contained—I am not sure, whether I fully agree with your conclusion about the mystical experience as a communal, theological framework in La Corona and A Litanie. This, however, would be in accordance with H. Grierson, who felt that much of Donne's religious torment may be attributed to the fact of his conversion, that he had not received faith, like Herbert for example, without the pangs of a private, personal, intellectual decision forced upon him. This is, of course, possible also, but the mystery still remains: why did he accept the 'self-less', communal, liturgical resolution in poems like La Corona and A Litanie, and found it impossible to accomplish a similar resolution in the majority, and in some of the most characteristically Donne-like or self conscious sonnets of the divine poems?

Thank you very much, again, for your very kind gift, and I wish I could send you anything in return. I cannot tell you, how pleased I am to find the affinity between our directions, the whole metaphysical approach, and often even the analytical methods we follow to reach conclusions. Would you be interested in any of my works, indeed in any book, essay or manuscript, I would be very glad to send it to you.

With warmest regards,

Erika Gottlieb

Dated: 26 July 1978

Dear Professor Ansari,

Thank you very much for your letter of 5th of July. I am delighted to hear that you published my article, and would be very glad to receive a copy of your journal. I have moved recently to Toronto, and my address is:

2 Shouldice Court,
Willowdale, Ontario
M2L 2S4
Canada

I am presently working on the preliminaries of a work on the Romantic Image of Woman, and intend to apply for a research grant for the year of 1979. What with the move and the difficulties of the first summer in Toronto, it was simply out of the question to think about the Wordsworth Conference this year.

I hope you are doing well, and engaged in interesting literary tasks as usual.

Please excuse me for this short note – I hope our next communication will be in greater detail. Looking forward to your reply.

With best regards and many thanks for your note.

Erika Gottlieb

Dated: 12 October 1978

Dear Professor Ansari,

Thank you very much for the articles – it was very kind of you to send me so many copies. Your Marvell Seminar sounds very exciting, and I may have an article on the "Garden" (in terms of the meditative tradition) –Right now I am on some kind of professional leave of absence, teaching one course only (on World Literature) and working on the preliminaries of a book on the Romantic image of woman. Our move to Toronto has not been an easy one, and it will take some time to get settled.

Hoping that your work is progressing well, with best wishes.

Erika Gottlieb

PS: Should you be interested, I also have an analysis of Wordsworth's "Westminster Bridge", entitled "The Romantic Poet in Meditation", and a study on the paradox in Donne's "Nocturnal". The latter would need some more work, but I would be glad to send you whichever you are interested in.

With best regards,

Erika Gottlieb

Dated: 11 April 1981

Dear Professor Ansari,

Thank you very much for your kind letter – I am indeed delighted to have my book on Romantic Tragedy published, and gratified by your offer to review it.

Please accept this copy as token of my appreciation: both I and my colleagues are looking forward to the newest issues of *Aligarh Journal.*

With best regards,

Erika Gottlieb

Dated: 15 April 1983

Dear Professor Ansari,

Thank you very much for the extensive analysis of *Lost Angels of a Runied Paradise* in the *Aligarh Journal.* One can rarely hope for such a thorough and impartial approach to a book in a scholarly publication. Although the reception of the book was quite good both in Canada and in the U.S., I cherish Mr. Wiqar Husain's review more than all the others, both for the depth of critical insight and its open-minded approach.

Dear Professor Ansari, I hope you will forgive me for not having written much earlier to thank you and to wish you and the Journal a very successful new year. Unfortunately, I suffered a heavy loss in my family and it has taken me quite a while to catch up with my correspondence and get back to normal. Although my teaching load is quite heavy, I have started a work on George Orwell's *1984.* I should have a thirty page article, "Room 101 Revisited: The Consistency Between Political and Psychological Dimensions in *1984*" ready pretty soon.

I have also completed an essay, "Silence to Sound" about a very promising Canadian writer, Joy Kogawa, whose first novel, *Obesan,* is a perceptive comment on the Japanese – Canadian experience during World War II.

I would be glad to send you either or both articles, should you feel interested. It seems to me the question of *1984* will be re-examined with new interest in the next year.

Thank you again for the excellent review.

With best regards,

Erika Gottlieb

Dated: 15 July 1983

Dear Professor Ansari,

Thank you very for your very much kind letter of the 26th of June. I would be delighted to see "Room 101 Revisited" included in your April issue on Orwell.

The paper consists of 34 pages (including footnotes) and I sent it to you in full. Should you, for any reason, consider it too long for your purposes, would you please recommend cuts, or if you may run out of time, consider editing it, depending on the requirements of your special issue. (Needless to say, I would much prefer seeing the paper published as it is, since I feel that each individual aspect is instrumental in establishing the central statement for an over-all interpretation of the novel).

Last week we have seen some very fine productions of *Macbeth, Richard II,* and *As You Like It* at our annual Shakespeare Festival in Stratford, Ontario. Have you ever considered a tour including the American and Canadian performance of Shakespeare? You may find the various traditions and experiments illuminating. *Macbeth*, for example, was presented in some kind of an early, Anglo-Saxon setting: earth colours, sackcloth, furs, long braids, no adornments – none of the sharp definition and clear line of the blacks, greys and reds one traditionally associates with the play. *As You Like It,* on the other hand, was presented in the costumes of late 18th and early 19th century Europe, and it even included some *fin-de-siecle* Viennese music at the end. Also, both *As You Like it* and *Richard II* made allusions to evil in its contemporary political associations: The costumes of the Bad Duke's followers and of the forces of Bolingbroke were to remind the audience of the Gestapo or the KGB – quite an Orwellian reinterpretation of evil as the tyranny of the police state, – we have also seen *Blake*, a one-man dramatization of Blake's Life, at the same time: you would have enjoyed the tasteful combination of anecdote, personal letters, prophetic works, and the inspired rendering of some of the best known pieces from *Songs of Innocence and Experience.*

Should you decide on a North American trip at any time, we would be delighted if you could visit us in Toronto. I hope both you and your family are well.

With best regards,

Erika Gottlieb

Dated: 04 May 1984

Dear Professor Ansari,

Thank you very much for your gracious letter. It must have been indeed a most pleasant surprise to find out that you will be honoured by your colleagues with the publication of a volume of essays. I consider it a great privilege to participate in their project.

Unfortunately, I am not a Shakespeare scholar, and therefore I would like to clarify a few questions with you or with the editor. Would it be appropriate to deal with Shakespeare's influence on the Romantics, for example, with the connection between *King Lear* and *The Cenci?*

Should this approach be inappropriate to your focus, I may be able to write something on Shakespeare's Renaissance attitude to the Chain of Being, a somewhat ambivalent attitude I find particularly interesting in his comedies, e.g. in *The Taming of the Shrew*. It seems to me the source of humour may be located in the author's attitude to the fixed relationship between man and woman, that is, in his awareness of a fixed relationship which in the comic situation may turn upside-down temporarily. Since I have a rather heavy teaching load (20 hours/week) and a long academic year, I would not be able to get started before July or August, but I hope I could complete a short essay by the Fall.

Please let me know what you think about these areas of exploration. Thank you for thinking of me, and please accept my best wishes for this exciting project.

Sincerely yours,

Erika Gottlieb

Dated: 29 September 1984

Dear Professor Ansari,

Thank you for your last letter in which you remind me of the deadline for the article for the Shakespeare volume. As I have expected, I have just been able to complete it. I am sorry that the typing is not any better, but since I was pressed for time, I had no opportunity to have it done professionally.

As you probably have observed, this has been an extremely interesting year for Orwell scholars; I have been to several Symposia and heard some extremely thought-provoking arguments. I would very much like to continue my work on Orwell, and I have also started working on some books in Canadian literature. My teaching load is as heavy as ever, and it takes quite a bit of organization to go on with one's writing. I am very much looking forward to your memorial volume. Please let me know what you think of my paper, if you have the time.

With best wishes to you and your family,

Yours sincerely,

Erika Gottlieb

Dated: 11 July 1985

Dear Professor Ansari,

This is just a note to inquire about the stage reached in the publication of the commemorative volume. Since I have not heard from you since October, I was wondering whether you had any difficulties with the publication.

I hope you are well, and neither you nor your family has been affected by the unfortunate events of the last year.

Are you thinking of going on with your research and the editing of your journal after retirement? Should you plan to visit our part of the world, please let us know: we would be very glad to see you and your family.

In a few days we are going off to Stratford (a less than two-hour drive from Toronto) to see a few plays. *King Lear, Measure for Measure* and *Twelfth Night* are playing there at the moment. Another centre for theatre is Niagara-on-the Lake, also a short driving distance for us, the centre for the annual Shaw Festival. So, you see, Canada may have its own attractions for the traveller interested in theatre.

Apropos theatre. Have you had a chance to see the films on Gandhi and *Passage to India*? I would very much like to hear your opinion. Both are extremely attractive visually, but I felt something was missing nevertheless. For a student of E.M. Forster *Passage to India* may leave a great deal to be desired.

Hoping to hear from you soon,

With best regards,

Erika Gottlieb

Dated: 02 January 1986

Dear Professor Ansari,

I was sorry to hear that you have not received my Curriculum Vitae by the 17th of December. I sent it along with a note right after I had received your previous letter. Also, if I remember it correctly, it was sent by SPECIAL DELIVERY – I cannot understand the reason for the delay.

It was with great interest that I heard you were called back form your retirement. This must have been a difficult decision to make, once you have made up your mind to give up academic work. I hope, however, you also find it gratifying to continue your excellent work with the journal for another while.

I hope you find the following few lines satisfactory for the "bio-data" you required. Should you feel that more information is needed, I send along another copy of my CV for your perusal.

I am greatly looking forward to the Commemorative Volume.

Erika Gottlieb received her Ph.D. in English Literature from McGill University and she taught in the English Department: of McGill, Sir George Williams University, and Loyola College, and in the Humanities Department of Dawson College, all of them in Montreal. In 1981 she published a study on Romantic drama, *Lost Angels of a Ruined Paradise: Themes of Cosmic Strife in Romantic Tragedy.* She also published studies on the Metaphysical poets, and on Women's Studies, and in 1984 gave lectures on Orwell's major novel at a variety of Conferences in Canada and the United States. Currently she teaches in the English and Communications Division of Seneca College in Toronto.

Thank you for your Season's greeting – I also wish you and yours a very happy New Year.

Sincerely,

Erika Gottlieb

Dated: 22 May 1986

Dear Professor Ansari,

This is just a note to let you know that I am looking forward to the publication of the Commemorative Volume. In your last letter you mentioned the middle of February as the date of dispatch. Since I still have not received it, I was wondering, whether it could have gotten lost in the mail. Would you please let me know whether I should have received it by now.

I have received a sabbatical for the next term and hope to be able to work on my book on Orwell, and possibly also on an earlier study on the Romantic image of Woman. How are things going for you? Will you be teaching next years?

Hope to hear from you soon.

With best wishes,

Erika Gottlieb

King's College Library
Cambridge

Dated: 26 November 1979

Dear Professor Ansari,

I am very sorry that this has taken so much longer to prepare than I originally thought. I hope that it is not yet too late, though I realize that this may well be the case. But I think that the diary-entry, which is almost wholly unpublished, is one of the finest and most moving pieces of Forster's later years, and I hope you will agree that its publication in your special number of the *Aligarh Journal of English Studies* would be at least worth considering, now that you have it before you, as a replacement for the lost talk on Dickens.

As regards copyright, Dr. Parry has given me permission to authorize its publication, in the form in which I have prepared it, in your special number. Any question of further publication, or any question of publication in any different form from the enclosed (e.g. abridged or with different notes), must be referred back to Parry, of course. If you are unable to include it in your special number, and do not wish to use it elsewhere, perhaps would be so good as to return it, or alternatively, to keep it yourself for personal reference.

Dr. Rylands and Dr. Parry ask me to convey to you their warmest good wishes for the special number of the *Aligarh Journal of English Studies*, to which I join my own. I hope that Forster studies and the Department of English in Aligarh will go from strength to strength:

Needless to say, if you have a spare copy of the *Aligarh Journal of English Studies* on Forster, whether or not you are able to use the little piece we have sent you, we should be delighted to receive a copy for a permanent home in our Archives.

Sincerely yours,

Dr. M.A. Halls
Modern Archivist

Dated: 06 January 1981

Dear professor Ansari,

In checking through my correspondence for the past year I find no record of my having thanked you for sending me the copies of the *Aligarh Journal of English Studies* and off prints, which I received last autumn. If this is indicative that I did indeed neglect to do so, then I am profoundly sorry. I was delighted to receive them, and I am most grateful that you should have sent me so generous a number of off prints, which have turned out to be most useful; I have distributed them where they are most needed and deserved amongst my colleagues.

The E.M. Forster special number was most impressive, and it must be a matter of great contentment that you should have been able to bring together such a splendid and valuable set of articles.

I hope that the *Aligarh Journal of English Studies* will continue to flourish in the New Year, and henceforward.

Very best wishes for the New Year.

M.A. Halls

Modern Archivist

E. Hanquart
University de Paris IV
Paris Cedex 05

Dated: 6 March 1979

Dear Professor Ansari

Thank you very much for your letter which arrived in due course. No, I had not forgotten our meeting in Jaipur, how could I have!

I was myself quite sorry to miss the Aligarh Forster meeting, but as I told you it winded exactly with my return to France. Anyhow I heard about it from Dr. and Mrs. Beer whom I saw at Cambridge last month.

Here is my contribution to the Forster Number of *The Aligarh Journal of English Studies*; I am afraid it is slightly shorter than what you expected, but for the time being I could not write on another subject, and this one could not be enlarged.

I am looking forward to hearing from you and send my best wishes for the journal.

Yours sincerely,

E. Hanquart

Professor D.W. Harding
Ashbocking Old Vicarage
Ipswich
England

Dated: 26 December 1988

Dear Professor Ansari,

Your letter has just reached me and I must answer at once because unfortunately I cannot accept your kind invitation. In the small amount of time I have for writing I am committed to finishing another piece of work and in any case I should have nothing more to say about the Eliot plays than I put in my early essay. But thank you for asking me; and my good wishes for the sources of such an interesting issue of your journal.

It was good to have my thoughts taken back to Anwar Ansari, whom I remember with respect and affection.

Your sincerely,

D.W. Harding

Dated: 26 April 1989

Dear Professor Ansari,

Congratulations on your very impressive Eliot Centenary issue of the *Critical Miscellany*. I do very much appreciate your kindness in sending me a copy. I have at present only skimmed through most of the essays, though I have read more carefully your study of *The Family Reunion* and greatly enjoyed it. There seems to have been some belittlement of that play (perhaps encouraged by Eliot himself) but I remember how important it was when it was first produced. You deal convincingly with the unsatisfactory quality of the conclusion.

The general discussion of Eliot's work has, I suppose inevitably, become largely religious and follows it into areas foreign to me. There may be some danger of forgetting how important the earlier work was before any religious concern became explicit or focused on Christianity. I cannot forget its importance to me when, under I.A. Richards' influence, I first met it as an undergraduate in 1926.

With best wishes and many thanks.

Your sincerely,

D.W. Harding

Dated: 02 November 1989

Dear Professor Ansari,

I would have written more promptly but I was very busy when the *Critical Miscellany* arrived. I am most grateful to you for sending it and I have now been able to make a beginning at it with great interest. The essay on stage versions of *Measure for Measure* was valuable – to me very informative and leaving me convinced that Shakespeare was vastly more interesting than the directors who exhibit their personalities so remorselessly through the modern productions. Present day acting seems to me to be at a very high level and on the whole willing to put itself at the service of the author, but the productions are too often pseudo-creative affectations.

I want to re-read your own deeply seeking and penetrating account of 'Little Gidding'. I have a blind spot for religion and for philosophy, and this, of course, creates difficulties for me with religious poets, whether Eliot, Hopkins or Donne – or Herbert – for all of whom – I have great and humble admiration. Although the religious beliefs and the philosophical conceptions are foreign to me, I cannot feel that I am altogether cut off from the experience – at least a great part of it – that finds expression in these poets' work, even when they are dealing explicitly with matters of their faith. It would be altogether too arrogant to claim that they are only using a different idiom to convey experience that I can share, and yet there is some way in which a non-believer and a non-philosopher can feel humanly at one with them. But how to argue that position convincingly I do not know.

I look forward to reading more in this issue of the *Miscellany* with great interest but meanwhile I want just to send you my thanks and my congratulations on producing it.

Yours sincerely,

D.W. Harding

Dated: 15 January 1990

Dear Professor Ansari,

I very much appreciate your kindness in sending me the Blake issue of the *Miscellany*. I am writing at once without having time to do more than glance-with a great deal of interest at the topics covered, because I have to go into hospital tomorrow for an operation which is not very formidable but will keep me inactive for some time. In the meantime I send my best wishes for the continuing rigour of the *Miscellany* and for your own satisfaction in the work it must entail.

Yours sincerely,

D.W. Harding

Department of English
University College of Swansea
Singleton Park
Swansea SA2 8PP
W. Glam. (UK)

Dated: 30 May 1987

Dear Professor Ansari,

Many thanks for your news that a copy of the *Aligarh Journal of English Studies* is being sent here with my article on 'The Theosophical Preoccupations of Blake and W.B. Yeats'. This has not yet arrived but I shall look forward to receiving it and hope the information and views there may be of help to your readers in their work.

I should be pleased to offer another contribution to your Journal, but doubt if this could arrive at Aligarh by this August. But for a later issue this could be quite possible.

Would you be interested in a discussion of Blake's religious ideas? I could expand on any early broadcast of mine called 'What did Blake Believe?'

I am hoping to get a contract for another book following *Hidden Riches* to help the general reader to get into this difficult work. I am hoping to get some encouragement from Dr. Northrop Frye who is paying a visit to London.

Many thanks, again, for your continuing interest.

Yours sincerely,

Desiree Hirst

Dated: 21 June 1987

Dear Professor Ansari,

Many thanks for your letter. This is just to confirm that the copy of *The Aligarh Journal of English Studies* has arrived, together with all the off prints. The chance of reading the other contribution is much appreciated.

I shall try to get a copy of my article on 'What did Blake Believe? to you as soon as possible after August.

With all good wishes.

Desiree Hirst

Dated: 17 December 1987

Dear Professor Ansari,

Enclosed is a copy of the sequel to my earlier article on William Blake's Belief, which I have titled 'The Problems Posed by William Blake's Religious Position', closed which I hope gets deeper down to some of the puzzling aspects of Blake's doctrine.

Some points have been taken up from the first article but I hope it does not contain too much repetition. It is a big subject to get round but I have tried to be fairly balanced. My plan is to work further on a book on the subject and I am still approaching publishers about this.

Another, more modern poet and artist, a friend of Kathleen Raine's, is David Jones, of Welsh extraction. He died over ten years ago, but was regarded by T.S. Eliot, his publisher, as one of the great figures of this century. I have been looking at his achievement for BBC Television, in the hope of a programme on his assessment of the present day situation. He was very critical of the increasing materialism and loss of tradition. Perhaps your readers might like to know more of this remarkable figure?

Yours sincerely,

Desiree Hirst

PS: Many thanks for sending on a copy of the very interesting last number of Journal.

Dated: 12 June 1988

Dear Professor Ansari

Many thanks for the copy of the collection on Professor Raleigh. I did not know that he had been at Aligarh University.

Are the Blake articles likely to be out in your Journal soon? I am being asked to list my publication which is why it comes to my mind. Still struggling with publishers over my project for a book on Blake's beliefs. Routledge tried but have put me on to a new imprint called 'crucible'. Piloo Nanavutty has found things disappointing too. It seems a bad time in the publishing world. Important to help literary standards promoted.

With all good wishes.

From

Desiree Hirst

Dated: 07 December 1989

Dear Professor Ansari,

Many thanks for the copy of Vol. 1 No. 2 of the *Aligarh Critical Miscellany*. No doubt my other Blake article will appear later? You may have heard this new firm, the Campbell Press, have given me contract for a revised edition of *Hidden Riches* & a study of *The Development of William Blake's Thought*. Have not heard whether Piloo Nanavutty has had any offer from them?

I did suggest this.

With best wishes for the next decade.

Desiree Hirst

5, Newton Villas,
Mumbles, Swansea 5A3 4SS
UK

Dated: 01 August 1993

Dear Professor Ansari,

Many thanks for your kind invitation to contribute to the Christopher Marlowe number of the *Critical Miscellany* for December, 1993.

I should be glad to send an article by the first week in December, as you ask, but I ought to explain that as I am not expert on Drama or on biography of the period, what my contribution is likely to cover will be a study of the impact of the Renaissance scene on Marlowe's personality and work, in a more general way. His role as a Renaissance Man, yet one still influenced by older attitudes from the Medieval background. Some comparison of his work with aspects of Shakespeare's would seem to be in order.

I hope this would be suitable for this special number. Just lately I have offered a paper for a collection from Uppsala University in Sweden on the background to a work on the Kabalah arriving at the Bodleian Library as a copy of an earlier MS from France and ultimately Spain. This has some bearing on questions on the climate of Thought of the time. So having been considering Renaissance attitudes, perhaps I could contribute something relevant to the problems of Marlowe's life and work in this very general way?

You may like to know that I am still researching for a sequel to my Blake source study *Hidden Riches* and will let you know what comes of this.

With kind thanks for the copies of the journal so regularly sent on here.

Yours sincerely,

Desiree Hirst

Dated: 16 January, 1994

Dear Professor Ansari,

Thank you for your letter of January 3rd. As you ask, I can extend the article on Marlowe and the Renaissance, though I cannot re-write it.

I am aware that articles for the *Miscellany* are usually longer than this one was, but I have been under great pressure and have to be very careful as I am dealing part of the time with other people's research.

Still, I shall do my best to let you have the extended version by the middle of March. Meanwhile I shall look forward to the copy of the next issue which you promise.

Yours sincerely,

Desiree Hirst

Dated: 23rd April 1994

Dear Doctor Ansari,

My last paper was sent off from here mid-March, but a better kind of postage seems to be needed. Another copy will be sent early next week by registered post and this seems to be the best I can do. There is no swift-air postage to India, apparently.

But if you can get another paper to put into the journal quickly it may be worth waiting for mine, as the contribution to the Forum on Renaissance Studies held at Uppsala University in 1993 will be in print by this June and reference with more detail to my research might make my paper for your *Miscellany* more interesting. The last paper will be sent in any case to save time.

It must be very trying for you if there is this trouble.

Yours sincerely,

Desiree Hirst

Dated: 25th April 1994

Dear Professor Ansari,

Here is the further copy of my article for the *Miscellany* number which you have been kept waiting for. The first copy did go off in good time to arrive by mid-March and I hope this registered postage will keep this one safer. I did not keep a receipt of the date when the last one was sent, unfortunately, but it ought to have arrived well before the end of March at the outside.

As I mentioned in my last letter of April 24th, if you can find another paper to put in soon to avoid more delay, the paper on my research for the Renaissance Forum held at Uppsala University in 1993 will be in print by June. The material there might add further interest.

I hope something can be arranged for the immediate future in any case.

Yours sincerely,

Desiree Hirst

Dated: ....

Dear Professor Ansari,

Thank you for your letter which reached me just before I went into hospital. By now I hope you have received my article on 'William Blake's Beliefs', but this was assembled in rather a hurry to get it off to you and it could do with some corrections. As I explained in my covering letter of September 20th, I would really like to follow this up to give a more general discussion of the significance of Blake's beliefs, after this rather factual account.

But enclosed now is a list of corrections which could make the present article clearer, if there is time to enter them; with page references.

If you can add any further references to Piloo Nanavutty's articles on Blake's Hindu allusions, I should be very grateful, as I have not been able to get at her work fully in this direction.

I hope all this is not too much trouble.

Yours sincerely,

Desiree Hirst

(Miss K.E.D. Hirst B. Litt. MA., Oxon. Lecturer in English)

Dated: 02 October 1994

Dear Professor Ansari,

In answer to your last letter all I could do was to send on this copy of my article in the proceedings of the 1993 Conference on Renaissance Studies at Uppsala University, Sweden.

You can see from this that it comes from my work on William Blake's early sources. It would be possible for me to contribute another article on that subject, especially as I am now working on a book on *Blake and the Bible*. This would be better than attempting anything further on Marlowe. Much new information has recently come up on Swedenborg's influence in the late 18th Century on Freemasonry. Let me know what would be useful.

Yours sincerely,

Desiree Hirst

Dated: 09 December 1994

Dear Professor Ansari

This is just a line to let you know I have in mind a paper based on the work I am doing for this study on *Blake and the Bible*. As this preceeds the idea for a paper will become clearer. The main thesis here concerns the influence of Jacob Boehme's interpretation of the Lutheran Bible, as it was beautifully translated into 17th century English, upon Blake's drawing upon biblical imagery, while he was using the 17th century authorized or 'King James' version' at the same time.

But just lately much material has surfaced on the early history of the Swedenborgian movement which attracted many Anglicans. It was closely linked to Freemasonry, which also had big political effects. But the Masonic Lodges preserved much Renaissance imagery, taken up by many notable and cultivated members, and passed on until the end of the 18th century. Emannel Swedenborg's family and friends were absorbed in the Kabbalah, in Alchemy and Neo Plantonism, as well as in the scientific theories of the Royal Society. His father conversed in Hebrew and had many learned Hebrewist friends. Swedish friend came to visit England a while after Swedenborg's death, promoting aspects of his teaching thought storage by others of his followers. So this could come into the paper. Kathleen Raine is interested, of course. I received and enjoyed last issue of the Miscellany.

With best wishes for the coming year.

Desiree Hirst

Dated: 02 October 1998

Dear Professor Ansari

In reply to your kind letters, I shall explain that I have been working on a book on an Irish poet, *Inspired Remember, A Study of the Poetry of John Montaigne,* for the Four Court Press, Dublin *expected 1999. Montaigne's* influence has had an effect on the Talks & Agreement in Northern Ireland.

However, I have also worked on the much earlier sources on Blake's work. This symbolism follows a line from Medieval Spain, into the 15th, 16th and 17th Centuries. Much needs to be tidy and far clearer, on the descent of such sources. Perhaps they may be of interest?

Desiree Hirst

Dated: 28 September 1999

Dear Professor Ansari,

I must warmly thank you for sending me a copy of your typescript of your new book *Minor Prophecies of William Blake*, with its Appended: Blake and the Kabbalah. And also to thank you for your kind dedication to James Ogden and myself. Why has nobody thought of appreciating Blake's Minor Prophecies in this way? It will be with real interest that I shall look at Blake and the Kabbalah in detail. But I am writing now to explain that there will be some delay before my reports get to you.

This is because I am working from my bed here, and after giving your valuable work my full attention, the reports will have to be typed out and mailed. As I tried to explain on the phone my recovery after an operation lasting seven hours at Singleton Hospital here, is bound to be very slow. This will not prevent me from giving your work justice, but inevitably there is still the battle with weakness.

My most recent study has been a piece of History of Ideas, *Discovering Images of Symbolic Thought: Enduring Throughout the Decades;* which bring some material from the Renaissance, through the sixteenth century, up to the seventeenth and finally on to the eighteenth century including, therefore, some aspect of Blake's sources.

But a study of the achievement of the Irish Poet John Montage for the Four Courts Press in Dublin, has been my main preoccupation. They are interested in the chapter I have sent, which they have wanted edited by my writer friend here, Mr. James McNamam. We shall have to go back to them soon, to find a way of ending the book.

Perhaps you can forgive me for this dreadful scribble and various spelling mistakes. But I thought you should know that my report will be with you as soon as my difficult present circumstances will permit.

With all good wishes for the continued success of the *Aligarh Critical Miscellany.*

Yours sincerely,

Desiree Hirst

Dated: 10th October 1999

Dear Professor Ansari,

Congratulations on gaining publication for your book with the Edwin Millin Press. Is this connected in any way with Lampeter University, the most high level quality of the Welsh Universities? But anyway your press is likely to be excellent. My problem is that my appreciation of *Blake's Minor Prophecies* with *Blake and the Kabbalah,* the appendix, is likely to be delayed. The reason for this is that I had an operation at Singleton Hospital here, lasting seven hours and I have been warned that it is unlikely that I shall be back to normal before December. My position is not so good as Kathleen Raine's, who undertakes so much at her advanced age! Alas! But you will get my response to your excellent work as soon as I can manage it, regardless.

Thank you very much for the copy of Vol. X No. 2 of the *Aligarh Critical Miscellany.* Your double perspective of *The Songs of Experience* is included, and that is much needed as serious reader of *the Songs*, which comprise both *Innocence* and *Experience*, ought to be able to grasp the work that has been done on so many of the other poems. Readers turn to the songs first and foremost. The article on the *Troubadoure* is fascinating.

Another difficulty over my situation is that postage as well as shopping has to be carried out from here by careers. I am really working under extreme obstacles. But I am keeping your deep thought over Blake's sources and achievements, carried out for so long in my mind, all the time.

Sincerely,

Desiree Hirst

The British Council
1 Beaumont Place
Oxford, OX1 2PJ

Dated: 03 February 1978

Dear Professor Ansari,

Thank you very much for your letter of 26.01.1978 and also for the latest issue of *The Aligarh Journal of English Studies*, How enterprising of you to print Leaves' 1969 lecture. And I was most interested in the review of Spender's *Love – Hate Relations*, which I read in November 1977 and which seems to be his best piece of criticism.

What I should really like to do is to send you an essay on Edward Thomas, but it would be much more satisfactory essay if I can have time to digest the new *Collected Poems* that is due to appear from OUP very shortly.

Provided that if comes out as announced, I could send you the essay in mid-May or early June.

Would this be acceptable?

I remember your visit with particular pleasure, and hope that we may meet again. You are more likely to revisit Oxford than I to revisit India. Let us look forward to a reunion here

Yours Sincerely

Robert C. Johnson

P.S. your essay on *Measure for Measure* gives much food for thought. It is a play I have always greatly admired once acting in it at the madder market Theatre, Norwich, and I recently saw a fine performance of it at the Birmingham Repertory Theatre. I have read your essay with much interest. It is indeed a grim play, and at Birmingham the 'happy' ending is shown in its true light. Isabella is left alone on the stage, puts off her nun's habit, and in utter weariness and resignation follows the Duke – he not in my view, an attractive character, and I do not think that he is meant to symbolize Providence. But of course the play offers no easy solutions.

Miami University
Department of English
Bachelor Hall
Oxford, Ohio

Dated: 12th August 1980

Dear Professor Ansari,

Enclosed is the article on Shakespeare you requested. I hope that you will be able to publish it in your journal. I did receive copies of the journal and the off prints. I thought the issue was excellent one, I especially enjoyed the perceptive study of *The Winter's Tale.*

I am again enclosing the international reply coupons. Since I cannot cash them in the States, you should use them for postage.

Sincerely,

Robert C. Johnson

Dated: 04th November 1985

Dear Professor Ansari,

I have just finished reading your excellent article on *Othello* in the recent issue of *The Aligarh Journal of English Studies*. Your emphasis on the loneliness of Othello and your analysis of the non-communication between Desdemona and Othello are perceptive and convincing.

I have neither received nor been able to locate in the local library your commemorative volume, for which I contributed an essay on *Titus Andronicus.* I was hoping to purchase two copies; could you inform me how I might do this.

Warm regards,

Robert C. Johnson
Professor of English

Dated: 21 July 1986

Dear Professor Ansari,

Congratulation on the publication of your commemorative volume. I received my copy yesterday and spent a splendid evening reading several of the essays. I am honored to be in the company of such a collection of scholars. I can imagine your pride of being honored in such a way.

Best wishes

Robert C. Johnson
Professor of English

Merton College
Oxford

Dated: 1 July 1976

Dear Professor Ansari,

My warm thanks for your present of the first number of the *Aligarh Journal*; it has followed me to Devonshire where I am spending the next three months, writing on Dostoevsky. You must forgive me for not writing earlier, but the College has been slow forwarding my mail.

I read your *Twelfth Night* essay with keen interest, and found your discussion of duality, irony and tension in that great play most rewarding. I also found much to admire in the writings of your colleagues, and I wish the new enterprise every success.

I shall bear in mind your kind invitation to contribute to the *Journal*. For the next year or so I am likely to be busy with the Russians. Thereafter – who knows?

Yours sincerely,

John Jones

Dated: 8 June 1990

Dear Professor Ansari,

Thank you so much for the current number of the *Miscellany*. I have read it as I have earlier numbers – with keen interest. I particularly enjoyed and admired your essay on William Blake, that great man.

Yours very sincerely,

John Jones

Dated: 17 July 1974

Dear Professor Ansari,

A note of hearty thanks for the *Essays on Wordsworth* which has just reached me on holiday. I am reading it in the evenings, when the day's work is done with great pleasure and profit.

Outstanding (I think) in your whole team of contributors, is Mr. M.H. Khan who has kindly sent me the book from the Birmingham Shakespeare Institute.

I was also pleased much by the contributions of Mr. Usmani and Mr. Ghosh – heartily, no doubt because their view of W.W. is akin to my own! The same (if I may say so) is true of your essay.

With warm thanks and congratulations.

Yours very sincerely,

John Jones

Dated: 12 August 1995

Dear Professor Ansari,

Heartily thanks for the *Aligarh Critical Miscellany*. As always, it was a delight to receive and to read. In particular, I found great pleasure and profit in Kathleen Raine's thoughts about Blake. (My little grandson lives within sight of Hercules Road in S. London. I sometimes call him. ("Hercules")

yours very sincerely,

John Jones

Dated: July 1996

Dear Professor Ansari,

How very kind of you to write.

I have indeed been receiving, reading, enjoying and profiting from the *Miscellany*. In fact the John Keats special number stands on a small bookshelf in front of me as I write to you.

If I have failed to thank you, I can only hope you will forgive me. The unpleasant condition of asthma has struck me at a surprisingly advanced – I would prefer to say mature – age, reducing the span of activities, even as regards ordinary but important courtesy.

I am heartened by your invitation. I don't feel robust enough to offer anything strictly new. But I think a chapter from my very recent *Shakespeare at Work* (OUP) might be acceptable. Perhaps the "Thomas More" chapter. Or the longer *Othello* chapter. The book has only been out a few months, but I feel fairly confident that Oxford would not press for any payment along the customary lines. I would of course be prepared to state forcefully that, as author, I am prepared to waive any right connected with copyright, and that I hope my publisher will do the same.

With best wishes, renewed apology and thanks

Yours sincerely,

John Jones

Dated: 8 August 1996

Dear Professor Ansari,

Many thanks for your letter. I am delighted that you think the Othello chapter of my *Shakespeare at Work* would be acceptable.

As I hope I explained, OUP has to give permission. I don't think this will be difficult, but one can see that the sale of the book would be affected if all and Sundry were allowed to reproduce parts of it. So they must be asked (OUP, Copyright Dept., Walton Street, Oxford). And of course I will send them a supporting letter if they ask for one. And of course no fee.

It shouldn't be difficult to get your hands on a copy. I'm sure the OUP office in Bombay would help.

I was touched by your kind words about my tiresome asthma.

Yours sincerely,

John Jones

Dated: 12 September 1996

Dear Professor Ansari,

Thank you for your letter. But I'm afraid I cannot manage any more, being unwell. Surely you can get your hands on a copy of my book. Oxford University Press has two offices in India.

Yours very sincerely,

John Jones

Dated: 20 October 1996

Dear Professor Ansari,

Many thanks for the recent *Miscellany*, gratefully received and already dipped into.

Also for your most kind thoughts about my asthma. About that I have good news; the inhalers I am now using have much improved my breathing.

I look forward to the *Othello* chapter and earnestly hope it gives pleasure. (I'm confident OUP will be friendly)

John Jones

MLA
Modern Language Association
of America
10 Astor Place
New Your, NY 10003

Dated: 20 February 1992

Asloob Ahmad Ansari

Dear Colleague:

The Modern Language Association is preparing to publish the seventh edition of the *MLA Directory of Periodicals,* which contains information on journals and series published in the fields of language, linguistics, literature, and folklore. We would like to include a listing for your journal, *The Aligarh Critical Miscellany,* containing the most recent information available.

Please review the enclosed questionnaire and note any changes or missing data. If all information we have listed is complete and correct, please state your approval by checking the appropriate line at the end of the questionnaire. We ask that you follow the enclosed instructions carefully so that your *Directory* listing will be as accurate as possible.

We must receive the completed questionnaire by **3 April 1992** to ensure that your corrections or additions appear in the next *Directory.* Please spend a few minutes now filling out this questionnaire so that your publication will be accurately listed.

Thank you for your cooperation.

Sincerely yours,

Kathleen Kent
Coordinator
MLA Director of Periodicals

King's College Cambridge
Postcode CB2 Ist
Telephone 0223350411

Dated: 23 March 1984

Dear Professor Ansari,

Thank you so much for the copy of your journal which, having been abroad, I have only now received. I wish I could comply with your request for a contribution on *Lear,* but I have so much else to write, all of it very remote from your topic.

With good wishes,

Yours sincerely

Frank Kermode

Lammas House
Brinkley, Newmarket,
Suffolk, Stetchworth 268

Dated: 14 February 1966

Dear Dr. Ansari,

Very many thanks for sending me your *Arrows of Intellect.* It is a very impressive performance. You have fruitfully related Blake to Bacon, Milton and the philosophers, and as Frye says, to others with whom there is no question and direct influence.

I am glad, though, that I did not attempt to read and criticize it before hand. You kindly call me in your letter "one of the greatest Blake scholars of our time". But this is exaggerating! I have never regarded myself as at all an Interpreter of Blake, being a very insufficient philosopher. I have worked in the humbler fields of bibliographer and edition for which I am more fitted.

Yours sincerely,

Geoffrey Keynes

The New Youk Public Library
Mid-Mauhattan Library
455 Fifth Avenne
New York-10016-0122
USA

Dated: 14 April 1990

Aligarh Journal of English Studies
Aligarh Muslim University
Department of English
Aligarh, Uttar Pradesh, India

Dear Mr. Ansari

The Literature and Language department of the Mid-Manhattan Library devotes heavy emphasis to primary and critical material on English literature from around the world. Consequently we are always on the lookout for new journals that would be beneficial to our readers. I was made aware of two journals that are published by your department: *Aligarh Journal of English Studies* and *Aligarh Critical Miscellany*. Could you kindly provide me with information on these journals for possible subscription? It would be wonderful if we can possibly review current issues of each of these journals. Thank you so much for your kindness.

Sincerely,

Stephen Kiss
Literature & Language Dept.

Prof. G. Wilson Knight
Caroline House,
Streatham Rise
Exeter EX4 4PE

Dated: 11 December 1965

Dear Dr. Ansari

Thank you for sending me your book on Blake. It only takes a very cursory inspection to see that it is a very able piece of work, deeply understanding and deeply instructive, and written with a fine command of English. I am so glad to see that you have had satisfying comments by F.W. Bateson and Northrop Frye.

I have not time to do more than glance at it here and there at present. I am getting a large number of books and off prints sent to me and I am coming to the point where I have to stop my own work in order to grapple with the influx of correspondence. In any case I would not be a good one to comment on your book because I have never specialized in Blake: When I do read it I shall read it not in order to pronounce a value judgment on it but in order to learn from it myself.

I do not know whether your university has anything like a literary laboratory that buys tape recordings. If it has I have three, two on Shakespeare and one on Byron, published by Seminars, 3402 Cincinnati 20, USA. They hope to sell them all over the world, but their price (ten dollars each) for buying, cheaper for hiring, may be prohibitive. However, it seemed as well to let you know.

With all my good wishes for Christmas and the New year and congratulations on your fine accomplishment.

Yours sincerely,

G. Wilson Knight

Dated: 01 June 1981

Dear Dr. Ansari,

I fear I cannot write anything new. I am fed up with commitments of various sorts. I have a collection of Shakespeare essays soon to be offered for publication, but they are mostly articles that have already appeared. I must remember, I am 83 years old, and it is very difficult to cope with correspondence, let alone new writing.

Your articles are a high standard. I congratulate you on them. I am only sorry that I cannot nowadays do all that people want.

Yours sincerely,

G. Wilson Knight

Dated: 19 July 1982

Dear Dr. Ansari

Thank you for the copy of *The Aligarh Journal* and the off prints of my article. The essays in it are fine and keep up a high standard. Mine is not so very good but it is the best I had available. Thank you for everything.

I sent my good wishes for future issues.

Yours sincerely,

G. Wilson Knight

Professor L.C. Knights
Queens College
Cambridge
England

Dated: 24 May 1967

Thank you very much for your book *Arrows of Intellect* which I am very pleased to have together with your kind letter. It is clearly a book that I shall wish to read and although it is impossible (for a multitude of reasons) for me to settle into it immediately, I shall certainly hope to profit from your insights when I return to work on Blake, as I hope to do before too long.

I am glad to know that you have found some of my own work stimulating. Since you mention *Hamlet* I wonder if I may say that an admirable book by Miss Eleanor Prosser called *Hamlet and Revenge* has just come out from the Stanford University Press. If you could persuade your library to get it I am sure that you and others would find it useful. Please accept my best thanks and kindest regards.

Yours sincerely,

L.C. Knights

United Republic of
Cameroon
Peace-work-Fatherland
Department of English
University of Yaounde
Cameroon

Dated: 06 November 1987

Prof. A.A. Ansari

Sir,

Article for Publication

I hereby forward to you an article, "The Archetypal Pattern of Wordworth's 'Lucy' (Poems)", for publication in your prestigious Journal.

While waiting to hear from you at your earliest convenience.

I remain

Yours sincerely,

John A. Lambo

Dated: 12 December 1992

The Editor

Object: Article For Publication

Enclosed is an article entitled "William Blake and Willam Wordsworth: A Study in Revolt as an Inevitable Response to Oppression" for publication in your Journal. In fact, the present article is a sequel to an article on Blake and Wordsworth which was earlier published in your Journal – Cf. Vol. 4, No. 2, November 1991.

While waiting to hear from you at your earliest convenience, accept my warmest greetings and respects.

Your sincerely,

J.A. Lambo

The University of Michigan-Dearborn
College of Arts, Science, and Letters
Humanities Department
Dearborn, Michigan 48128

Dated: 04 April 1988

Dear Professor Ansari,

I was delighted to receive your letter of March 12, accepting my article "The Infernal *Macbeth*" for publication in *The Aligarh Journal.* I look forward to reading the issue in which my article will appear; will you kindly send me a copy of the *Journal* when it is printed?

Since last corresponding with you, I have discovered two minor errors in the manuscript I sent you:

P. 8, paragraph 3, line 7: "as Dante as conceived it" should read "as Dante has conceived it".

P. 12, footnote 3: the final sentence should have quotation marks at the end, i.e. "... his brows against his Maker, well may all sorrow proceed from him]."

I do hope it is not too late to include these small corrections and I apologize sincerely for any inconvenience I may have caused you.

Thank you again, Dr. Ansari, for your kind letter of acceptance. I look forward to our continued correspondence and to a close association with your fine journal.

Yours sincerely,

Jacqueline E. Lawson

1424 Golden Avenue, # 2
Ann Arbor, Maulvi 48104

Dated: 19 February 1988

Dear Professor Ansari,

My colleague Melita Schaum suggested I submit the enclosed article, "The Infernal *Macbeth:* A Comparative Study of Shakespeare and Dante", for consideration by your editorial board.

Thank you. I look forward to hearing from you.

Yours sincerely,

Jacqueline E. Lawson

Department of English
University of York
Heslington, York
Telephone 59861

Dated: 15 March 1967

Dear Mr. Ansari

I am sorry you should have felt neglected, but I am a far less leisured and privileged person than you suppose. I for the last 18 months have been peculiarly hard driven -commuting weekly between the Universities of Cambridge and York. (I am in my seventies). I have many things sent in for comment, and it is impossible to find time to read and criticize them all. And I have endless correspondence and no secretary.

Last year I had to go to America (to prepare for the visit) and I have just finished giving the Clark Lectures at Cambridge, a commitment that has weighed heavily on me. I am tired, but at last free from immediate pressure. So I can make myself acknowledge your letter.

Just consider how many hours it must take to read and comment on you book! Actually, I *had* read it and marked it in the margins. I can say that I read it with pleasure and profit. *It is* one of the books I have read on Blake that I don't dismiss as pretentious, muddled and not of much use. To say that one doesn't expect to find a satisfactory book on him is not to be supercilious, or to say that no book can be useful. He is a very difficult subject - a complex one. One may know where the *center* of one's interest lies, but in order to articulate one's interest critically one has to acquire knowledge, outside one's own field (mysticism, metaphysics, Swedenborg and Christian theology.........) Reading a book like yours helps one to get a firmer grasp on those areas of knowledge that one intends to exclude from one's own critical essay (to write which is a supremely difficult thing) By "exclude" I mean the process that results in the boundary line, the boundariness of which gives the relevant presence of what is left.

Blake was (partially) a mystic, but it's the poet - the *creative* artist I try to stress on. There is no mystery about his hatred of Locke and Newton (Dr. Joshua Reynolds). He is the protest of life against the positivist culture of the 18th C. (See Eliot's Introduction to ...; he insists that life is inescapably creative. Newtonian science restricts the real to what can be mathematically treated. Locke ignores the creativity of perception (the retina is not photographic plate – see ...... Art and Pleasure). Blake insists that there is continuity from the creativeness of perception to disciplined creativeness of the artist.

I am not a Christian, but I think you ought to know a little more about Christian theology (than I do!). A book that has helped me to strengthen my grasp on some points (e.g. pantheism, agnosticism, mysticism from the Christian point of view - Blake's') is I.G. Davies' *The Theology of William Blake* (Cambridge U.P.). Don't misunderstand me: I want to get Blake's theology' out of the way.

The only criticism I would make – a minor one – is that you bring too many authorities in. There is no point for example in citing B. Willey or W. Wallace: they don't matter.

Congratulations on your book and thank you. I am very tired, hence this scrawl.

Best wishes

Your sincerely,

F.R. Leavis

Dated: 15 February 1974

Dear Professor Ansari

I'm not on the staff of York University and have never been. I am in my 79th year. As one with no proper pension, I am badly menaced by inflation, and I'm (with my wife) more than ever dependent on my royalty income. In any case there are still a number of books I am impelled to write – I know I shan't live forever.

Many people in the course of the years send me copies of their books on many subjects (I have never posed as a specialist), and intimate that they would like my comments. If I satisfied their expectations, I should have time for nothing else. As things are, there are many claims on my time and energy that I have strong reason for responding to favourably: e.g., I have just returned from Oxford where, I addressed an important audience.

You will see that I can't write you a satisfying answer.

Yours sincerely,

F.R. Leavis

---

12 Bulstrode Gardens
Cambridge

Dated: 16 January 1978

Thank you for the magazine, which I have shown to my husband and which he has received with pleasure. The above formula will tell you that he is now an invalid confined to bed, not surprising as he is 82½ years old. I am glad to have this copy of his unpublished lecture which I didn't even get to hear at Milan because I was myself lecturing at the time elsewhere in the University.

Your sincerely,

Quesir D. Leavis

Katholieke Universiteit
Instituut Engels-Amerikaans
Nijmegen, The Netherlands

Dated: 05 June 1983

Dear Professor Ansari,

I am writing to you because my co-literary executor of the Leavis Estate, Professor G. Singh, has communicated to me that you have a valuable letter from my father in your possession. As perhaps you know, Professor T.A. Bissell of Niemeyer University, one of the few surviving '*Scrutineers*' is the person we have chosen to edit and collect my father's letters and he has arranged for the edition to be eventually published by the Cambridge University Press.

I am very interested in my father's letter to you and would be extremely grateful if you felt that it was possible to send me a photocopy of it so that I could pass it on to Professor Bissell. I have been working with Professor Bissell in collecting and sorting copies of my father's letters, and we have acquired quite a body of material, but we want as much variety of topic and style as possible.

Yours,

Robin Leavis

Dated: 23 June 1983

Dear Professor Ansari,

Thank you so much for sending the photocopy of your letter. It is indeed a most valuable and interesting letter, and I will do my best to get it included in the collection-though of course the ultimate decision rests with Professor Bissell. I have deliberately refrained from having anything to do with the volume officially as I have prejudice against sons who further their careers by means of their famous fathers! Also the reception in England to anything connected with my father's work by the press is so militantly hostile that I did not want to give any number of reviewers a chance to use the 'sneer' "filial piety" to suggest that the collection was not worth publishing.

I suspect that Professor Bissell will need no urging from me about your most valuable letter's inclusion in his volume.

Yours in gratitude,

Robin Leavis

PS: It was lucky that the letter arrived at all, for someone had slit your envelope completely open somewhere in transit.

Professor (Dr) M. Lehnert
DDR 1170
Belin-Kopenick
Gutenbergstrabe 6

Dated: 07 April 1985

Dear Colleague,

Thank you very much indeed for sending me the valuable and very interesting Volumes 6 (1981, Special *Hamlet* Number), 8 (1983, Special *King Lear* Number) and shortly Vol. 9 (1984), No. 1 with your own attractive contribution on "Political Man in Shakespeare's English History Plays'. We are presently preparing the annual Shakespeare Day at Warmer, the foundation place of the time honoured German Shakespeare Society in 1864, the oldest Shakespeare Society on the Continent whose President I have been more than twenty (exactly 22) years. I am sending you with the same post a copy of our Shakespeare journal for 1984. The next volume 121 for 1985 will appear in the end of April. Hoping to meet you once again in Stratford- upon- Avon, Britain or elsewhere (possibly in India).

I am sending you all my best wishes.

Yours,

M. Lehnert

The University of Sussex
Professor of English
Laurence Lerner
Brighton

Dated: 05 January 1982

Dear Professor Ansari,

You may, if you wish, use the enclosed in the *Aligarh Journal of English Studies*. It has not been published, but it will appear in my forthcoming volume of essays, *The Literary Imagination,* to be published by the Harvester Press. I expect the book to appear in the course of 1982, so you will have to use the essay, if you want it, in your next issue. Please add a note saying that it will appear in my forthcoming volume, and give name and publisher.

Sorry about the mistakes in the typescript. The top copy went to the printer, and I hope this version is quite clear. You may want to add translations of the quotations from Sartre's play. If you do, and have any difficulty in getting them, let me know and I will supply them.

I enjoyed my visit to Aligarh. Please give my greetings to your colleagues.

Yours sincerely,

Laurence Lerner

Dated: 14 June

Dear Professor Ansari,

I'm afraid it's quite impossible for me to write something specially for your *Commemoration Volume*: my commitments for the next year or so are too heavy. Nor have I any essay on Shakespeare conveniently to hand.

There is a good deal on Shakespeare in my book *Love and Marriage* and if you are very keen on having me in the book I could probably extract a reasonably self-contained piece. But it would not of course be a new article.

I'm sorry I can't be more helpful, but I really have too much on my plate. Good luck for the Volume.

Yours sincerely,

Laurence Lerner

Vanderbilt University
Nashville, Tennessee

Dated: 11th February 1986

Dear Professor Ansari,

Your letter was forwarded from Sussex, and took a long time to reach me, so I'm afraid my reply will be too late to be any use to you. I don't really mind what you say (or have said!) about me in the Notes on Contributors. If you still want suggestions, I'd say:

> After many years as Professor of English at the University of Sussex, Laurence Lerner now teaches at Vanderbilt University in Tennessee, but still lives in England. His most recent books are *My Grandfather's Grandfather* (a novel) in 1985, *Selected Poems* and *Chapter and Verse (Bible Poems)* in 1984. His most recent critical books are *Love and Marriage* in 1979 and a collection of his essays, *The Literary Imagination* in 1982.

Best wishes,

Laurence Lerner
William R. Kenan Professor of English

Goegia Melchiori
Via Capodistria, 900198
Rome, Italy

Dated: 8 July 1981

Dear Professor Ansari,

I must apologize for the long delay in sending my contribution to the Hamlet issue of *The Aligarh Journal of English Studies*. I tried several times to start a completely new study of the play, but didn't get very far. When my old friend Professor Singh called last week with your greetings and a pressing reminder of my undertaking, I made up my mind, and finding that after all the Italian introduction I had written for a bilingual edition of Hamlet and the problem plays had its merits, I have adapted it in English. The essay, as it stands, has never been published in English, and I think that, though still introductory in character, it makes one or two original points – but this is up to you to judge.

I shall be very grateful if you'll think it worth publishing, because it is my first attempt to put forward to a non-Italian audience some basic ideas and principles of mine on the inner structures of Shakespeare's plays, a subject on which I am planning to write a book.

I shall be in England for the whole of August (first in Stratford, then in Cambridge, and finally in Yorkshire). I suggest that the address that is most likely to find me during that month is that of relatives that can readdress the post:

C/o Mrs. H.R. Arnett
126 Beverley Road
Kirkella North Humberside. (England)

From the beginning of September I shall be back at my usual private address in home. Thanking you for your forbearance, and looking forward to hearing from you,

With all best wishes,

Yours sincerely,

Giorgio Melchiori

Harrison T. Mereole
Texas and SM University
Department of English
College Station
Texas 77843-4227

Dated: 7 September 1978

Dear Professor Ansari

Thank you for your letter of 21 August, for the copies of AJES, and for the brief abstracts of a number of articles on Shakespeare. You will be pleased to know that your articles on "The Ambivalence of Caliban", "Fools of Time in *Macbeth*" and "*Measure for Measure* and the Masks of Death" are all indexed and abstracted in the World Shakespeare Bibliography for 1977 which is now in press with a projected publication date of 15 November, 1978.

All best wishes.

Sincerely yours,

Harrison T. Meserole
Editor
World Shakespeare Bibliography

Dated: 11 January 1989

Dear Dr. Ansari

First let me thank you for sending the copy of Volume 1, No. 1 (1988) of *The Aligarh Critical Miscellany*. It is a handsome new scholarly publication which we shall add to our Master List of publications to be covered for the World Shakespeare Bibliography, and of course we shall list all the Shakespeare materials in the Bibliography for 1988 on which we are now working.

May I ask you, please, to correct your address record for me? My correct address is on this letterhead. The copy you sent to The Pennsylvania State University was forwarded to me here and consequently was measurably delayed in reaching me despite the fact that you sent it airmail. That Pennsylvania State University address has not been a viable one since 1985, and that may account for the fact that I never received copies of the *Aligarh Journal of English Studies*, Volume 11, No. 2 (1986) and Volume 12, No. 2 (1987). Would it be possible for you to send me those missing copies, via sea mail of course, so that I can be certain that our coverage of Indian scholarship in that journal was complete?

I shall look forward to receiving Volume 1, No. 2 of your new journal. If the articles contained in it are as stimulating as those in your first issue, you will have won a major scholarly audience.

Thank you very much for your cooperation in making these publications available to us for our bibliographical work on Shakespeare.

Sincerely yours,

Harrison T. Meserole,

Harrison T. Meserole
Editor
World Shakespeare Bibliography
Distinguished Professor of English
Abell Professor of Liberal Arts

Associate Professor of English
Department of English and Fine Arts

Dated: 02 February 1987

Professor A.A. Ansari
Department of English
Aligarh Muslim University
Aligarh
India

Dear Professor Ansari

Thanks for the copy of the Journal, the offprint, and your letter. You are most welcome to review *Shakespeare's Rome* in your journal and thank you for the kind words about it. I can't promise a new submission by August since I don't have anything at hand just now, but am working on a few pieces which might prove suitable. I am honoured by your kind invitation and shall certainly send something along if a good piece materializes.

Thanks again for your interest in my work.

Sincerely yours,

Robert S. Miola

Kenneth Muir
6 Chetwynd Road
Oxton
Birkenhead, Merseyside
L43 2JJ

Dated: 16 November 1983

Dear Professor Ansari,

Thank you for your letter and the copy of the *Aligarh Journal.*

I could revise a lecture I give at the Folger Shakespeare Library last year on the controversy about the text of *King Lear* (whether a modern edition should print those passages omitted from the First Folio) if you think that would be suitable. It would be about 20 pages.

Yours sincerely,

Kenneth Muir

Dated: 21 February 1984

Dear Professor Ansari,

Thank your for your letter.

I will gladly contribute to your Commemorative Volume. I haven't yet chosen a topic but I'll think of one in the next few weeks.

Best wishes,

Yours sincerely,

Kenneth Muir

Dated: 12 April 1984

Dear Professor Ansari,

The Harvester Press are publishing a selection of my recent articles, mainly on Shakespeare, and the volume is due to appear in 1985. Have I your permission to include the piece on the text of *King Lear*, which you are publishing shortly?

Yours sincerely,

Kenneth Muir

Dated: 13 June 1986

Dear Professor Ansari,

Thank you for your letter. Your volume arrived safely a few weeks ago, and I've enjoyed reading it. I would have written before but I've been writing a book for Penguins on *Antony and Cleopatra*, and was struggling to complete it on time – June 1st.

Best wishes,

Yours sincerely,

Kenneth Muir

Dated: 26 September 1988

Dear Professor Ansari,

Congratulations on the first number of your new Journal, which I have much enjoyed. It may be some days before I can post this, as they won't reopen the mail boxes until they have cleared the millions of letters delayed by the strike.

I was sorry not to see you at the Stratford Conference last month, although the performances at the theatres were disgracefully bad, especially compared with the new company which has been touring with *Much Ado* and *Hamlet*.

Ann Mackenzie and I have finished another Calderon translation *Jealousy the Greatest Monster* and are busy with another. Otherwise I'm trying to revise a book on Dickens drafted nearly 30 years ago, but now very much out of date. This, I expect, will be my Swan-song.

Yours sincerely,

Kenneth Muir

Dated: 6 November 1988

Dear Professor Ansari,

Thank you for your letter. I have written to Mr. Usmani to say how much I have admired his essays. I feel sure that he well deserves promotion.

As for *Bleak House*, I'll be glad to send you an article, but it will be some time – three months – before I can start it. I've promised an article for a collection before the end of the year and I have to meet a deadline for another translation of a Calderon play. Will it suit you for the Dickens?

Yours sincerely,

Kenneth Muir

Dated: 26 April 1989

Dear Professor Ansari,

Many thanks for the Eliot number of your *Critical Miscellany*. It is very good, I think, and I admired nearly all the contents.

I had been meaning to write for several months because I had not finished my promised article on *Bleak House*. I had to put it on one side because of unexpected and inescapable jobs – contribution to three *Festschriften* and revision of my translation of a Calderon play because of a revision of the Spanish text.

I have now finished *Bleak House* – it needs only to be typed and if you at all want it, I'll let you have it as soon as I hear from you.

By chance there's a television programme tonight on the question of Spontaneous Combustion – whether it is scientifically possible.

Best wishes,

Yours sincerely,

Kenneth Muir

Dated: 14 September 1989

Dear Professor Ansari,

Thank you for the *Critical Miscellany*. Another good number. I liked particularly the articles by Nagrajan and yourself. Is the *Journal of English Studies* still being published? It must be a year since the editor acknowledged an article of mine on *Hamlet*, and I thought it would have appeared by now.

Best wishes,

Yours sincerely,

Kenneth Muir

Dated: 8 December 1989

Dear Professor Ansari,

I think your colleague must have misunderstood me. It must be nearly thirty years since I lectured on Eliot as a poet – my piece on Eliot as a dramatist is about to appear. I looked for my notes on Eliot but I must have thrown them out when I retired 15 years ago. So I'm afraid I can't send you an article on Eliot in the near future. At the moment I'm struggling to finish my translation of another Calederon play – the one about Herod which has been foolishly compared with *Othello*. If, as I hope, I finish this in January, I could let you have an article later in 1990. But not on Eliot.

Best Wishes.

Yours sincerely,

Kenneth Muir

Dated: 2 January 1990

Dear Professor Ansari,

I gave a lecture last year to the Scottish Renaissance Society on "King James and Shakespeare'. I could, if you like, turn it into an article for your *Miscellany*. Let me know.

With New Year greetings,

Yours sincerely,

Kenneth Muir

Dated: 10 February 1990

Dear Professor Ansari,

Thank you for your letter. I'm sorry that I have nothing more to say about *Othello* – I still agree with my theories in *Shakespeare's Tragic Sequence* and my edition of the play. All I could do would be to compare *Othello* with Calderon's *Jealousy the Greatest Monster* – a play about Herod I have just finished translating. If you would like this I could write it (probably) in May or June. When is your deadline? I much enjoyed the Blake issue – some excellent articles.

Best wishes,

Yours sincerely,

Kenneth Muir

Dated: 11 February1992

Dear Professor Ansari,

I had a short stay in hospital – nothing very serious but in attempting to recover lost time, I find that I have missed some letters – I have found letters written to me in 1926, but not these. As a result I don't remember whether it was you or the Journal of E.S. which solicited an aricle on *Othello.* I sent one comparing it with Calderon Herod. If it was you who asked, can you let me know if you are printing it fairly soon. I ask because our edition of the Herod play should appear before the end of the year.

I hope to see you at the Stratford Conference in August.

Yours sincerely,

Kenneth Muir

Dated: 12 February 1992

Dear Professor Ansari,

Many thanks for *ACM* IV(1). A good number! I enjoyed your article on Urizen, Roberts' and Jean Brook's on Ophelia particularly. The copy must have been on the way when I wrote my last letter.

Best wishes.

Yours sincerely,

Kenneth Muir

Dated: 7 July 1992

Dear Professor Ansari,

Thank you for your letter. I'm very sorry about the Conference. I suppose Stanley wants to vary the Indian delegates from year to year, though this means we shall miss the best.

I'll try and send you something for the *Critical Miscellany* (1). I have drafted an attack on the Penguin translator of Racine and Cornville for plagiarism and incompetence. (2) I have to prepare a lecture on Wilfred Owen for his centenary next March and I could write on Owen and the poets of the 1914-8 war(3). I have an unpublished article on Shakespeare and the Trojan War. I think No. 1 is too specialized for your purposes, but one of the others might be suitable. No. 2, unwritten as yet, I ought to finish in September or October. In November I go to Roven to talk on Lope de Vega and Shakespeare (but this will be published in their *Proceedings).*

Best wishes,

Yours sincerely,

Kenneth Muir

PS: Looking for no. 3 I have come across an unpublished piece on Keats' Odes, updating my previous article on the subject.

Dated: 23 August 1992

Dear Professor Ansari,

I consulted Stanley Wells and Roger Pringle at the Stratford Conference and they agreed with me that you ought to mention both the libraries – the Institute and the Centre – in your application and state what will come out of your study. (Presumably a book or series of articles?).

There would then be no difficulty in getting the backing you need for a travel grant. You could use me or Wells or Pringle as referees.

My article on 'Shakespeare and the Tale of Troy' is being typed and should reach you in September.

Best wishes,

Yours sincerely,

Kenneth Muir

Dated: 7 October 1992

Dear Professor Ansari

Thank you for your letter. I'm very sorry about the family tragedy.

You should by now have received "Shakespeare and the Tale of Troy". It was posted last month. The Keats article needs some revision and I'm busy with festschrift articles at the moment and with two lectures for the Wilfred Owen centenary. About your Stratford visit you should, I think, write 3 letters.

1. To the British Council in India, outlining your proposed book on Shakespeare and saying how necessary it is to spend some time in the Stratford libraries you can say that I will gladly act as a referee as I know many of your articles.
2. A letter to Standley Wells, asking if he will let you use the library at the Shakespeare Institute. I'm sure he will.

3. A letter to the Director of the Shakespeare centre. I spoke to him about your project and I know he will be delighted to welcome you to the library. His name is Roger Pringle.

I hope all goes well.

Yours sincerely,

Kenneth Muir

Dated: 11 January 1993

Dear Professor Ansari

Thank you for your letter and the *Critical Miscellany* which arrived by the same post. I've not read it yet, but I was glad to see you've printed the third part of Harold's article on Gray and Blake.

I'm sorry that the British Council hasn't replied. They have not yet asked my opinion, but they decided ten years ago that I was too old to travel to America, so perhaps that's the snag but they ought to write. I'll ask the Stratford people when I see them if they have been approached.

About the Wilfred Owen lectures. I'm delivering them from brief notes; and if I have time to write them up as articles I promised the centenary committee to let them publish then if in the end they wanted to. I'm so busy with other urgent jobs, it would be some time. Later this year I've agreed to speak on the 400th anniversary of Marlowe's death.

Best wishes for 1993.

Yours sincerely,

Kenneth Muir

Dated: 12 February 1993

Dear Professor Ansari

I am very sorry that the British Council refused your application, though it is true that the government has (foolishly) cut their budget as I told you I'm busy with the Wilfred Owen centenary and I'm giving numerous readings of his poems in addition to the lectures. These go on till June. But I'll send you an article when I get time.

Best wishes,

Yours sincerely,

Kenneth Muir

Dated: 28 July 1993

Dear Professor Ansari

I am sorry if I neglected to acknowledge the receipt of the last number of the *Critical Miscellany*. It arrived when I was terribly busy with the Owen Centenary, several lectures, a day school, an article and more lectures and readings to come. I have also lectured at the Cambridge Conference on Marlowe, and I could make an article out of my lecture. But I promised to wait a while until they know if they are to publish proceedings of the Conference. If this project materializes, I don't suppose it would reach publication until 1995. But I will write to ask them if they would object to your publishing it first. If there is an objection I could perhaps provide you with a shortened version. I'll let you know as soon as I hear from them. (The theme is 'Marlowe: Atheist or Heretic?' I argue and I think prove, that he was a Socinian.

Best wishes

Yours sincerely,

Kenneth Muir

Dear Professor Ansari

Many thanks for *ACM. III. 1*. There are some excellent contributions, including of course, yours; and the two on Wordsworth.

I hope to see you at Stratford in August.

Yours sincerely,

Kenneth Muir

Dear Professor Ansari

Thank you for *ACM IV. 1.* and your article on R III an R II. I was interested to see that you have got two more Liverpool contributors. I was also glad to see your interview in *AJES*. I admired Leavis at one time but I now feel that his pupils have been disastrous – arrogant, narrow-minded, offensively rude and often ignorant. L.C. Knights, although he owes a lot to Leavis, is a much nicer man. But they both hated the stage.

How is your Marlowe number progressing?

Yours sincerely,

Kenneth Muir

Dear Professor Ansari

Many thanks for *ACM IV.2*. I liked your review of Barbara Everett. My knowledge of Iqbal is too slight for me to appreciate fully your article. I liked, too, Brooks and Barfoot.

Best wishes,

Yours sincerely,

Kenneth Muir

Dated: 9 June

Dear Professor Ansari

I'm very sorry I didn't acknowledge the receipt of the *Raleigh Collection*. I enjoyed them and thought that together the articles gave a useful and valuable account of his books. The archivist is very pleased.

My excuse for not writing sooner is that I had a phone call from New York asking me to send a copy of one of my Calder'on translations as quickly as possible. It was in manuscript and without final checking and had to be typed. It was sent off yesterday, thank goodness.

I hope to see you at Stratford.

Yours sincerely,

Kenneth Muir

Dated: 16 June

Dear Professor Ansari

Many thanks for the recent number of the *Aligarh Journal*, containing your admirable article on *Timon*. My delay in answering was due to my 80th birth celebrations and the 120 letters I had to write afterwards to contributors to my *festschrift* and others.

Best wishes

Yours sincerely,

Kenneth Muir

Dated: 14 August

Dear Professor Ansari

Thank you for your letter. I'm leaving for Stratford on Sunday and I'll consult Stanley Wells about the best way of approaching the British Council. I think you should give some indication of what you intend to write as a result of your time in Stratford and I suggest that you make use of the Shakespeare Centre as well as the Shakespeare Institute.

I'll write again when I return from the Conference and I'll send you one of the promised articles when I have had it typed.

Best wishes,

Yours sincerely,

Kenneth Muir

Dated: 10 September

Dear Professor Ansari

Thanks you for your letter. I had read the article on Edmond but I was confused by the date on the cover (1988) which was presumably a misprint.

I read the article with great interest but with a number of reservations. I think that the author underestimates the sheer wickedness of Edmand and gives him excuses not justified by the text (e.s. the sentence on p. 159 arguing "He wishes to become more powerful …"\ I would have preferred more distinction between the good bastard in *King John* and Edmund. And I'm sure Albany never regarded Lear and Cordelia as in need of pardon (p. 168).

But I agree that Edmond undergoes a partial conversion at the end. As he is dying, there's no point in having Cordelia killed. He does not speak immediately while Goneril is alive, but his realization that he was "beloved" by the two sisters is the thing that motivates his wish to do good.

I thought the Stratford Conference was disappointing this year, and there was a good deal of acrimony – and a tendency to applaud only those papers with which one happened to agree. The feminists cheered the feminists, the Marxists the Marxists, the homosexuals their fellows. Shakespeare was reduced to a weapon in a war with which he was not concerned.

Best wishes,

Yours sincerely,

Kenneth Muir

Dated: 12 September

Dear Professor Ansari

Thank you for your letter. *A.C.M.* arrived safely just before I went on holidays. When I returned, I imagined I have acknowledged the receipt. Evidently I was mistaken and I'm very sorry (I enjoyed particularly Harold's article on *The Waste Land* and yours on *Richard II*). You will have noticed that I am wrongly said to belong to Birmingham University; and I expect it has been pointed out that it was Dr. Johson who refuted Berkely, by striking his foot against a large stone. (Boswell in1763).

I've just been admiring your article on the existentialist Shakespeare. I'm writing a foreword to the anthology in which it is to appear, and could not do this without reading the contents.

I look forward to receiving the issue containing my article on *Othello* and *Herod*. I have another coming out about the same time on *Lope de Vega* and Shakespeare.

With best wishes,

Yours sincerely,

Kenneth Muir

Dated: 24 October

Dear Professor Ansari

Many thanks for your Journal and for your article on *The Merchant of Venice*, which I like. I've not yet read the other contents as I wanted to say that I've written an article on Walter Raleigh, and it is now being typed. You may find it unsuitable for your purposes as I argue that Raleigh did not live up to his early promise because of defects of character. But I include an interesting letter from the Liverpool University archives defending academic freedom and unsuccessfully appealing for a French colleague who was dismissed.

Yours sincerely,

Kenneth Muir

Dear Professor Ansari

No one here seems to know Marian Ellot's address, but his surname is illegible in your letter.

I'm glad you liked my article.

Professor Bate (in his inaugural lecture) spoke about Professor Raleigh and agreed with my article on the subject which he had not then read.

My other colleague, Kelvin Everest, spoke warmly of his visit to Aligarh

Best wishes.

Yours sincerely,

Kenneth Muir

Carleton University
Ottawa
Canada K1S 5B6

Dated: 18 March 1988

Dear Professor Asnari,

Thank you for accepting my article on *Hamlet* for your Journal. Please let me know when it will be appearing, along with the volume, date, and page numbers, and whether you will be sending me the proofs for proof-reading.

Best wishes in all your endeavours.

Yours sincerely,

Thomas G. Nollet

Depart of English
Carleton University
Colonel By Drive,
Ottawa, Ontario
Canada
K1S 5B6

Dated: 09 August 1988

Dear Professor Ansari,

I am writing to you about my article, "Nothing Either Good or Bad': Sophistry and Self-delusion in *Hamlet*" which you accepted for publication in your letter to me of 2.3.88, and which I replied to. Would you please let me know as soon as conveniently possible when it will be published, if the proofs will be sent to me, and when a copy of the article will be sent as well?

Thank you in advance for your consideration of this matter.

Yours sincerely,

Thomas G. Nollet

Department of English
Hugh Owen Building
The University College of Wales
ABERYSTWYTH
Dyfed SY23 3Dy

Dated: 13th December 1983

Professor A.A. Ansari
Chairman,
Department of English
Aligarh Muslim University
Aligarh-202001
India

Dear Professor Ansari,

Many thanks for sending me your Special Hamlet Number of *The Aligarh Journal of English Studies*, a valuable publication if I may say so. Thanks also for your letter about your forthcoming issue on *King Lear*. I hope to send a contribution by the middle of January. As Professor Slay has no doubt told you, it will be a short essay on the ending of the play.

Best wishes,

Yours sincerely,

James Ogden

Dated: 4 January 1984

Professor A.A. Ansari

As I promised in my previous letter, I enclose my essay on *King Lear*, for *The Aligarh Journal of English Studies*. I am hounoured by your request, and have been glad of the opportunity to put my ideas in some order. I have read much criticism of the play, and am conscious of the difficulty of saying anything original and illuminating. However, when I was an undergraduate (1954-7) criticism tended to be literary rather than theatrical, and Christian interpretations held sway. I have emphasized theatrical effects, and have supported recent critics (mentioned in my notes) who have taken a more humanistic view. I believe such an approach is more likely to do justice to the universal appeal of *King Lear*. I look forward to reading what your Indian contributors think about the play.

The late Professor Nosworthy was a good friend of mine. I know he left unpublished manuscripts, but I believe these relate chiefly to nineteenth-century topics. If you are interested in publishing these, do please write to his literary executor, Jamea C. Bulman, 636 Madison Avenue, Meadville, PA 16335, USA, and if you like mention my name,

Best wishes,

James Ogden

Dated: 28 January 1984

Dear Professor Ansari,

Thank you for your letter. I was glad to hear that my articles on *King Lear* had been thought worthy of publication. I have mentioned to my colleague Ned Thomas, who wrote book on Orwell in the "Writers and Critics" series, that you are interested in publishing something on *Animal Farm*. He says he has turned against Orwell to some extent since writing his book, but anyway he is thinking about it. Also, I have written to my old friend Jim Bulman, Professor Nosworthy's literary executor, telling him to expect a letter from you. I have not yet received *AJES* Vol.8. No. I, but there may have been some disruption of the mails here, on account of snow.

It was good of you to mention, in your previous letter, that you knew my book on Isaac D'Israeli. I tried to get your book on Blake, *Arrows of Intellect*, but the library does not seem to have a copy. However, a colleague has promised to lend me his. I am afraid that in my book I was unable to throw much new light on the relations of D'Israeli and Blake, but I was able to give the only correct version in print, so far as I know, of D'Israeli's letter to Thomas Frognall Dibdin about his collection of Blake's drawings. Dibdin himself published it with some grotesque errors, and some modern authorities have simply followed Dibdin. I cannot claim to know much about Blake, but I frequently use his well-known poem "And did those feet" as an example in a lecture on the theory and practice of criticism.

Best wishes,

James Ogden

Dated: 15 February 1984

Dear Professor Ansari,

Many thanks for your letter of 8 February and for the copy of AJES Vol. 8. No. 1, both of which came today.

I am sorry to say that my colleague Ned Thomas does not feel he can write anything new on *Animal Farm* by the end of April. He feels he has said most of what he has to say on Orwell in his book, published some years ago. But he would have liked to have supported *AJES*, and I dare say that, given a little more persuasion, he will send you something eventually. His present interests are in Mathew Arnold and Anglo-Welsh literature.

With best wishes,

Yours sincerely,

James Ogden

Dated: 22 February 1984

Dear Professor Ansari,

Thank you for your letter of 1 February. I am greatly honoured at being asked to contribute to your Commemorative Volume. I hope to be able to write something worthy of occasion in the time allowed. Among several possible contribution, the one I am most likely to complete is an essay on the interpretation of *Troylus and Cressida*. If I can be of assistance in approaching other contributors, please let me know. It is unfortunate that the two Shakespeare scholars I know best, Jim Nosworthy and Clifford Leech, have both passed on in recent years – "expiring amid their volumes", as Isaac D'Israeli put it. I was also acquainted with the late F.W. Bateson, having attended his seminars at Oxford, 1959-61. I particularly admire his work on the relationship of scholarship and criticism.

With best wishes,

Yours sincerely,

James Ogden

Dated: 23 May 1984

Dear Professor Ansari,

My copy of the *King Lear* issue of *The Aligarh Journal of English Studies* arrived today, with off prints of my essay, and I must immediately write to thank you. I congratulate you on assembling so many distinguished contributors and valuable articles, and I congratulate myself on appearing alongside them. I immediately sat down and read Professor Muir's article, which alone should mean that your journal is sought after by Shakespeareans in many countries. I also re-read my own essay, and was pleased with the accuracy of the printing. I will probably write again when I have read all the articles. In reply to your last letter: I am afraid I don't know Professor Thomson, and indeed now that Jim Nosworthy and Clifford Leech have passed on I do not know anyone eminent in Shakespeare studies, except of course by reputation. I could approach some young hopefuls, if you like.

Best wishes,

James Ogden

Dated: 20 July 1984

Dear Professor Ansari,

Thank you for your letters of 4 June and 12 July.

I beg you to accept my apologies for not writing sooner. I was very busy in June with teaching and examining. These duties have been especially heavy this year, because my department is suffering a 25% cut in staff as a result of the British Government's reduced funding of Universities.

I would still like to contribute to your commemorative volume, but I fear I have been relying excessively on your promise that I could take six or eight months. I see now that the time will run out sooner than I had calculated.

I have written the first draft of an essay on *Troylus and Cressida*. I have asked the department's secretary to make a fair copy of it, which I hope to send with this letter or in a few days' time. I must emphasise that it is only a first draft, which I am only submitting because time is short. It is a critical study opposing the fairly widespread view that Shakespeare's treatment of the lovers is unsympathetic, but I have not read enough recent criticism to assess its originality. I doubt if it is really worthy of the occasion. However, if you think you would like to have it, I could have a somewhat improved version ready for you in September.

Please let me know what you think about this. I will not be in any way offended if you decide that in view of the delay, and the inadequacy of my contribution, you must proceed to publish the commemorative volume without it.

About the *King Lear* number of *AJES* I thought that as a whole it presented an interesting variety of approaches, dealing as it did with textual problems, sources, theatrical effects, and what may be called the "philosophy" of the play. The essay by Professor Muir, giving the views of so eminent an authority on matters currently of great interest, was particularly valuable. His criticisms of Steven Urkowitz's book must temper my enthusiasm for it. I was surprised at the degree of indebtedness to Nashe, Montaigne and Harsnett demonstrated by Tobin and Salingar in their essays, and I should imagine that future editors of the play will have to take note of them. I found Professor Thomson's "*King Lear* and the Actors" stimulating.

I count myself fortunate that my own essay appeared in the company it did, especially as my views evidently somewhat opposed to your own. It may be that my argument needs expanding into a full-scale interpretation of the play, if it is to suggest the possibilities of compromise between your reading and the sentimentalizing of Bardley and others. Perhaps it is very much a Western view, but I cannot avoid the feeling that great art is essentially positive, not nihilistic.

I notice that a number of articles by yourself and others in *AJES* have been mentioned by David Daniell in the "Shakespeare" chapter of *The Year's Work in English Studies*. Your special number of *Hamlet* is favourably received in the volume just published, *YW* 62. If you have not already sent Dr. Daniell a copy of your special number on *King Lear* it would be a good idea to do so (address: English Department, University College, Gower Street, London WCI). I will write to him in due course and mention it.

Well, as I said, I hope to send a draft of an essay on *Troylus and Cressida* either with this letter or after a few days, when it has been typed. I then go away on holiday for two or three weeks. I will be back here by about 25 August at the latest. I would then be able to do some more work on my essay if you thought it was likely to be acceptable. I would not cause much further delay, as during September I must begin writing my chapter for *YW* 64; I must either finish or abandon my essay before that.

I hope this arrangement is satisfactory to you? I look forward to hearing from you.

With best wishes,

Yours sincerely,

James Ogden

Dated: 5th September 1984

Dear Professor Ansari,

Thank you for your letter of 21 August and for some additional offprint of my essay on *King Lear*, which came recently.

I am glad you liked my essay on *Troylus* and *Cressida*, and will certainly send a revised version before October.

I have written to David Daniell about the special *King Lear* number of *AJES*, and will write to Jim Bulman reminding him of your interest in the late Professor Noswrothy's papers.

I enclose a photocopy of the page (p. 194) of *YWES* Vol. 62 where the special *Hamlet* number is mentioned. And a leaflet about *YWES*, hoping that you may subscribe!

Best Wishes,

James Ogden

Dated: 14 September 1984

Dear Professor Ansari,

I have now revised and somewhat reauthored my essay on *Troylus and Cressida* for your *Festschrift* and I am sending a copy with this letter.

I habitually write for the intelligent reader rather than the specialist. I hope you do not mind being told that the Quarto of *Troylus* was published in 1609, which I am sure you know or can easily find out. Anyhow, if the date seems otherwise, it can easily be deleted.

You should by now have received an earlier letter of mine, with information about the coverage of *AJES* in *YWES*.

Best wishes,

James Ogden

Dated: 01 July 1985

Dear Professor Ansari,

I am at present compiling my entry for the *Annual Bibliography of English Language and Literature* published by the Modern Humanities Research Association. I have recorded the essays and reviews in *The Aligarh Journal of English Studies*, vol. 8, and vol. 9 no. 1. If vol. 9 no. 2 is now available I will record the work in that too, if you will kindly forward a copy. However, I think it would be better if in future this work were done by ABELL's Indian representative, P.S. Guptara, whose address unfortunately I do not have, or by somebody else who is on the spot and could perhaps cover other Indian Journals and books. I am not expecting to contribute to *ABELL* much longer myself.

I wonder whether your *Festschrift* has been published yet?

Best wishes,

Yours Sincerely,

James Ogden

Dated: 14 August 1985

Dear Professor Ansari

Thank you for your letter of 23 July, and for sending *AJES*, vol. 9 no. 2. I was very glad to have it, and I look forward to seeing your *Festschrift* when it is ready.

I was interested in your review of *The Leavises.* I always had great admiration for Dr. Leavis myself, heard him lecture on a good many occasions, and met him when he was a Visiting Professor here in the early seventies. It is rather sad that you did not visit him in Cambridge when you were a student at Oxford, as I am sure you would have been treated well. In my experience Leavis was always courteous in conversation, and those who took offence generally did so because to have done anything else would have been to acknowledge Leavis's intellectual superiority. I offer an anecdotal illustration or two.

I first heard Leavis lecture at Durham in 1956, when he spent an hour or so explaining why he believed that critics, as distinct from philosophers, had to exemplify, rather than define. He said something to the effect that he could not define literary greatness in a manner that would satisfy a philosopher, but he supposed nobody would disagree if he asserted that *Anna Karenina* was a great novel. To me as an undergraduate the line of argument was perfectly intelligible. In the discussion after the lecture a Professor (of Modern Languages) stupidly asked what Leavis *meant* by saying *Anna Karenina* was a great novel. Leavis courteously restated what he had said in his lecture. The Professor persisted: Dr. Leavis still had not explained what he meant by such a statement. Leavis replied: "Have you ever read *Anna Karenina?*" The Professor: "I do not share Dr. Leavis's familiarity with Russian". Leavis said something to the effect that experts had assured him that the Aylmer Maude translation was perfectly adequate for his purposes; and that if, as seemed to be the case, the Professor had not read *Anna Karenina,* then it would be impossible to explain to him why it was considered a great novel. The Professor said no more, and was later reported to have been deeply offended. It seemed to me, though, that he had been asking for trouble all along.

When I was first introduced to Leavis the following incident took place. He was talking to some colleagues, and I joined the group. "This is Mr. Ogden", somebody said, "But perhaps you have met before?" We shook hands, and Leavis said, with a hint of a smile to me, "I do not know. I meet so many people you know." Many English academics are very conceited and would have taken offence at this; I just grinned. "Now where were we?" asked Leavis, getting back to more important matters. "Ah yes, Wordsworth. I sometimes think he fulfilled Carlyle's definition of genius you know." He paused. Everyone tried to look as if they remembered it, but I do not think any of us did. Leavis supplied the definition himself, and went on. Many academics would have taken offence here, they had been made to feel a trifle foolish, though they would have done better to have reflected that they ought to have known Carlyle's definition ("The infinite capacity for taking pains") and that they had just heard a most interesting and probably valid application of it. I am sure Leavis was not trying to score off us. It was simply that his mind was not trying to score off us. It was simply that his mind was full of such ideas and information, and they simply flowed out in his conversation, as he strove to do his best with any topic that arose.

A colleague of mine, knowing that Leavis had (in *Revaluation)* expressed dislike of Swinburne, supposed that in fact Leavis would not know much about the poet. It was generally supposed in this country that Leavis knew little about poets of whom he expressed disapproval. This colleague professed to admire Swinburne and to know something about him, so he tackled Leavis on the subject. Leavis replied by quoting poem after poem verbatim, and after each quotation making some adverse criticism. I am glad to say that my colleague, who told me the story himself, did not take offence; but many would have hated Leavis after an incident of that sort.

Perhaps these anecdotes will explain why I think that if I were you I would value Leavis's qualified praise more than Northrop Frye's exuberant commendation.

I am sure you are right that Leavis was religious by temperament. This is sufficiently evident in the writings on Blake, Dickens, and Lawrence, to which you allude. I would add the essays on Bunyan, especially the one in *The Common Pursuit,* and the quotation and comments on the last page (p. 210 in my edition). I was also interested to see that you seem to feel that Leavis's comments on "the malaise of the present age" have some relevance outside what we are pleased to call Western civilization.

About Mrs Leavis you are perhaps a little harsh, though she was undoubtedly guilty of "cussedness". I wrote to her on Leavis's death. She replied by sending a copy of the printed version of a lecture on Wordsworth Leavis gave her. I was very glad to have it. But I *was* rather offended when she claimed to have been unable to read the signature on my letter; as you know, it is always perfectly legible.

Yours sincerely,

James Ogden

PS: Do you by any chance know anything about a Ph.D thesis to be submitted at the University of Calcutta by Sri Arun Kumar Sarkar on "The Intellectual Quest in the Works of Samuel Butler"? I have been asked to act as external examiner, and have replied that I cannot accept till I know whether the thesis is about the seventeenth or the nineteenth century Butler. No need to answer this question if the matter has nothing to do with you.

Dated: 03 December 1985

Dear Professor Ansari

Thank you for your letter.

My entry in your notes on contributors in your commemorative volume:-

James Odgen, M.A. (Dunslon) B. Litt. (Oxon) Senior Lecturer in English, University College of Walves, Aberystwyth, UK.

I hope that is sufficient, and I look forward to assessing the volume.

I have received the recent issue of *AJES*, and will write again later, Very busy at present.

Have heard no more from Calcutla about Samuel Butler.

Best wishes,

James Ogden

Dated: 26 April 1986

Dear Professor Ansari,

Thank you for your letter. I am sorry to have been so long in replying. I thought I would wait while I received my copy of the commemorative volume, which I was expecting some time in March, but it still has not arrived. This is just a brief note to say that if you visit UK in the last week of August, and if you think it worth making the considerable journey from London to Aberystwyth to see me, my wife and I would be very happy to accommodate you at my house.

Best wishes,

James Ogden

Dated: 20 May 1986

Dear Professor Ansari,

Thank you for your letter of 6 May. It is most kind of you to send me a second copy of the *Essays on Shakespeare*. The one sent by air came today, and when the earlier one comes I will donate it to the college library, as you suggest, and in your name.

The volume is a handsome one, and you have got together some excellent contributors. The volume should be in demand for academic libraries, and I hope you have some means of publicizing it outside India, especially in the States.

I was interested to see that Sir Walter Raleigh was the first to hold the Chair of English in your University. I have his book on Shakespeare in the "English Men of Letters" series. Some of the critics of that generation are rather understated, and I look forward to reading Mr Khan's essay on Dowden.

So far I have only read the contributions of Professor Muir and myself. It is good to have Muir's thoughts on the very topical subject of women's parts in Shakespeare. In my own contributions I noticed one or two printing errors:

> p. 223 line 5; should be *Troilus*
> p. 224 line 3; should be Menelaus
> p. 225, 10 lines from the bottom: should be lady, and

p. 226, 4 lines from the bottom: should be Ulysses
p. 226, 3 lines from the bottom: should be proponents
p. 227 beginning of 2nd paragraph: should be the lovers
p. 228 middle of page: should be: not so much because she is trying to conceal things from him as because she is embarrassed.
p. 229 line 13: should be gives (not givas)
p. 229 line 21: should be: be (not ba)

There are more of these than I thought when I started compiling the list. I do not mention them in any carping spirit, but if there is a need for a reprint, as seems perfectly possible, I hope they can be corrected.

I wish I had given a few more personal details, as the other contributors have done. I am afraid I did not realize what was expected. I could have mentioned that I have written a book, *Isaac D'Israeli* (Oxford, 1969), and have contributed to several learned journals, including *The Year's Work in English Studies, English, The Critical Quarterly* and of course *The Aligarh Journal of English Studies.*

I am honoured at having my essay included in your admirable volume. I will write again when the second copy arrives. Do come and see us, if you have time, when you are in England.

Best wishes,

James Ogden

Dated: 30 January 1987

Dear Professor Ansari,

Thank you for your letter of 14 January, about your collection of articles on Sir Walter Raleigh. I am quite interested in this project, though I do not yet know whether I will be able to contribute to it.

I knew from John Gross's account of Raleigh in *The Rise and Fall of the Man of Letters* that he had been a Professor at Aligarh. I gather from Raleigh's collected *Letters* that he was fascinated by Indian and Arabic culture, but thought that the worst features of the London University B.A. scheme had been exported to India.

His views on University education generally are of some interest and might make a suitable subject for an article. They were expounded in various addresses including one at Aberystwyth in 1911.

I have a copy of Raleigh's book on Shakespeare, and have borrowed his book on Milton from the college library. The Milton book is somewhat more incisive, I think, and may be somewhat more influential too. William Empson's *Milton's God* begins with a handsome tribute to Raleigh, anyway. Raleigh's own estimate of the Shakespeare book, that "it gets going, sometimes, for a page or two, and then switches off, and stops", seems fair enough. Raleigh's British Academy lecture "Shakespeare and England" is a strange affair. He had become very patriotic during the 14-18 war, and the lecture is as much about the War as it is about the Bard. Later he became the official historian of the Royal Air Force, a strange way for a Professor of English to end his career.

As you probably know there is a bibliography of Raleigh's writings at the end of the collected *Letters.* I have not yet had time to study this thoroughly and to find out whether all the writings are available here. So I must beg for more time to think about a possible contribution, and I think Raleigh's Milton may prove a better subject than his Shakespeare. I suppose that in a volume of this sort one is not expected to be too critical!

My colleague Richard Brinkley has a copy of the *Catalogue of the Bulk of the Library of the Late Sir Walter Raleigh,* which was sold by Blackwell in 1922. Some 2000 volumes are listed and the catalogue gives some idea of Raleigh's literary interests. I could probably persuade Brinkley to send you an account of it for your book if you like.

Best wishes,

Yours sincerely,

James Ogden

Dated: 04 June 1987

Dear Professor Ansari,

Thank you for your letters of 4 and 20 May, about the Sir Walter Raleigh commemoration volume. I was rather surprised by both, especially the second, in which you say I have consented to write an essay on Raleigh as a Milton critic and send it by the beginning of May.

I have before me your letter of 14 January, which asks me to write an essay for the commemoration volume, but makes no mention of an early deadline. As I recall, in my reply I only said I was considering the possibility of writing an essay on Raleigh as a Milton critic. I mentioned some other points of interest, for instance that my colleague Richard Brinkley has a copy of the sale catalogue of Raleigh's library, and could perhaps write an article about it. I had no reply to my letter till May, so you will perhaps appreciate that I failed to sense any urgency.

I had perhaps better explain that I have had personal problems this year, on account of the illness and death of my mother, and I have not made much progress with any of my research projects. I am sorry to say I have nothing ready on Raleigh, so I think you had better go ahead without me. I hope I will be able to make a further contribution to *AJES* eventually.

I am glad to say that I have received *AJES* vol. 10 nos. I and 2, and have reported on them for the *Annual Bibliography of English Language and Literature*. I had a letter from the editor only yesterday, thanking me for my "interesting" contribution. I take this to refer to *AJES*, which is not so well known here as the other journals on which I report. The articles on Blake by Kathleeen Raine and Desiree Hurst are of course especially valuable, and when scholars find them in *ABELL* they will want to consult *AJES*, and will no doubt be attracted by other articles in it.

I am sorry I have been unable to help with the Raleigh commemoration volume.

Best wishes,

Yours sincerely,

James Ogden

Dated: 06 July 1987

Dear Professor Ansari,

Thank you for your letter of 11 June.

It is now the summer vacation here, and I can think about contributing to your volume of essays on Professor Walter Raleigh. I will try to write something on his book on Milton, and to let you have it before the end of the vacation, that is, in September at the latest. Some 4-5000 words. Nor many wanted? I am sorry to say I cannot do better than that, and I hope it will not interfere with your timetable for publishing the volume.

One of the difficulties about writing for a volume designed to commemorate Raleigh is that he has attracted a great deal of powerful adverse criticism. There was Virginia Woolf's essay in *The Captain's Death Bed,* followed by Q.D. Leavis's comments in her essay "The Discipline of Letters", published in an early number of *Scrutiny* and since reprinted. The accounts of Raleigh in John Gross's *The Rise and Fall of the Man of Letters* (1969), Chris Baldick's *The Social Mission of English Criticism* (1983) and Terry Hawkes's *That Shakespearian Rag* (1986) are all basically unsympathetic. Some of these critics go so far as to accuse him of seeing English studies as an adjunct of the British Empire, and most believe he helped to establish a view of the subject with which they profoundly disagree. I hope that some of your contributors are familiar with these criticisms and can do something to moderate them. The criticisms seem to have been directed mostly at Raleigh's work on Shakespeare and his influence generally, so that in writing about his book on Milton I will partly sidestep them.

I have asked my colleague Richard Brinkley to consider writing something about the catalogue of Raleigh's books, but he has been on holiday and I have not seen him for some time. Have just seen him again. He is definitely working on Raleigh Library. Have told him September at the latest.

I was interested to hear about your plans for future issues of *AJES*.

In case you think I am allowing myself an excessive amount of time for the completion of my essay, perhaps I should add that I have to write my chapter for *YWES* vol. 67 this summer vacation too.

Best wishes,

James Ogden

Dated: 10 July 1987

Dear Professor Ansari,

I hope you have by now received my reply to your letter of 11 June. In my reply I promised to write an essay on Raleigh's book on Milton for your commemoration volume, but said I did not expect to have it ready before September.

I am glad to say that I now expect to send you the essay before the end of the present month. Some of the preliminary work I did when I first heard about your project in January has proved more useful than I thought. I have set aside all other work, and now have the draft of an essay of some 4000 words, including the footnotes, just about ready for the typist.

I have called the essay "Raleigh's 'Splendid Handbook' on Milton", taking the quoted phrase from Empson's *Milton's God*. Raleigh's book is not really a handbook in the usual sense, but it was obviously handy for Empson, as he borrowed examples from it when writing *Seven Types of Ambiguity*. I hope I have done enough in my essay to show what Raleigh's book is about and why it has been influential. I am quite pleased with the way my work has developed, and I hope you will be.

I was rather sorry that I could not find a suitable place in the essay for the information that Milton was one of the authors Raleigh lectured on at Aligarh: see his *Letters*, ed. Lady Raleigh (1926) i, 43. I have included this in a footnote. But it occurs to me that you may like to use it yourself, if you are writing a general introduction to the volume!

My colleague Richard Brinkley is keen to write something on the sale catalogue of Raleigh's library, but as a librarian he has other duties, and he is a rather slow writer. Can you please let me know if it will be all right if his essay is ready by September, or shall I urge him to get a move on?

Best wishes,

James Ogden

Dated: 23 July 1987

Dear Professor Ansari,

Thank you for your letter of 15 July. By now you should have my essay on Raleigh and Milton, which I sent off a week ago. I hope it will be all right. You ask me to photocopy some adverse commentaries on Raleigh I mentioned in an earlier letter. I think two of these were by Hawkes and Baldick, and the third probably by John Gross. I will try to photocopy the relevant parts of the books concerned, though this will not be very easy in the case of Baldick especially.

Best wishes,

James Ogden

Dated: 09 November 1987

Dear Professor Ansari,

Thank you for your letter of 28 October.

I have urged Mr. Brinkley to get on with his article on Sir Walter Raleigh's books. I will keep mentioning the matter to him, and I hope he will finish it by the end of the month. He says he has not received your letter.

Thank you for sending copies of *AJES*. I have issues up to and including Vol. 11 No. 2. I look forward to getting Vol. 12 No. 1. I am still reporting on *AJES* for the *Annual Bibliography of English Literature*. The most recent volume of *The Year's Work in English Studies* covers work published in 1984, and I am afraid it does not make much reference to *AJES*, so far as I can see.

Best wishes,

James Ogden

Dated: 10 February 1988

Dear Professor Ansari,

Thank you for your letter of 1 February.

I was glad to hear that the Raleigh commemoration volume was so near to publication, and I very much look forward to receiving a copy.

You could put something like this about me in your list of Contributors:

James Ogden is a Senior Lecturer in English at the University College of Wales, Aberystwyth, UK. His publications include a book, *Isaac D'Israeli* (Oxford, 1969), and numerous articles, such as 'Milton's Ideal of Innocence' (*Critical Quarterly*, 1982) and 'Lear's Blasted Heath' (*Durham University Journal*, forthcoming, 1988).

Some time ago Professor Munir Ahmad wrote, asking for my comments on *AJES* and contributions to future issues. I repeated what I had written to you, that I quite admired Professor Maqbool Khan's essay on Raleigh's Shakespeare criticism. I have circulated his letter round this department, with a note from me asking for contributions, but unfortunately I haven't had any yet. Advance notice of any special issues dealing with particular authors or subjects might be helpful.

With best wishes,

Yours sincerely,

James Ogden

Dated: 29 April 1988

Dear Professor Ansari,

Mr. Brinkley and I received our copies of *Eassys on Sir Walter Raleigh* earlier this week. Many thanks.

Congratulations on conceiving and carrying out this project. The volume includes some very interesting contributions, particularly your own introduction and essay on Raleigh's book on style, and Professor Muir's essay. I have not had time to do very much more than glance at the other contributions, but I do look forward to reading them. Some of the quotations in Professor Singh's essay on Raleigh's letters are appetizing.

Best wishes,

Yours sincerely,

James Ogden

Dated: 28 June 1988

Dear Professor Ansari,

Thank you for your letter about *The Aligarh Critical Miscellany.*

I do not think I can contribute anything on T.S. Eliot, but I have alerted colleagues, and something may be forthcoming from them. Please let me know of plans for later issues.

And I am sorry to say I do not think our library will subscribe. Owing to financial difficulties caused by Government policy, we are having to cut back on subscriptions to periodicals. My request will almost certainly be rejected by the committee.

I continue to contribute to the *Annual Bibliography of English Language and Literature,* and to the *Year's Work in English Studies.* I expect to spend a good deal of time in the next year or so editing *The Country Wife* for the New Mermaid series. I enclose an offprint of an article I have had published in the *Durham University Journal.*

With best wishes,

Yours sincerely,

James Ogden

Dated: 27 September 1989

Dear Professor Ansari,

I received today *The Aligarh Critical Miscellany,* vol. 2 no. 1. I was very pleased to get it, not only because I will enjoy reading some of the essays, but also because I had not heard from you for some time. I have not heard from the editor of *The Aligarh Journal of English Studies* either, and I had begun to fear that the Salman Rhushdie affair had come between us.

I am glad to say that I have been able to report on the *Miscellany,* vol. 1, and the *Essays on Sir Walter Raleigh,* for the *Annual Bibliography of English Studies.* The *Essays* will and thus achieve some prominence when the volume eventually appears. I have, I think, treated it as a *Festschrift,* greatly reduced my contributions to *The Year's Work in English Studies,* and hence also my influence with its editor, but I would hope that if you continue to send your miscellanies and other publications to the English Association some of them will be reviewed.

I wrote some time ago a critical introduction to Benjamin Disraeli's novel *Sybil,* which was not published, partly I think because the prospective publishers, Penguin Books, obtained an introduction by R.A. Butler the distinguished politician, which would no doubt sell the book better than anything I wrote. If you would like to consider my essay for your *Miscellany* I will revise it. I must add that a new session is about to begin, and it is unlikely that I could complete the revision very quickly. I have a "light term" from January to March, and that is when I would probably finish it.

Best wishes,

Yours sincerely,

James Ogden

Dated: 09 January 1990

Dear Professor Ansari,

Many thanks for your last letter and for sending *The Aligarh Critical Miscellany* vol. 2 no. 2, which has just arrived.

I was glad to hear that you would like an essay on Disraeli's *Sybil* for the *Miscellany*, and I have been revising my work. I will write again about his, certainly well before the March deadline. I would like if possible to get a colleague to read my essay before sending it off.

In answer to your query, I did receive your T.S. Eliot centenary number, which I read with interest and reported to *ABELL*. I look forward to reading the special William Blake number. You have certainly assembled an exceptionally strong team of contributors for the latter.

I was interested to hear that you are to devote a forthcoming number to *Othello*. I do not think I can offer a contribution. My views are no doubt excessively influenced by those of T.G.A. Nelson and Charles Haines, 'Othello's Unconsummated Marriage', *Essays in Criticism* vol. 33 (1983) pp. 1-18. I have not seen a convincing refutation of this essay, though if Nelson and Haines are right, it seems odd that nobody thought of their explanation before they did. Perhaps one of your contributors can show how they go wrong.

Best wishes,

Yours sincerely,

James Ogden

Dated: 25 March 1991

Dear Professor Ansari,

I am sorry I have not written for some time. As you will see from the letter heading we have a new Head of Department, and consequent changes in the syllabus have distracted me from research.

If I have not thanked you before, may I say many thanks for sending *The Aligarh Critical Miscellany*, vol. 3 no. 1. I have just been reporting it for the *Annual Bibliography of English Language and Literature*, and noticing again that it contains some valuable articles. I do not seem to have a copy of vol. 3 no. 2, and assuming it has been published I would be most obliged if you could send one, for *ABELL*.

You may be interested to hear that my edition of Wycherley's *The Country Wife* for the New Memaids will be published soon, the publication process having taken well over a year.

Best wishes,

Yours sincerely,

James Ogden

Dated: 30 May 1991

Dear Professor Ansari,

I have been deeply saddened by the assassination of Mr. Gandhi and by the violence during your General Election. Of course I cannot assess the merits of the various political parties, but no cause justifies terrorism, and terrorism achieves little or nothing. India is engaged in a great effort to achieve and maintain political stability and economic progress. Your country has many friends who pray that this effort will succeed, for the sake of your own people and humanity in general.

Many thanks for sending *The Aligarh Critical Miscellany,* vol. 3 no. 2, on which I have reported for *ABELL.* Of course you have done well to obtain and publish the articles by Kenneth Muir and the late Harold Brooks. I read these and your own essay on "The Power Nexus in *Richard II*" with great pleasure. I am inclined to think that Shakespeare meant us to see Richard as a more tragic figure than you seem to allow, giving him a fine speech in Act V, and allowing him to kill two of his assassins. Bolingbroke is diminished in comparison, yet we are not to lose sympathy with him, so he is to be a forceful, eloquent, and sad figure in the two parts of *Henry IV*. So as you say there is "ambivalence" in *Richard II*; that is certainly the word for it.

Best wishes,

James Ogden

Dated: 27 June 1991

Dear Professor Ansari,

Thank you for your recent letter.

With regard to Northrop Frye, there are two possibilities. Firstly, my colleague Mr. Tim Woods is willing to write a short essay – some four pages, he suggested – on Frye's standing as a critic today. Secondly, Professor Richard D McGhee of Kansas State University visited us recently and gave a talk on Northrop Frye and Harold Bloom. Some of his material on Frye would probably be suitable for publication.

If you are interested in publishing an essay by Tim Woods, please let me know as soon as possible. It will have to be written during the coming long vacation. If you want to get in touch with Professor McGhee, please write to him at:

Department of English
Denison Hall
Kansas State University
Manhattan
Kansas 66506-0701
United States of America

and mention my name.

I will try to write an article for a forthcoming issue of your journal. I have in mind something on *Measure for Measure.*

Best wishes,

Your sincerely,

James Ogden

Dated: 13 September 1991

Dear Professor Ansari,

Many thanks for your letter of 3 September. I was glad to hear that Professor McGhee had sent you his paper, and that you had found it worthy of inclusion in your journal. I have told my colleague Tim Woods that you would like him to write an article, rather than a note, on Northrop Frye as a critic, and that it will not be needed before February 1992. He said he was glad to hear this, as he has not made as much progress on it as he hoped this summer, but he thinks he will have some spare time during the Christmas vacation and January. As for my promised article on *Message for Measure,* a change in our teaching arrangements means that it must be delayed. I had expected to lecture on the play during the coming term, and hence to complete an article in November or December, but I will not now be lecturing on it till next term, and hence will not complete an article till February or March, probably too late for the February deadline. Other changes in our arrangements mean that I will have a disagreeably heavy teaching burden this year. You will perhaps infer from this last sentence that I have just re-read *Pilgrim's Progress.* It is of course one of the most universally admired works of English literature, and I would be interested to know how it is regarded by Moslems.

With best wishes,
James Ogden

Dated: 12 March 1992

Dear Professor Ansari,

I am sorry I have not written to you for some time. As I may have mentioned before, we are teaching a new syllabus here, and all this session I have been unusually busy, and in the evenings very tired. I have been feeling my age: fifty-six this year. However, I should have written to you sooner, to thank you for your new year greetings, for a copy of your *Miscellany* vol. 4 no. 1, and for an earlier letter about my colleague Tim Woods's proposed contribution.

Mr. Woods is on study leave this term, and I do not see him very often. When I received your earlier letter I got in touch with him, and I gathered that he was doubtful if he could complete his article on Northrop Frye. He said he would write to you and explain his difficulties, and I gave him your address. I understood that he had written to you, and I will be annoyed with him if it turns out that he has not. I will get in touch with him again as soon as possible. So you see my conscience is fairly clear, but I am still truly sorry that you seem to have been misled.

I have one piece of good news. My article on *Measure for Measure* is almost ready. This busy term ends on 27 March, and I should be able to produce the final version soon after that. I hope you will find it worthy of inclusion in your *Miscellany.*

Best wishes,

James Ogden

Dated: 19 April 1992

Dear Professor Ansari,

Thank you for your letter of 25 March, and for sending *The Aligarh Critical Miscellany* vol. 4 no. 1. I am sorry my colleague Tim Woods has not yet contributed anything on Northrop Frye, and I hope that by now be has written and explained himself. I know he has been busy finishing his Ph.D., and no doubt working against a deadline. I see that you have again been able to call on some distinguished contributors to your miscellany. I have not yet read all the articles but I did enjoy reading Jean R. Brooks's on Hamlet and Ophelia. I have completed my essay on *Measure for Measure,* and I hope to send it with this letter, though there will be a little delay, as the college is on holiday for Easter, and I may be unable to gain access to a photocopying machine. Also, I feel tempted to make some stylistic changes.

Best wishes,

James Ogden

Dated: 14 July 1992

Dear Professor Ansari,

I am sorry I have not written for some time. The summer term which has just ended has been unusually busy and difficult. But I did send off my essay on *Measure for Measure* for the *Critical Miscellany* before the term began, and as I have not heard from you about it I begin to wonder whether it arrived safely?

I have received that *Critical Miscellany* vol. 4 no. 2. Many thanks. Here are a few points arising from your review of Barbara Everett's book on Shakespeare's tragedies.

I agree with you in thinking Barbara Everett a perceptive critic, and with your objection to what she says about Othello on p. 217 of your review.

I have not got her book to hand, and in places I am not sure whether you are summarizing her views or your own. If what is said on p. 218 about the ending of *King Lear* is your own view, it was good of you to print my essay on the subject in the *Aligarh Journal* some years ago, as my view is quite different. Lear not only suffers, he also challenges.

Enter King Lear with Queen Cordelia in his arms.

Lear Howl, howl, howl; O, you are men of stones… Lear has recovered his physical strength, and ability to dominate the stage. He is not howling, but demanding that the courtiers should howl. They do not know how to respond.

I killed the slave that was a-hanging thee. The courtiers' faces express disbelief.

Gentleman, 'Tis true, my Lords, he did.

Lear. Did I not, fellow?...

This is an important incident, preserved in both texts. Later Albany tries to make the sort of speech that usually ends Shakespearean tragedies, but he is upstaged by Lear's death, and I think is overcome by a sense of his own inadequacy. Finally nobody quite knows what to say, but either Albany or Edgar makes the concluding speech. I think it should be Edgar, though in either case the character has learnt something from his harrowing experiences.

I also take a more sympathetic view of Cressida than Everett seems to do, in my essay in your *Festschrift.*

I am not "familiar" with the line "O that this too sallied flesh would melt" (p. 223 of your review); I know "sallied" has been suggested by editors but it has not been adopted in any of the texts I use. The idea that it means sexually assaulted is new; but spoken by a man, does not make much sense. The Folio's "too solid" is the only version of the line that makes sense of the repeated adverb and the metaphor: his flesh seems much too solid, so he wishes it would melt.

I am afraid I cannot comment very helpfully on the matter of Tim Woods and Northrop Frye. I wish you would take it up with him, if you still want an essay. I know he has been busy completing his Ph.D, which he has now been awarded. Like me, he has been busy with teaching too, as we have begun to implement a new syllabus. I think he is still not unwilling to write something on Frye for you, but feels that the occasion for it may have passed.

My own future plans include a book on Milton and a collection of essays on *King Lear*, which I am editing in collaboration with Professor Arthur Scouten, formerly of the University of Pennsylvania. This is meant to cover the textual controversy, recent interpretations, and performance history. We are having difficulties in finding women contributors – very necessary in the West nowadays – and somebody to write on the play in the enema and on television. I would be interested to know whether there have been Indian adoptions.

Best wishes,

As ever,

James Ogden

Dated: 4 January 1993

Dear Professor Ansari,

I was delighted to receive your *Critical Miscellany* today. I am sorry I tried to get my colleague Tim Woods to contribute something on Northrop Frye, partly because I fear that has delayed the appearance of this issue, and partly because I see now that Woods, who is a Marxist, could not have written anything appropriate. You have a much better appreciation of Frye than Woods will ever have, your essay is a worthy memorial to his work on Shakespeare.

I must say I agree with what you say on p. 23, that Frye is right in thinking that Christianity as an institutional religion is incapable of the tragic vision. His further statement quoted there seems to be an attempt to claim this vision for the individual Christian. But really, as my teacher the late Clifford Leech emphasized in his book *Shakespeare's Tragedies,* the Christian who believes in the resurrection of Christ and associated doctrines cannot consistently hold a tragic view of life. And Leech would have agreed with you against Frye, as I do myself that the experience of tragedy, though terrifying, can be energizing rather than debilitating. All this, of course, is not to deny that there are valuable insights in Frye's work as a whole.

These considerations bring me to what I was trying to say in a letter to you I began and gave up a month ago. My dear fellow-scholar: we live in deeply troubled times. I am disturbed by the news from India of attacks by Hindus upon Moslems, and from many parts of the world of similar tragic conflicts between people of different persuasions in religion. With some, these persuasions may be nothing but excuses, and with others they may be no better than dogmas. These unhappy probabilities will support arguments against religion by its materialistic enemies. It is clearly a time for all who believe in the essentially spiritual nature of human life to hold together. May your spirit be strong now and at all times.

Best wishes,

Yours sincerely,

James Ogden

Dated: 2 March 1993

Dear Professor Ansari,

As you know, T.S. Eliot completes *The Waste Land* with the words "Shantih shantih shantih" and explains in a note that "our equivalent to this word" is "The peace which passeth understanding". Repeated in this way, he says, it is the formal ending to an Upanishad.

Hence while listening to the radio commentary on the recent one-day cricket match between India and England at Jamshedpur, where there was much crowd trouble and at one point an invasion of the pitch, I was surprised to hear the words "Shantih shantih shantih" over the public address system. Possibly they did have some effect in calming the crowd. I wondered whether they still had their religious connotation? I do not think it occurred to Eliot that they could be used in very different contexts.

I hope you have received my letter thanking you for the recent *Aligarh Critical Miscellany.* I have also recently been sent the *Aligarh Journal of English Studies,* vol. 14 no. 2, 1989 – falling behind schedule, if this is their most recent issue; But I am grateful to Mr. Tariq for sending it, and will try to write when I have read one or two essays. At present I am busy writing a book on Milton.

Best wishes,

James Ogden

Dated: 2 July 1993

Dear Professor Ansari,

I am now indebted to you for a letter and a copy of your *Critical Miscellany* vol. 5 no. 2.

I am sorry I have not answered your letter sooner, but I feel sure you will understand that I was disturbed by your expression of despair at the recent turmoil in India, and did not know what to say. We have similar troubles, especially in Northern Ireland, but on a much smaller scale. In response, academics can only vow not to cease from mental fight, and take pains to promote better understanding of the spiritual needs of mankind. Your *Miscellany* itself encourages the "vitalizing processes of interaction" to which you refer in your review-article, which makes me feel I must re-read Blake, especially to understand his assimilation of Milton and Shakespeare's *King Lear.* This is a very good issue of the *Miscellany;* I think Vincent Newey's article, in particular, will be much sought after.

My projected book on Milton proceeds slowly. I will bear in mind your suggestion that parts may be suitable for publication in your *Miscellany.* Please may I have your permission to reprint my essay on Raleigh and Milton from your *Essays on Sir Walter Raleigh?*

Best wishes,

James Ogden

Dated: 02 August 1993

Dear Professor Ansari,

Many thanks for your letter of 9 July, and for permission to reprint my essay from your *Essays on Sir Walter Raleigh*. The source will of course be fully acknowledged.

I am applying for early retirement, but do not yet know whether I will get it on reasonable terms. If I do, I may have time to think about an essay on Marlowe by mid-December, but I fear it is doubtful whether I will have anything of much value. If I do not get early retirement, I am sorry to say I will certainly not have time. I will write again on this subject.

I have compiled a list of the essays on Shakespeare in the *Aligarh Critical Miscellany,* a copy of which I enclose. I hope you will not mind if I send a copy of it to my friend Thomas A. Pendleton, editor of *The Shakespeare Newsletter,* in the hope that he will publicise your *Miscellany* in his journal?

Best wishes,

James Ogden

Dated: 18 February 1994

Dear Professor Ansari,

I am very grateful to you for sending your *Miscellany,* volume 6 no. 1, and to Professor Maqbool Khan for sending the *Aligarh Journal,* volume 15 nos. I and 2. Their arrival here roughly coincided with the beginning of Ramadan. I will of course be writing to Professor Khan separately.

In your *Miscellany* I was especially interested in your essay on Richard III and Richard II, in Professor Singh's on Leopardi, and in Dr Beatty's on Byron. I believe Shakespeare could see Richard III as a tragic figure, but had some difficulty in portraying him as such, because his rival Richmond was none other than the reigning Queen's grandfather: to show Richard's downfall as anything other than Richmond's triumph was to question received wisdom in a manner that could have cost Shakespeare his head. Nevertheless Richard is presented as the most interesting character in the play, and we may be left feeling that we pay a high price for political progress in the alienation and destruction of the individual. In writing about Richard II Shakespeare was freer to say what he liked, as the Wars of the Roses belonged to a relatively remote period of history, and Richard is allowed a heroic death, with a fine soliloquy in prison and an act of self-assertion against his murderers. Bolingbroke's assumption of power is not represented as an unequivocal triumph.

I must admit I am not much interested in Shelly, and I do not know Mr. Everest, but the fact that he is currently engaged on the Longman annotated edition of that poet shows you are able to attract some of the best scholars to publish in your *Miscellany.* I suppose it is a good idea to publish the best essays you can get, even if necessary to the exclusion of some native Indian scholars. But I was pleased to see that the *Aligarh Journal* has got going again, and is providing an outlet for some of their work. I read Professor Khan's editorial and interview with you with great interest. I was sorry to hear that many Indians study Western literature before they have any real knowledge of Indian literature, and I would think it should be a great object of your education system to remedy this defect.

Best wishes,

Yours sincerely,

James Ogden

Dated: 15 October 1994

Dear Professor Ansari,

Many thanks for sending the special Marlowe number of *The Aligarh Critical Miscellany*. It is some years since I had to lecture on Marlowe, and I fear my knowledge of his work has faded. But I have read your essay and Professor Muir's with great interest, and I look forward to reading the others. I know something of Desiree Hurst's and I think Professor Viswanathan was an interesting subject. I know one should be contented with what has been done, and not complain about what has not been done, but I was hoping you would find somebody familiar with the history of relations between Muslims and Christians to write about *Tamburlaine*.

Marlowe's view of it in the second part of the play (II. i-iii) is not unfavourable to the Muslims, and he seems to represent Tamburlaine's fatal illness as retribution for burning the Koran (V.i). I wonder where Marlowe got such ideas, and how they were received, but I was too ignorant and to busy with other work to tackle the subject myself. I am glad to report that the anthology *Lear from Study to Stage* is now with the Edwin Mellen Press, and will probably be published by them next year. Would you like me to ask them to send you a review copy? A little publicity in India would be welcome.

Best wishes,

James Ogden

Dated: 1 November 1994

Dear Professor Ansari,

Many thanks for your letter of 12 October, which seems to have crossed my last letter in the post. I wrote about a fortnight ago thanking you for the *Critical Miscellany* special Marlowe number, I received some weeks earlier.

I think I may be able to supply an article for the forthcoming special Keats number. I have given lectures on our literary theory course, under the title "From Works to Texts", dealing mainly with critics who regard literature as works written by authors compared with those who regard it as texts read by readers. The former make claims to objectivity, and the latter are often frankly subjective. I have used critical discussion on a single stanza of Keats's "Ode to a Nightingale" as an example. I enclose a copy of my lecture notes. I hope the abbreviations do not make it hard to read:

w = with, o = of, t = the, tt = that, wd = would, & c.

All fairly obvious really. I am thinking of writing up these lectures for an essay in literary theory, but I hope you will agree that an expanded version of this section on the "Nightingale" ode would be suitable for your special number. I will somewhat expand the references to Gradman, White and Bennett. I will avoid attacking Talbot by name, as he has not actually published his views.

If you find an article on these lines acceptable, I may at some later date have to ask you for permission to reprint some of it. That reminds me that I am sorry if I forgot to thank you, in my last letter, for permission to reprint part of my essay on "The Ending of *King Lear*" in the introduction to *Lear from Study to Stage* (Edwin Mellen Press, forthcoming). I am truly grateful.

Best wishes,

James Ogden

Dated: 30 November 1994

Dear Professor Ansari,

I am obliged to you for two recent letters. In the first of these, which crossed my last letter in the post, you kindly agreed to review *Lear from Study to Stage* in *ACM*. I will arrange for a review copy to be sent to you, though I am sorry to say that publication may be delayed till 1996. In the second, you accepted for *ACM* my projected essay on "Keats and the Responsive Reader". I will probably write again about this essay during the Christmas vacation, when I see it taking shape. I have in mind adding something on the interpretation of Keats' "Ode on Melancholy" which does not really have much to do with what I have written about his "Ode to a Nightingale".

But, more important than all that, I hope your elder daughter is well, and I hope I can congratulate you on the birth of a grandchild?

Best wishes,

James Ogden

Dated: 05 May 1995

Dear Professor Ansari,

I enclose a copy of an essay on Keats, which I have written for your projected issue of the *Aligarh Critical Miscellany* to celebrate the bicentenary of his birth. The essay is along the lines we discussed earlier, and I hope it is suitable. I also hope it is not too late. During recent months I have found myself busier than I expected to be.

Best wishes,

James Ogden

Dated: 9 July 1995

Dear Professor Ansari,

Thank you for your recent letter. I was glad to hear that you liked my essay "Response and Responsibility". I am sorry you are having difficulty getting essays on Keats, and sorry I cannot be much help. The only Keats scholar known to me personally is Professor Ian Jack, the author of *Keats and the Mirror of Art*. He was my research supervisor many years ago, and can be reached through Pembroke College, Cambridge, but I know he is currently busier with Browning than with Keats. Mention my name if you write to him. He may know some younger scholars who would be willing to contribute.

I asked my friend Professor Anne Barbeau Gardiner if she had anything on Keats, but she has not, and as a Roman Catholic herself she finds Keats's whole attitude to life unattractive. She is an authority on Dryden, who will perhaps be commemorated in the year 2000.

Many thanks for sending the *Aligarh Critical Miscellany* vol. VII no. 1, which came while I was away last week. Once again you have assembled an interesting collection of essays, some of which will certainly be cited by other scholars. I met Professor Vincent Newey about a year ago when he came here to lecture on Thomas Gray, and I look forward to reading his essay.

We have had hot weather here in the last few weeks, and it seems to have affected my old typewriter, making some letters stick disconcertingly,

Best wishes,

James Ogden

Dated: 18 August 1995

Dear Professor Ansari,

In your letter of 20 May you said you were short of material for the Keats number of the *Aligarh Critical Miscellany,* and asked me for help. I think I said in reply that I would mention your problem to one or two colleagues in other universities. Now my friend Professor Stuart Sillars tells me he is expecting to read the enclosed paper at a big Keats conference at Harvard in September. He says he will be happy for you to publish the paper if you think it is good enough, and I am sending it with this letter. I have read it myself, and made a few minor corrections, but in general I think Stuart has brought to bear his knowledge of fine art very effectively, and has produced something interesting and original. Stuart is quite well known for his books on art and literature, and he has contributed an essay on paintings and drawings of *King Lear* for my forthcoming anthology *Lear from Study to Stage.* Unfortunately I cannot remember which American university Stuart currently teaches at, but I have his home address and will get this information for you.

As ever,

James Ogden

Dated: 8 September 1995

Dear Professor Ansari,

Thank you for your letter of 28 August, which reached me today. I was very pleased to hear that you like Stuart Sillars's article, and I will relay your comments to him.

If you need to write to Sillars, or need an address to put at the end of his essay, he is Slattery Professor of English, Incarnate Word College, San Antonio, Texas. I suppose with a name like that the college must be a Roman Catholic foundation, but Sillars himself is not a Papist.

Your *Miscellany*, vol. vii no. 2, came a little earlier this week. I look forward to reading the Shakespeare essays in particular, as it is likely I will take a course on Shakespeare this term. I notice Professor Paris says "the shift in Shakespeare's treatment of Brutus remains a mystery". Perhaps it is if you want Shakespeare to be entirely self-consistent; but he was a practical dramatist, I think, and wanted an effective conclusion in the theatre. Anyway, I will have to read the whole essay.

Best wishes,

James Ogden

Dated: 16 November 1995

Dear Professor Ansari,

Thank you for your letter of 3 November and for sending an offprint of "Time in Shakespeare's Sonnets". I hope you will not mind conveying my thanks to Professor Maqbool Hasan Khan for sending *AJES* vol. 10 nos. 1 & 2, which came a little earlier, though I will probably write to him eventually.

I enjoyed reading your essay. It probably makes no difference to your general argument, but I think I understand Marvell's "Definition of Love" differently. I believe Marvell's tone is that of somebody making the best of a bad job, so that we read with a wry smile and shrug of the shoulders:

> Therefore the Love which us doth bind,
> But Fate so enviously debars,
> Is the Conjunction of the Mind,
> And Opposition of the Stars.

After all his general argument in this poem is: I am desperate for love; but at least that proves my love is spiritual. The more ingenuity he puts into his proof that his love is spiritual, the more desperate we feel he is behind the smiles and shrugs. But I am sure you are right in thinking that "the marriage of true minds" (Shakespeare) "a love … inter-assured of the mind" (Donne) and "the Conjunction of the Mind" (Marvell) are similar ideas.

I am flattered that you want to reprint my "Dryden's Satirical Tendency" in your *Miscellany*. I have no objection at all, and I do not think the editor of *Forum* will have either, but I think you should ask permission by writing to

Professor A. H. Ashe
Forum for Modern Language Studies
University of St Andrews
Buchanan Building
Union Street
St Andrews, KY16 9PH
Scotland, UK

I will myself write to Professor Ashe, probably next week, and mention that you want to reprint my essay. I ought to write anyway, because *Forum* sent no less than fifty off prints, and I sent them all over the world (well, India, New Zealand, Hawaii, America, Germany), and have had some pleasing replies.

Best wishes,

James Ogden

Dated: 10 February 1996

Dear Professor Ansari,

Many thanks for sending *The Aligarh Critical Miscellany* Special John Keats Number. I am sorry I have been rather slow in acknowledging receipt of the *Miscellany*, but I have been preoccupied with family problems. My daughter Rachel, who has Down's syndrome, has been suffering from deafness, and my mother-in-law has become unable to look after herself, and has moved into an old people's home. I have not been very well myself, but I think I am recovered.

I have read most of the *Miscellany* with much pleasure. I do not think anyone will disagree with your statement that "To Autumn" is "the most flawless of the Odes", except perhaps by suggesting that there cannot be degrees of flawlessness. In some moods most of the odes can seem excessively poetical, with their frequent references to Lethe, Dryads, Psyche, Phoebe, Vesper and so forth, but probably the "ode to a Grecian Urn", and "To Autumn" certainly, would escape this criticism. The conclusion of the "Grecian Urn" has seemed to some critics to be either nonsense in itself or unsupported by the poem as a whole, but I think Cleanth Brooks disposed of such criticisms in *The Well-Wrought Urn.* In the case of "To Antumn" it is hard to think of any way in which the poem might be improved. I was interested to see that you thought of the gleaner here as being a male person. Probably most English readers would see the gleaner as female and perhaps associate her with Ruth. I wish I had pursued this point in my article.

I was interested in the suggestion that British Council representatives were all Keats enthusiasts. I wonder where they got this enthusiasm from? It is an aspect of Keats's influence I had not thought about before.

I have sent photocopies of my own article to some friends, and hope it may arouse interest in your *Miscellany*.

Best wishes,

James Ogden

Dated: 01 July 1996

Dear Professor Ansari,

Many thanks for your letter of 21 June. I was delighted to hear that my article on "Dryden's Satirical Tendency" is to be included in your *Miscellany,* and I look forward to receiving a copy. The publication of your daughter's book is likewise very good news, and I will gladly review it for you.

My anthology *Lear from Study of Stage* should be ready soon and I will ask the publishers to send you a review copy. One of the contributors, Stephen Philips, tells me he is writing an essay on *Hamlet.* I have suggested to him that you may consider it for your *Miscellany,* and that he should either get in touch with you directly, or send the essay to me first.

Best wishes,

James Ogden

Dated: 01 April 1997

Dear Dr. Asnari,

I enclose a review (4 pages) of your daughter's book on the last plays of Shakespeare. I fear there are some signs of haste, resulting from my efforts to meet your deadline. I have tried to express a favourable but balanced judgment.

On the first page I have altered "first scene" to "early scenes": I was of course forgetting that Edmund appears in the very first scene of the play as well as the second, and I hope your printers can read my writing. I have throughout referred to your daughter as "Dr. Ara": if this form is incorrect or unconventional, please supply the correct or conventional form.

Thank you for asking me to review this book. I sincerely hope your family will not suffer the vicissitudes of the families in the last plays.

Best wishes,

James Ogden

Dated: 15 December 1997

Dear Professor Ansari,

I was pleased to hear that you have another book on Blake ready for publication. I think the best thing I can do to help is put you in touch with the Edwin Mellen Press, Lampeter. This is actually an international publishing company which happens to have its UK branch here in Wales. I have already spoken to them on the telephone, and they will send me some literature which I will forward to you with this letter. The founder of the firm, Professor Herbert Richardson, is a liberal-minded theologian who is likely to be interested in a book on Blake. The only other publishers known to me in Wales are the University of Wales Press, but I think it virtually certain that they would not be interested, unless you undertook to prove that Blake was a Welshman.

In answer to the other query in your letter: yes, I have received your *Miscellany* vol. IX no. 1, with my review of your daughter's lively book on Shakespeare's last plays. This issue also included your tribute to the late Professor Kenneth Muir and some of his last thoughts on Marlowe and Shakespeare. I read these contributions with particular pleasure. I met Muir once or twice, and wish I had known him better.

You do not mention whether you have received from Associated University Presses *Lear from Study to Stage,* a collection of scholarly essays I have edited which you agreed to review in the *Miscellany?* I asked them to send you a copy and could if necessary repeat the request. Alternatively, you might like to write to the AUP yourself, requesting a review copy, and mentioning that you are seeking a publisher for your book on Blake? The address is: Dr. Thomas Yoseloff, Associated University Presses, 440 Forsgate Drive, Cranbury, New Jersey 08512, USA.

While we are on the subject of addresses, please note mine at the head of this letter. I am now fully retired, and while the Aberystwyth English Department will forward mail, there is generally some delay, so it is best to write to me here. The address may sound peculiar: "Tegfan" is the name of my house, "Llandre" the name of the village, and "Bow Street" the name of the postal district, not a street in the ordinary sense at all.

Best wishes,

James Ogden

Dated: 29 December 1997

PS: Unfortunately the literature for you from the Edwin Mellen Press did not reach me till today. The delay was no doubt caused by the Christmas festivities. As you will see from the leaflet you have a choice of sending your book proposal to *Mrs. Iona Williams* at Lampeter or to Mr. John Rupnow in America. I have met both of them but if you were to mention my name in correspondence perhaps you would do well to remind them that I was a Senior Lecturer in English at Aberystwyth. I know no advantage in dealing with the New York rather than the Lampeter branch, but you might – if you were thinking of visiting the USA for example. Make clear that you are proposing a monograph of interest in the fields of literature, history and religion.

Dated: 25 February 1998

Dear Professor Ansari,

Thank you for your recent letter. I think all you need to do is send the Mellen book proposal form to Mrs. Williams in Lampeter. You can say I suggested that you should do so. I have already mentioned your work to her but will do so again at the next opportunity. Mrs. Williams manages the Lampeter branch and puts proposals before Professor Herbert Richardson on his regular visits. I do not think you need to send copies of *ACM* at present, if at all. If you send anything other than the proposal form, let it be a brief covering letter outlining the scope and probable readership of the book: a study of the prophetic books of William Blake, likely to interest students of literature and religious thought, or whatever seems to you the best description.

Glad to hear you have received the *Lear* book, and will review it in *ACM*. I have seen only one review so far, in *Choice* (which as you may know is an American journal that briefly reviews academic books on all subjects). The reviewer finds the book "useful" but does not say (as Arthur Scouten and I could have wished) that it should be in every library.

I look forward to receiving the current *ACM*. Please do not apologize for its late appearance; you do well to keep it going. As for Aligarh being like a village, I know what you mean, but villages are the most civilized communities on earth.

Best wishes,

James Ogden

PS: I do not like leaving this space blank. It is not for me to tell you how to write your review, but I would be pleased if you would mention that part of my introduction was first published in *AJES*.

I know you are now – like me – retired from teaching, but I wonder if they now make much use of videos in Indian schools and Universities? We have found them very useful in the last ten or twenty years. Most of Shakespeare's plays are available on video, and there are some excellent productions in this form. I am thinking of writing an essay on *Twelfth Night* which would make reference to the Renaissance Theatre production by Kenneth Branagh (distributed on video by Thames Television International).

Dated: 20 January 1999

Dear Professor Ansari,

Many thanks for your letter of 19.09.1998 and for your more recent one, which I received today. I did not reply to the first letter because it presumably crossed in the post one of mine, in which I said that unfortunately I had nothing both suitable and ready for the *Critical Miscellany.*

In reply to today's letter, I was glad to hear that vol. x. no. 1 of the *Miscellany* is now ready, and that it includes an article by Professor John Jones. I attended his lectures to the B. Litt class at Oxford in 1959-60, and if you are in correspondence with him I would like you to give him my regards, though you may have to explain who I am! I quite enjoyed his lectures, but the subject was not one that allowed scope for his great abilities. I look forward to reading what he says about *Othello,* and what you say about the *Lear* anthology.

As I probably said before, I am now busy editing *She Stoops to Conquer* for the New Mermaid series. It is proving more difficult than I expected. First, I had to get a microfilm of the manuscript from America, and then I had to compare it with the text of the first printed edition. Now I am trying to decide which readings of the manuscript are acceptable. Next I must write an introduction explaining what remains interesting about the play itself. To attempt anything else at present would be too much of a distraction, but please believe me when I say I have not forgotten your request for something for the *Miscellany*.

I would be interested to hear what progress you have made with publishing your book on Blake.

Best wishes,

Yours sincerely,

James Ogden

Dated: 25 February 1999

Dear Professor Ansari,

Many thanks for your letter of 13 February and for the three copies of your *Miscellany*, which have just reached me.

I am very grateful to you for taking the trouble to review *Lear from Study to Stage.* I was glad to hear that you thought Arthur Scouten and I did a good job in collecting the essays, and that you found much to interest you in the essays by R.A. Foakes, Richard Levin, Carol Rutter and Stuart Sillars. I am sorry to say that, however interesting the association of the "heath" and Salisbury Plain may be, it is not my idea; I only reported (p. 141) that the actor Macready seems to have had that idea in 1838.

I feel sure the publishers will be pleased with the review, and I will send them copies, as you request in your letter. However, I think they will be satisfied if I send them photocopies. I will then be able to give the *Miscellany* to people who will be interested not only in your review but also in other articles. I hope that is all right with you.

The only one of the other articles I have had time to read as yet is Professor John Jones's on *Othello,* which I enjoyed, though I was not fully convinced that all differences between Q and F here are to be understood as improvements by Shakespeare. I started reading Professor Viswanathan's essay on *Richard II* but only got to his suggestion, perhaps not very seriously intended, that in Elizabethan English there could have been a distinction between "u" and "non-u" in respect of the words "(looking-) glass" and "mirror". Here is what I thought:

Mirror (= glass)	*glass* (= mirror)
13th century onwards	13th century onwards
French origin	Teutonic origin
Mentioned by Tamburlanine,	*looking – glass*
Marlowe's play Part I,	16th century
Act V scene I	English origin
Called for by Richard II	Called for by Bolingbroke
	Called for by Lear, V. iii
In 20th century, "non-u"	In 20th century, "u"
i.e. middle class	i.e. upper class
In my understanding,	In my understanding,
something large,	something small,
on a wall or stand	held in the hand

As the general idea of the abdication scene in *Richard II* is that the King retains a moral advantage over Bolingbroke, it is unlikely that Shakespeare would think of him as using a middle class term, and Bolingbroke an upper class one. It is possible he thought of his as asking for a mirror, and being provided with nothing but a hand-glass.

Have you read Nabil Matar, *Islam in Britain, 1558-1685?* Said to call in question much of what Edward Said argued in his *Orientalism*. Matar's book is published by Cambridge University Press – you may want to review it, or get in touch with the author.

Best wishes,

James Ogden

Dated: 16 November 1999

Dear Professor Ansari,

Many thanks for sending the *Aligarh Critical Miscellany,* vol. x no. 2, which has just reached me here. I have enjoyed reading the articles by John Jones, Professor Naqi Husain Jafri, and yourself. As I may have said before, I am interested in Shakespeare's revisions, and I congratulate you on reprinting more of John Jones's book. There was much in Professor Jafri's article that was unfamiliar to me, and it makes a contribution to better understanding of different literary traditions. Your own article sent me back to Blake's "Songs of Innocence and Experiences", some of which I have now been puzzling over for 45 years. I agree with what you say about the nightmare vision of "London" and find I have to re-read Wordsworth's "Westminster Bridge" to cheer myself up. Perhaps things in general are not as bad as Blake sometimes suggests, though they are bad enough. I will read the other articles in the *Miscellany* later. I hope you have made good progress with your book on Blake, which you were hoping to publish with the Edwin Mellen Press. I also hope to hear good news of your daughter, whose book on Shakespeare's last plays I had pleasure in reviewing for you some years ago. During the past year I have been busy editing Goldsmith's *She Stoops to Conquer* for the "New Mermaid" series. If all goes well, it should be published next year. I am not perfectly sure what I will do next. I may return to my book on Milton, in which I would like to incorporate my contribution to the *Essays on Sir Walter Raleigh* which you edited, if that is all right.

Professor Jafri may be interested to know that Isaac D'Israeli was an enthusiast for Oriental literature (as of course was his son Benjamin) and published a volume of *Romances* (1799), which included "Mejnoun and Leila, The Arabian Petrarch and Laura", based on a Persian source. This particular romance was reprinted at Calcutta in 1800 I believe. I unfortunately know no more about it than I said in my book *Isaac D'Israeli* (Oxford 1969).

Best wishes,

James Ogden

Dated: 31 March 2000

Dear Professor Ansari,

I have just received *The Aligarh Critical Miscellany* vol. XI no. 1. I was very pleased, partly because I have not heard from you for some time, and I was beginning to wonder if you were keeping well. I think I may infer that you are, as you have found time and energy to give a lecture on Shakespeare's sonnets, write an essay on "The Marriage of Heaven and Hell", review Harold Bloom's book, and of course edit the *Miscellany*.

I thought I would reply immediately because you will be anxious to know that the journal has arrived safely. I have read rapidly through various articles, particularly your lecture on the sonnets, Professor Singh's essay on Leavis, and your review of Bloom. You have chosen an inspiring topic for the lecture, and I imagine it must have been well received. I think Bloom's book is rather less original than you seem to suggest at certain points, but it is certainly stimulating, as you say. Professor Singh's concluding reference to prophets brought to mind another Biblical saying, "a prophet is not without honour, save in his own country", as Leavis is more often criticized than praised here. On looking at your essay on Blake I see I have given you high praise, in my first paragraph, in crediting you with "energy". Altogether, this looks like another excellent issue of your journal.

I hope to hear soon that your book on Blake is being published.

As I mentioned before, I have been busy editing *She Stoops to Conquer* for the New Mermaid series. I finished that before Christmas, but recently I have had to make many minor corrections of the text which were suggested by the copy editor. My main efforts recently, however, have been directed at a book on Milton, incorporating if possible all my previously published essays. These include my essay on "Raleigh's Splendid Handbook on Milton", published in *Essays on Sir Walter Raleigh.* I hope I may have your permission to reprint this essay, probably without much alteration?

As I cannot bear to leave the rest of this paper blank, let me add some comments to yours on Bloom on p. 98 of your review. (1) The theory that Othello did not consummate his marriage was put forward by T.G.A. Nelson and Charles Haines in *Essays in Criticism*, vol. 33 no. 1 (1983). (2) If Lady Macbeth has had no children by her first husband, is she lying when she says she knows how tender 'tis to love the babe that milks her (I, vii)? – it does not sound like lies. (3) I do not know who first suggested that Bassanio's marriage upsets Antonio because he has homosexual feelings for his friend, but it has frequently been played that way. (4) A more favourable account of the Duke's role in *Measure for Measure* is possible, and was suggested by me in the essay you kindly published in your *Miscellany*, vol. 5 no. 1.

I hope all is well with you and your family.

Best wishes,

James Ogden

Dated: 03 May 2000

Dear Professor Ansari,

Thank you for your recent letter about your problems in getting your book on Blake published by the Edwin Mellen Press.

I was sorry to hear about these problems, but did not fully understand what they were, so I wrote to Mrs Iona Williams at the Edwin Mellen office in Lampeter. She has just replied by phone. As I now understand things, you need two letters of recommendation, and have only one, owing to the sad demise of Miss Desiree Hirst. You have asked me to write this second letter, and the Edwin Mellen Press would be happy to accept me as a referee and will if necessary send me a copy of the typescript.

Firstly, I would urge you, if possible, to get this second letter from a recognized Blake scholar, or at least somebody with a better knowledge of the subject than I have myself. I have of course read some of your work in the *Aligarh Critical Miscellany*, but I must confess that I do not always follow what you are saying, owing to my lack of familiarity with most of Blake's prophetic books. If the letter of recommendation is to be more than a formality, as I think it must be, it would be much better if it came from somebody with more authority.

However, if you are unable to get anyone else, I will write a letter, if you will give me some help. It would be very helpful indeed if you could let me know the title, publication details, and general scope of your previous book on Blake. I believe it was commended by Dr. Leavis? There is no copy available here. It would also be helpful if you could list your publications on Blake, or better still, a complete list of publications as I know you have various other interests. Finally, and most important, could you please send an account of the main points of interest of the new book, which I could possibly use as the basis of my own letter? I will of course read through the typescript, and make my comments as personal as possible, but still it would save time if I knew what I was looking for.

I hope these requests do not seem unreasonable. I would not make them if I felt I could easily read and recommend the typescript. Also, the more information and explanation I have from you, the more quickly I can go ahead, always assuming you are unable to find somebody better than me.

Best wishes,

James Ogden

Desired data

1. Information on your previous book
2. Information on your interests, career, publications
3. Brief account of main points of interest in new book
4. Anything else you think could be helpful

Dated: 03 July 2000

Dear Professor Ansari,

Thank you for your letter of 26 June. I was delighted to hear that your Blake book had been recommended by Dr. Kathleen Raine. You could not have a better recommendation, I think, and there should be no further difficulty with the Edwin Mellen Press. I will, however, ask Mrs Williams about the book's progress.

I was also pleased to hear that you have dedicated the book to the late Miss Desiree Hirst and to me, though I feel I hardly deserve the honour.

I will try to provide you with an essay on Dryden for the *Miscellany* (My essay will probably be on Dryden's criticism, with special reference to his views on Chaucer, Shakespeare, and Milton.) before the end of this year. I will also write to my friend Professor Anne Gardiner, and ask if she will contribute. As you may know, she has published extensively on Dryden, and she is still very active in research and attendance at conferences. She may know others who will be interested in contributing to a volume of tricentenary essays.

As I may have mentioned before, a possible contributor to the *Miscellany* especially on Dryden, is Professor Nabil I. Matar, author of many publications on links between Western literature and the Muslim world in the seventeenth century. Unfortunately I cannot immediately tell you his present address, but it may be in the list of members of the American Modern Language Association.

I myself expect to be busy, during the next two months, with the proofs of *She Stoops to Conquer*, and with an article on John Langdon Down, after whom Down's Syndrome was named.

I hope your trip to the States went well.

I will be in touch again, when I have more definite news on any of these matters.

Best wishes,

Yours sincerely,

James Ogden

Dated: 13 September 2000

Dear Professor Ansari,

Thank you for your letter of 19 August.

I was sorry to hear that your problems with your book on Blake are not resolved. I have phoned the Edwin Mellen Press at Lampeter. I did not speak to Mrs Williams but to another lady. She said it seems you need to fill in your "AIF Form", and to suggest three possible titles for the book. They also need your own biographical details, and any outstanding "permissions" for quotations – I doubt if any will be necessary, unless you have quoted at length from copyright material. They have three photographs, which the lady thought were of Blake, one of his artistic works, and yourself. They needed captions for these, and a clearer idea of their purpose – possibly the photo of Blake could go on the paper cover. I suppose you already have these things in hand. I had the impression that the Mellen people would not delay matters further once they were resolved.

You should by now have received my essay on "Dryden as Critic of English Literature" – now my preferred title. I sent it by airmail on 22 August. There was a missing footnote, which is

11. *A History of English Criticism* (Edinburgh and London, 1930), pp. 130-1. I would be obliged if you would add this to the list of notes at the end of the typescript.

I enclose, for consideration for another issue of your *Miscellany*, a note on 'Isaac D'Israeli on Blake", which concerns a letter from D'Israeli to Thomas Frognall Dibbin about Blake. I believe all modern works on Blake which quote this letter print Dibdin's text, which is plainly incorrect at various points. My note gives a correct text and a little discussion. I think you would do both D'Israeli and Blake some service by printing a correct text.

I hope to hear pretty soon that you have received both the Dryden essay and the Blake note.

Best wishes, as ever,

James Ogden

Dated: 14 October 2000

Dear Professor Ansari,

Many thanks for your letter of 27 September. I was pleased to hear that you have received my essay on "Dryden as a Critic of English Literature" (my preferred title) and my notes on "Isaac D'Israeli on Blake", and that you will publish them in the *Aligarh Critical Miscellany.* I was especially pleased to hear that the note will appear in the issue you expect to publish this month, and I look forward to seeing it.

I was sorry to hear about your continuing difficulties and anxieties regarding the publication of your book on Blake by the Edwin Mellen Press. I fear almost all scholarly publishing tends to be slow, and we all must be patient, though I find myself that patience does not come easier with age. I get the impression that at the Lampeter office of the Mellen Press Mrs Williams has only managerial responsibility, and is reluctant to take any decision without the authorization of the Director, Professor Herbert Williams. As far as I know, Herbert is still based in Canada, and only visits Lampeter a few times each year. However, I have written to him, and to Mrs Williams, pointing out that your book could not have a better endorsement than that from Dr. Kathleen Raine, and urging him to give the process of its publication his personal attention. The Edwin Mellen Press should be proud to publish the book.

It will not be much comfort to you perhaps, but I found when publishing the book of essays on *King Lear* you so kindly reviewed that the publishers would do nothing about securing permissions for illustrations, and I was obliged to do without many that were desirable. Quite possibly in many cases permission was unnecessary, and would have been given without question, but as an independent scholar with no secretarial assistance I just did not have the time and energy for the task. In your case, if the Blake painting has been reproduced in a book, the publishers should make no difficulty about it being photocopied. The illustrations that *did* appear in my *Lear* book were all done that way.

I have been busy with the proofs of my edition of Goldsmith's *She Stoops to Conquer,* which will not now be published till next year, somewhat to my disappointment. There were problems with illustrations here as well, though A. & C. Black, being commercial publishers, do not mind doing some of the work. I hope to get back to my book on Milton, which I promised to the Edwin Mellen Press some years ago – in fact, ten years ago, now I come to think about it.

I wonder whether the fame of R.S. Thomas has reached India? Until his death recently he was the most famous of the Anglo-Welsh poets, and indeed one of the most distinguished poets writing in English. As he was for a time a Fellow of the Aberystwyth English Department I knew him slightly. I have been trying to write an essay on him.

Hope you and your daughter are well.

Best wishes,

James Ogden

Dated: 05 December 2000

Dear Professor Ansari,

Many thanks for your recent letters, and for sending your *Miscellany* vol. xi No. 2, with my note on Blake.

I cannot remember if I wrote to say I had written to Herbert Richardson, the Director of the Edwin Mellen Press, and to Mrs Williams, about your book. Mrs Williams later phoned to say the book had now gone to America, where it would be printed and published about next June. It is kind of you to attribute this development to my influence, but I rather think they just proceeded in their usual way. All publishing is pretty slow, in my experience.

I must immediately make an exception, to that generalization, as here is my note on Blake which I sent to you only about two months ago. I like the typeface, which is very clear and readable. Unfortunately there are some printers' errors. I would not mention these, or ask you to print corrections, but the point of the note was to give a correct version of D'Israeli's letter, and Blake scholars might say "Ogden complains of us getting it wrong, and then gets it wrong himself". So I hope you will not mind printing corrections, perhaps along these lines:

Isaac D'Israeli on Blake (*ACM* vol. XI no. 2): Corrections

p. 143 1. 10, *for* Frongnall *read* Frognall
p. 144 1. 07, *for* of *read* or
p. 144 1. 13, *for* covey *read* convey
p. 145 note 4, *for* 1936 *read* 1836

Obviously the correction of "covey" to "convey" is the most important, and I really would like to see that, at least, corrected.

I enclose an article from *The Times* which may be of interest.

I am most grateful for the *Miscellany* and look forward to reading the other articles and your review.

I am afraid my essay on R.S. Thomas will not be suitable for the *Miscellany*, as it assumes some knowledge of the poet, and interest in him. However, I will think about making a further contribution on a subject of greater interest to your readers, possibly on Shakespeare.

At present we are preparing for Christmas – our Prophet's birthday. Perhaps I can wish you the compliments of the season, and say I hope that some day all people of different creeds will be reconciled.

Best wishes,

James Ogden

Dated: 22 January 2001

Dear Professor Ansari,

Thank you for your letter of 8 January. I am writing again to say I think the following corrections really ought to be printed in the next issue of your *Miscellany*. It is only because I have complained that bad texts of D'Israeli's letter to Dibdin have been preserved in modern Blake scholarship, and the purpose of my note was to correct them, that I feel I must repeat this point.

Vol. XI (1998) No. 2, "Isaac D'Israeli on Blake", pp. 143-5.
p. 143 *for* Frongall *read* Frognall
p. 144 *for* power of sublimity *read* power or sublimity
for covey *read* convey
p. 145 *for* (1936) *read* (1836)

In general I can live with the occasional misprint, but in this particular note I feel I should show the concern for accuracy I have said has been wanting in others.

In your letter you mention that you understand my hesitation "in writing on the author you promised earlier". This was R.S. Thomas. I think if you look through previous correspondence you will find I did not promise to write for you on R.S. Thomas. I just mentioned that as he died recently I was writing an essay incorporating some reminiscences of him, which I thought might be suitable for one of the Welsh literary journals. I guess there is not much interest in his poetry in India, so what would be needed, though I do not feel competent to write it, would be a general introductory essay. I do assure you I am contemplating another essay on Shakespeare which I hope may be suitable for your *Miscellany*. Also, I am looking forward to seeing my essay on "Dryden as a Critic of English Literature" in print.

I am at present engaged in some difficult correspondence with the publishers of *Lear from Study to Stage,* concerning royalties. However, I suppose there would be no harm if you wrote to them, pointing out that you reviewed that book in your *Miscellany*, and now wondered if they would be interested in publishing your book. I would give it a title, if I were you, such as *Shakespeare: An Existential Approach,* and of course you should send a list of probable contents. The address, which is actually on the back of the title page of the *Lear* book, is:

> Associated University Presses
> 440 Forsgate Drive
> Cranbury, NJ 08512
> USA

Most of my correspondence has been with the Director, Julien Yoseloff. Frankly, although the *Lear* book has been reasonably successful, I am not sure whether it would be helpful if you mentioned my name.

Best wishes,

Yours sincerely,

James Ogden

Dated: 02 February 2001

Dear Professor Ansari,

My friend Professor Tom Craik has sent me the address of another publisher who may be interested in your book on Shakespeare from the existentialist point of view. This is:

Palgrave Publishers Ltd
Brunel Road
HoundmillsBasingstoke
Hampshire, UK
RG21 6XS

Palgrave Publishers are I understand the academic division of Macmillan, who have representatives and branches throughout the world, and who would therefore be easier to deal with than the Associated University Presses of Edwin Mellen.

Many thanks for your letter of 29 January, which has arrived this very minute. If you have already written to the Associated University Presses you may feel obliged to deal with them, but there can surely be no harm in contacting other publishers at this stage. As I have probably mentioned, it may not be easy to publish another book on Shakespeare, when there are already so many, so it seems advisable to have ready a striking title, indicative of the point-of-view, an outline of the contents, and an idea of the likely readership.

I was glad to hear that you will publish corrections to my little note on D'Israeli and Blake in the next issue of your *Miscellany*. I assume this issue will be the special Dryden one, which I am very much looking forward to seeing. I hope there will not be too many printing errors in my essay on Dryden's criticism of English literature, because I am hoping to send photocopies to one or two friends, and perhaps thereby arouse interest in your journal. I assume further that the issue for which you are urgently seeking contributions will be the one after that. I am sorry to say that I am not qualified to write an introductory essay on R.S. Thomas, but I will write to an acquaintance of mine who may be able to help. I may try my hand at something on *The Merchant of Venice*, though I fear I have nothing very original to say. Again, I will ask acquaintances if they have anything suitable, though as you know I have made such appeals before without much success.

That reminds me that Richard Brinkley, who contributed to your collection of essays on Professor Walter Raleigh, has died recently, and I am quite upset about it, as he was only about sixty years old, and seemed to have many years of useful work ahead.

With best wishes,

Yours sincerely,

James Ogden

Dated: 28 February 2001

Dear Professor Ansari,

Thank you for your letter of 14 February, which clarifies your schedule for publishing your *Miscellany*. Please do not expect a piece on R.S. Thomas from me. However, from what you say there should be time for me to write something on Shakespeare for the second issue of 1999. I know I specified *The Merchant of Venice,* but having started writing my essay I realize I do not have enough to say about it. I am hoping therefore to write something on three problematic characters: Shylock in *The Merchant*, Hero in *Much Ado*, and somebody else, possibly Henry V. As you can see, this essay is at a very preliminary stage, and I would not write it at all, except that I would like to help you out. I wish you luck with the publishers of your book on Shakespeare. I do not know the one you mention on Shakespeare as an existentialist dramatist, but I feel sure yours will be quite different, and you should have no difficulty in finding a distinctive title. I fear I have not read the book on Leavis by your friend Professor Singh either. I was surprised and pleased to hear that it includes my message of condolence on Leavis's death. I well remember writing it, but I suppose Mrs Leavis must have received such messages from people of greater distinction than me. It seems a long time ago. My attitude to Leavis has changed a bit over the years, and my projected book on Milton will include an attempt to refute some of Leavis's opinions, but I still think of him as a major critic of literature and society. His influence in Universities was sometimes excessive but its passing has left them, in my view, much weaker. Before my retirement I noted that people were pulling in many different directions. We really need people to pull together, and I am sorry I cannot help with R.S. Thomas, but I will try to help with the other article.

Best wishes,

James Ogden

Dated: 25 March 2001

Dear Professor Ansari,

I am sorry to say that I cannot write an essay on a Shakespeare subject for one of the 1999 issues of your *Miscellany*. The essay I was trying to write, on some problem characters in his plays, would be unworthy of your journal and I have abandoned it.

However, I can offer something else. As I think I have mentioned, I have for some years been writing a book on *The Milton Tradition,* mainly on the editing, reputation and criticism of his poems. The essay on Raleigh's Milton criticism which you published will, I hope, form a chapter. I have recently completed a chapter on "Milton's Sonnets", and this might be suitable for your journal. It will be about 12 to 14 pages in my usual typescript. It briefly surveys the impact of the sonnets on critics, poets, and readers generally, and explains their present interest and status. Please let me know if you think you will want it. I should by then have a nice typescript ready.

I am sorry I cannot promise a Shakespeare essay. The more I wrote, the more I felt that it had nearly all been said before. Also, I must now concentrate on the Milton book, and get it finished and published. I am not getting any younger.

I hope reasonable progress is being made with your own books on Blake and Shakespeare. I know you have had to be patient. That is another reason for me concentrating on the Milton book; isn't it – the gap between acceptance (always supposing somebody wants it) and publication can be years.

Best wishes,

Yours sincerely,

James Ogden

Dated: 6 May 2001

Dear Professor Ansari,

Thanks for your recent letter. I was very sorry to hear that you are losing sight in your left eye. I pray that the condition can be alleviated and that you will recover sufficiently to carry on your scholarly work. Your daughter's assistance is a great blessing: please give her my thanks and best wishes.

On page 1b there is a table headed "Milton's Sonnets: Identification". Its purpose is to give information on their publishing history, and to enable readers to identify sonnets in their own editions, by number, opening words or title. The printing of tables is sometimes a problem, so I will add a note which you can if necessary cut off and give to the printer.

Best wishes for your recovery from your present distress.

Yours sincerely,

James Ogden

Please note that the typescript of "Milton's Sonnet" actually has 13 pages, numbered thus: pp. 1, lb, 2-12. I would like the table on p. lb headed "Milton's Sonnets: Identification to be printed, if possible on the second page of the text. It need not necessarily follow the second paragraph (as it does in the typescript)

Thanks,

James Ogden

Dated: 24 May 2001

Dear Professor Ansari,

I have just received your *Critical Miscellany,* vol. XII no. 1, and I have rapidly read through it. I thought your friend Mr. Singh's essay on the value of silence was both original and profound. It is some years since I studied either *Julius Caesar* or *Macbeth*, but your essays made me feel I should return to these plays with renewed interest. I have read Dr. Leavis's essay on Blake before, but I have not a copy here at home, and I dare say many like me will be glad to see it reprinted.

Regarding your essays one after the other I was struck by the parallels between the two plays. In both, the heroes are not absolute villains, but become deeply involved in crime, and suffer in consequence. There are similarities of detail, for example neither of them has the *time* to mourn the death of his chief partner in crime, Cassius in the one case and Lady Macbeth in the other. At the end there may seem to be big differences: Brutus is said to have been the noblest Roman of them all, Macbeth nothing but a dead butcher, but we can accept neither of these verdicts. I think Shakespeare may be said to have developed Brutus's character further when he came to Macbeth. There is an essay on this subject in G. Wilson Knight's *The Wheel of Fire,* as no doubt you know.

I am very grateful to your for printing the corrections to my note about "Isaac D'Israeli and Blake" I realize now that with your failing eyesight you may find great difficulty in spotting such typographical errors. I would not have made so much fuss about them, but as my note by implication criticized other scholars for overlooking errors, I felt I must not commit any myself. Well, I do hope your eyesight has not deteriorated further, and that you can get help with proof-correcting and similar work.

You should by now have received my essay on "Milton's Sonnets" for the *Miscellany,* and I hope it will be found sufficiently interesting. I have tried to solicit contributions from friends, but alas; we are all getting older. Some have stopped writing altogether, and others confine themselves to a few specific projects. I will be sixty-five myself at my next birthday, but hope to be spared to complete my book on Milton, and to see my edition of *She Stoops to Conquer* in print. At present I am busy with the third and I hope final set of proofs of the latter.

By the way, I noticed in "The Sunday Telegraph" of 20 May a review by Jonathan Bate of *The Stranger from Paradise: A Biography of William Blake* by G.E. Bentley Jr., published by Yale University Press at £25. According to Bate the book is "a permanently valuable resource" for scholars, as might be expected, but not the best place for others who may want to understand Blake. It is to academic.

Best wishes,

James Ogden

Dated: 18 September, 2001

Dear Professor Ansari,

I hope you are well, and able to pursue your scholarly interests despite your eye trouble.

I recently received a copy of *The Aligarh Journal of English Studies,* with a note from the editor, Professor S. Wiqar Husain, inviting me to send contributions to forthcoming issues of the journal.

I have written to Professor Husain, to say that I have within the last year or so contributed essays on Dryden's criticism and Milton's sonnets to your *Miscellany*. I had to tell you, I added, that at present I have not got anything that seems suitable for your future issues. I am in fact concentrating mainly on my Milton book, and some reviews. I am also thinking about publishing some poems.

However, I have told Professor Husain that I would like to help him if possible, and if I can do so without giving offence to you. So I hope you will not mind if I write something for him, perhaps next year. Of course Professor Husain may have circularized many scholars and received more than enough material – I hope so.

At this time of terrible international disputes, I feel that scholars should set an example of mutual respect and co-operation.

Best wishes to you and your daughter.

Yours sincerely,

James Ogden

P.S. Here is one of my poems, about my mother and aunt Mary.

A Sister-in-Law

Mary came down again last Saturday,
Her usual apologetic self.
She sunbathes here in that playsuit, and looks
As if she's been poured in but failed to set.
Our back lawn's private, she believes, while hers
Has nosey neighbours all around: God knows
What Mrs Thornton thinks. She did had her tea,

She said, and wanted nothing for herself,
But pressed on me some ham and eggs and cake,
The kind her mother called goloptious.
"Nay Mary, do not be so damn daft", I said,
Upset us both a bit. But soon she laughed
And had her tea, and cake, and last words too:
"I feel so awful Hetty coming here
Without an invitation every week"
I have known her since she was a slim young lass
Some fifty years ago, for goodness sake.
One day I will crown her with her own cream cake.

Dated: 03 February, 2002

Dear Professor Ansari,

Thank you for your letter of 18 December and for your *Miscellany* XII 2, which came yesterday. I delayed replying to the former in anticipation of the latter.

I was very sorry to hear about the difficulties you faced last year, especially your deteriorating eyesight. We must hope and pray that it will not deteriorate further. In writing about Milton's sonnet "When I consider how my light is spent" I did not fully appreciate its relevance to your situation, but I must say now that I think the lesson "They also serve who only stand and wait" is a hard one to learn. I doubt if I could be so philosophical myself.

On looking again at your letter I see you were still wanting contributors to the Dryden issue of the *Miscellany*. You may remember that you asked me about this before, and I wrote to the few people I know who might be willing to contribute something, but had some disappointing answers. My friend Anne Gardiner is writing articles on Dryden commissioned by other editors, while Tom Craik and Stuart Gillespie had nothing to offer. I do not think Anne would mind if you wrote directly to her – it may be that she can think of others who would be interested. Her address is 5 Ferndale Road, Brewster, NY 10509-5621, USA.

I suppose the principal Dryden scholars in this country, not known to me personally, are Professor Paul Hammond, English Department, University of Leeds, and

Dr. David Hopkins, English Department, University of Bristol. They may have research students who would be glad to get something published, if nothing else.

Do write again about this problem, if it is not solved soon, though I have no idea what to do about it at the moment.

I have read most of the current issue of the *Miscellany* with pleasure. It was a good idea to reprint Leavis's "Memories of Wittegenstein", which are interesting and not well known. I am not sure that I fully understand your essay, as I have always found existentialism difficult, but I will make another attempt at it. Professor Viswanathan seems to have found an original angle on *Hamlet*, and Professor Nagrajan's notes on *King Lear* are well worth pondering. I may have more to say on these later. The review of the book on Leavis reminds us how much he lived for the literary criticism which Wittegenstein urged him to give up. What he really should have given up, I think, was Cambridge.

I was glad to see my essay on Milton's sonnets in print so soon after it was written, and that my references in it to Leavis fit rather well into the *Miscellany* as a whole.

Best wishes,

Yours sincerely,

James Ogden

Dated: 06 April 2002

Dear Professor Ansari,

Many thanks for sending a copy of your book on *William Blake's Minor Prophecies*, which came today.

I do not know how to thank you for dedicating the book to me as well as to the late Desiree Hirst. I fear I have done much less than she did to promote the study of Blake in this country. However, I was happy to help you get your book published by the Edwin Mellen Press and I think they have done a reasonable job on it. I know you would have liked to have had illustrations, but so far as I can see these are not essential to your commentaries, and anyway nowadays most academic and many public libraries can supply them for interested readers. I have not, of course, had time yet to do more than read Kathleen Raine's foreword and your introduction, but I promise to read or re-read the rest of the book in due course, and to re-read the work of the poet himself. You are very fortunate to have the enthusiastic recommendation of Miss Raine, and I am sure she is right in thinking "spiritual illumination" the aim of all religions. Perhaps it is also the aim of all literary studies, properly understood.

I hope you have by now received my letter thanking you for the *Critical Miscellany* vol. XII no. 2, the one including your essay on Shakespearean characterization and mine on Milton's sonnets.

I very much hope to hear, in your next letter, that the doctors have been able to do something to arrest the deterioration in your eyesight.

I was interested to discover, from the back of the book, that you read for Honours in English at Oxford. From your high regard for Dr. Leavis I had vaguely supposed you were at Cambridge. I myself was at Lincoln College, Oxford, 1959-61, reading for a B. Litt, and at that time I attended classes by F.W. Bateson and John Jones, and lectures by Wallace Robson.

To conclude, congratulations on your book. I hope you get some good reviews.

Best wishes,

Your sincerely,

James Ogden

Dated: 02 December 2002

Dear Professor Ansari,

A few lines to say that I have just received the tercentenary Dryden number of *The Aligarh Critical Miscellany*, and to congratulate you on yet another valuable contribution to the study of English Literature.

You have done well to reprint T.S.Eliot's famous essay, and to obtain contributions from Anne Gardiner and Paul Hammond, especially as Hammond is now our leading Dryden authority. With the contributions of Professor Viswanathan and yourself, these give the *Miscellany* an international scope appropriate to the subject, Dryden himself having a more positive interest in both America and India than any other early writer.

I have not yet had time to read any of the contributions properly, but as I know you will be anxious to hear that the *Miscellany* has been safely and appreciatively received, I think it may be worthwhile writing straight away. Although I know you think highly of F.R. Leavis's criticism, as indeed I do myself, I was a little surprised to see you have included his essay on *All for Love,* which is rather unfavourable to Dryden, but I dare say Hammond's essay on the same play will redress the balance. I very much look forward to reading the essays by Professor Viswanathan and yourself. I read Dryden's odes for St Cecilia's Day on the day itself, 22 November; they are two poems I always very much enjoyed, as it happens.

I hope the appearance of the *Miscellany* may be evidence that your eyesight has not deteriorated further?

I have just finished writing my book on Milton, which will incorporate "Dryden's Satirical Tendency" (which you reprinted some years ago), "Raleigh's 'Splendid Handbook' on Mliton", (which I wrote for your collection *Essays on Sir Walter Raleigh)* and "Milton's Sonnets" (which you published recently). I hope you do not mind me reprinting the essays on Raleigh and on the sonnets.

I have had the good news that my editions of *The Country Wife* and *She Stoops to Conquer,* in the New Mermaid series, are reprinting.

In general I am pretty well, and I hope you and your daughter are well too.

Best wishes,

James Ogden

Dated: 01 May 2003

Dear Professor Ansari,

Thank you for your letter of 18 April. My wife and I were very sorry to learn that you have been feeling "very miserable" and that you fear you may go blind.

You ask me advice. I think I know what you *should* do, though I do not know what you *can* do. You should have an operation to reattach the retina as soon as possible. The procedure I had was called a vasectomy, though I believe there are other operations depending on the condition of the eye. There is little or nothing to fear about the operation itself, assuming you have access to a qualified surgeon and proper facilities. You may need an additional operation or operations for the cataract or cataracts but this operation I am told is quite straightforward. I say I do not know what you can do because I do not know anything about the health service in India; whether it is free but rather slow like our National Health Service, or quick but rather expensive like our private health care.

As I may have explained, I was fortunate in that once my condition was diagnosed I was immediately operated on at Shrewsbury hospital, about 75 miles from here. I only stayed in the hospital one night, then had nine days in bed at home. If it had been impossible to have the operation done quickly on the National Health, I would have thought it worthwhile to pay to have it done privately. Incidentally this specialist who diagnosed my condition was an Indian, Mr. Varghese, a very good man, but they do not have facilities for the operation in Aberystwyth, so he arranged for me to go the Shrewsbury.

Of course I am not an eye specialist myself, but my advice is that you need an operation on the retina as soon as possible, and that as the operation has a very good chance of complete success it would be worth paying for it if necessary. You are not very far from Delhi, and there must be specialists in that great city who can save your sight at this stage, even if there are none in Aligarh itself.

I think you have done well to keep the *Critical Miscellany* going for so long, but I fully understand that you now feel forced to bring the series to an end. I am sure you have helped many young scholars to get their work published. I am honoured to be asked to contribute to the last issue, and I will certainly send something within the next two months, though just now I am not sure what exactly it will be. It must be something already fairly well advanced, on Shakespeare, Milton, or perhaps literary theory. I suppose Shakespeare would be ideal but unfortunately my work on him is not very original. While I am on this subject, I would be interested to know whether the *Aligarh Critical Journal* keeps going? The most recent issue of that to have reached me was vol. 21 no. 2, 1999.

You are very fortunate in having such talented and I believe affectionate daughters. As I said in my letter to Roshan, I have difficulty in understanding abstract thought, so my progress in reading her book has been slow. I think I agree with much of what she says about communication and relationships in chapter iv: that good relationships are characterized by reciprocity, and bad ones by domineering. Hence it seems to me that Jaspers and Sartre are at odds, not in agreement, if Sartre is demanding that "the beloved makes of the absolute end" (p. 76) Perhaps the argument could have been clearer, or perhaps I could give it more thought.

As I may have also said, my daughter Rachel has Down's syndrome, and lives in a Camphill community. The Camphill movement is international but I do not think it has branches in India. Its thinking is ultimately based on the philosophy of Rudolph Steiner (1861-1925), who believed that man's innate capacity for spiritual perception was dulled by the materialism of the modern world. Jaspers must have known something of Steiner's thought, which has inspired a number of successful educational and therapeutic enterprises.

I hope to be in touch again fairly soon, but do write and let me know what you are doing about the eye condition.

Yours as ever,

James Ogden

Dated: 14 May 2003

Dear Professor Ansari

I found and re- read your letter of 18 December 2001, in which you said that you had an eye operation during that year, and that it had not been successful. So I now appreciate a little better your difficulties and worries during the past three years or more. However, I don't know what exactly their cause is. If you have had an operation for retinal detachment which has not succeeded, it should be possible to repeat the operation. It may not be possible to restore your eyesight to what it was, but there should be no further visual loss. If you have developed cataracts, which is quite likely, dealing with them is comparatively straightforward, and after that operation your eyesight should be much improved. I do hope that you can obtain satisfactory treatment.

I am sorry to say that my own recovery from the operation I had in January has not been quite as good as I at first thought. I can see well enough for reading and for driving a car, but I tire very easily, especially when reading. I can't read for more than an hour at a time, or for more than one or two hours a day. Consequently I have made no further progress on reading Roshan's book, and not much with my promised article for the last issue of your *Miscellany*. I must ask you to allow me as much time as possible for the article.

I would like to write something on Shakespeare, but most of my ideas require more reading and thought than I had envisaged. I will, however, persist with these ideas for the present. If the time comes when you say you must have an article immediately, I will either do my best to complete the Shakespearean article, or send an essay on "Poets' First and Second Thoughts", which is more or less finished, but which I had intended for another journal. Either way, I still expect to have something for you, but in your letter of 18 April you specified "the next couple of months" and it will be difficult for me to meet the implied deadline of 18 June. I should have explained that there have been other projects that have needed attention, notably a revised reprint of *She Stoops to Conquer*. And I still have not quite finished with my Milton book.

There is also, at his time of the year, work to be done in the garden: "What we by day/Lop overgrown, or prune, or prop, or bind,/one night or two with wanton growth derides/Tending to wild". The advantage of this work is that it does not tire the eyes. Well, we must muddle through.

The Shakespeare plays on which I am most likely to write are the romantic comedies *The Merchant of Venice, Much Ado about Nothing,* and *Twelfth Night*. I may look at back issues of the *Miscellany* to see if you have published articles on these before.

It occurs to me that the completed series of some thirteen volumes should have an index. I would be very happy to compile one for you. It could be quite short and could be included in the last issue. Please let me know if you would like me to go ahead. But perhaps you already have this matter in hand? I think there should be two short indexes, ideally, one of contributors, and one of subjects. No need to specify page numbers – volume and issue numbers will be enough to identify everything.

Above all, do let me know what exactly your eye condition is, and what treatment is being attempted. I may be able to give better advice.

Best wishes,

Yours sincerely,

James Ogden

Dated: 04 June 2003

Dear Professor Ansari,

I have written an article for you entitled "Notes on Shakespeare's Comedies", about 16 pp. double-spaced. It is mostly about *The Merchant of Venice, Much Ado* and *Twelfth Night*, with some reference to other plays. It is rather less miscellaneous than this description may suggest. I need to do a little more work on it, but I can send it off fairly soon.

I have also, as I hinted that I might in my last letter, compiled an index to the *Aligarh Critical Miscellany*; it will be useful for my own purposes even if you do not want it. At present it is only in draft form, mostly because I have not a copy of vol. IX no. 1, 1996, and of course I do not yet know the contents of vol. XIII no. 2. I assume vol. XIII no. 2 will be the last issue.

So, if you would like me to complete this index for insertion in the last issue, please send a copy of vol. IX no. 1, or failing that a photocopy of the contents page, and let me know the authors and titles of everything in vol. XIII no. 1. As soon as I have this information I can complete the index in a day or two. The index runs to just over 4 pp. double-spaced, and is in two parts, (1) contributors, (2) subjects, including authors of books reviewed.

The longest entry is of course that for Shakespeare, where I have used the sub-divisions: comedies, histories, sonnets, tragedies, general.

I hope to hear that you have had some more reassuring advice about your eye trouble. It is not perfectly clear to me what the nature of the trouble is. I think if you have had an operation for retinal detachment which has not been successful, you can have another operation, with a reasonable chance of saving your eyesight, though the quality will not be as good as before. And I will venture to say that I do not believe it is simply the will of Allah that you should lose your sight at this stage, though looking back over your career you must be pleased with the amount of scholarly work and publication you have been permitted to achieve.

As for my own eye trouble, I am glad to say that my vision is almost as good as it was before my operation. But as I have no doubt mentioned, I find I tire easily, particularly when reading academic books and articles. I am still contributing to *The Year's Work in English Studies* on Restoration drama.

Best wishes,

James Ogden

Dated: 11 July 2003

Dear Professor Ansari,

Thanks for your letter of 31 May. I was glad to hear that you are again consulting your ophthalmologist, and I hope to hear that some more effective treatment has been adopted. From what you say I deduce that your condition differs from mine. The cause of my retinal detachment is unknown, whereas the cause of yours is apparently diabetes. I think you must be suffering from advanced diabetic retinopathy. This condition can in many cases be stabilized, I understand, by a type of laser treatment known as pan-retinal photocoagulation, or alternatively by vasectomy, the treatment I had myself. Of course I do not know whether either of these treatments would be recommended in your case, or what their chances of success would be. May depend on age. As I may have mentioned, I am sixty-seven this year, and my vasectomy seems to have been wholly successful.

Since you last wrote, I have posted to you a letter (6 June) and a copy of my "Notes on Shakespeare's Comedies" (7 June), which I fear may be unworthy of your journal, but it is the best I can do at present. In my letter I explained that I cannot finish my index to *ACM*, because my set is incomplete. So I would be grateful if you could send a copy of the table of contents of vol. ix no. 2 (the issue itself would be even more welcome) and a list of contributors and titles of contributions to vol. xiii no. 2.

In compiling as much of the index as possible, I noticed that the poet and Blake scholar Kathleen Raine made four contributions, and her work was often reviewed. As you probably know, Kathleen Raine died on 6 July aged ninety-five. I enclose obituaries from *The Times*, *The Guardian* and *The Independent*. May I suggest that it would be appropriate for the last issue of *ACM* to include a tribute to this extraordinary lady, and that if you have any letters of hers, they would be well worth publishing?

I have put in a new typewriter ribbon for this letter. Hope you can read it. Regards to your wife and daughters.

Best wishes,

James Ogden

Dated: 28 August 2003

My Dear Ansari,

I hope you are well. I fear the association of your retinal degeneration with diabetes must make its treatment more difficult, but I still hope to hear that something can be done to arrest it.

You will be interested to hear that my old friend Professor Tom Craik the Shakespeare authority has also suffered a retinal detachment this year, and that it seems to have been satisfactorily treated under a local anesthetic by the consultant surgeon Mr. Ingles by at Sunderland Eye Infirmary. I myself was treated under general anesthetic by Mr. Andy Callear at Shrewsbury hospital. Mr. Callear has recently told me that I need not see him again, but should keep in touch with my optician.

Many thanks for sending the copy of the *Aligarh Critical Miscellany* volume IX number 2, which came today. I immediately read your friend G. Singh's essay on Dante, and greatly enjoyed it; I hope you can convey this message to him. I look forward to reading the other contributions to this lively issue. I will of course incorporate the names of authors and subjects into my indices, but cannot complete them till I know the contents of volume XIII number 2, though I appreciate that these contents may not yet be fully known. When I have a complete set I will eventually donate it either to the Aberystwyth University Library or to the National Library of Wales. As I have probably said before, by discontinuing the journal you will at least save time and money, which I think you should divert more to your own needs. At present I am busy finishing my book on *The Milton Tradition,* which will incorporate my essays on Raleigh and the sonnets, which you have published in *Essays on Sir Walter Raleigh* and the *Miscellany.* Full acknowledgment will be made in the preface, not only of your interest in these essays, but also of your encouragement of my work generally. You will no doubt know the biblical saying, "a prophet is not without honour, save in his own country". I have sometimes thought the same of my scholarly efforts, which have aroused at least as much interest in America and India as at home. The Bible adds a phrase which is not usually quoted, "and in his house", but I hope I am somehow honoured in mine, as I feel sure you are in yours.

Best wishes,

James Ogden

P.S. We are threatened here with postal strikes, which I fear may delay correspondence in both directions.

Dated: 23 October 2003

Dear Professor Ansari,

Many thanks for sending *The Aligarh Critical Miscellany*, vol. XIII no. 2, which came yesterday.

I thought this number was to be the last, but there is no announcement in the number itself, in fact on the inside of the front cover you are still asking for contributions. So I wonder if you have found some way of continuing? I think it is a good number. I am glad to see that you have written an obituary for Kathleen Raine, and have published two of her letters. You mention your sense of personal loss. I believe there are others who will carry forward her work, perhaps in ways not wholly anticipated. I wrote somewhat similarly to Mrs Leavis on the death of her husband, and I hope I was not altogether wrong. I think Dr. Leavis and Kathleen Raine would have broadly approved of the *ACM*, for instance, including the present number. She would have liked your essay on *Four Quartests,* and he would have been pleased to see his work on Wordsworth given proper recognition. I was present when Leavis gave his lecture on "Wordsworth: The Creative Conditions", and I remember the strong impression it made, especially on some who were unfamiliar with his mode of thought. Two other essays call for immediate comment. You have done well to secure one from Professor Jonathan Bate, and he is especially interesting on the subject of Shakespeare's response to Islam. And I was glad to see that the very first essay was your daughter's on Wittgenstein and Heidegger. There is much in it that I do not understand, but I am sure she is right to emphasize the dangers of people identifying with their social roles (p. 112). If she teaches her students nothing else, she will do well. But I am glad to say that I have known people who have insisted on being themselves, even within the academic community. I hope I am right in thinking that your own contributions show that your eyesight has not deteriorated further.

I am at present rather busy, completing my annual contribution to *The Year's Work in English Studies,* and revising my book on Milton. The latter will include a concluding section on "Two Modern Critics", who will be Raleigh and Leavis. Raleigh anticipated Leavis in a way I had not considered, unfortunately, when I wrote the essay you kindly commissioned. Progress on revision is rather slow.

With best wishes,

James Ogden

Dated: 14 May 2004

Dear Professor Ansari,

Many thanks for sending your *Aligarh Critical Miscellany*, vol. xiv no. 1. I have added all authors and subjects to my index to the journal, and if vol. xiv no. 2 is really to be the last issue, I must ask you to send details of authors and subjects as soon as you have them, for completion of the index. If there is not time for that, I could send the index in its present form, and you could add final details in ink before sending it to the printers. However, you may have found means of continuing the journal, under a different editor? I should imagine Roshan Ara could do the job.

It is another good number. I look forward to reading the essays on Shakespeare, and hope to comment on them in my next letter. I have tackled Roshan Ara's essays on Solipsism and Cloning. I think it is most important that philosophers should discuss such important ethical problems as cloning, and I would agree that it is hard to foresee circumstances in which human cloning would appear justifiable. I was very pleased to see that you have found an intelligent and enthusiastic reviewer for your book on *Blake's Minor Prophecies*.

I was glad to see the *ACM* for another reason .We have been a little out-of-touch lately, and I had been wondering about your eyesight and health generally. I hope it is a reasonable inference from the appearance of the *ACM* that you are at least as well as can reasonably be expected. I myself have not been at my best, having been found to have high blood pressure; fortunately, with medication, this seems now under control.

I have managed to complete my book of essays and studies of Milton, and have sent it off to prospective American publishers. I have also completed a booklet of poems, which will be published here later this year. I will send a copy.

I have recently been made a fellow of the English Association .This learned society has been in existence for almost a hundred years. It seeks to promote the study of English language and literature at all levels – primary, secondary, and higher. To this end it publishes a number of journals, organizes conferences, and seeks influence on all educational bodies. The fellowships are an innovation of the past few years. People from all over the world are honoured in this way, and with your permission I will put forward your name, as your contribution to English studies in India and beyond has been outstanding. The fellowships are essentially honorary, and carry no obligations.

Having been away for a few days – to attend an English Association reception for new Fellows – I came home to find the *ACM* waiting, and felt I must write to you immediately. Unfortunately I found many other matters waiting attention, so I must conclude this letter now, but I hope to write again fairly soon.

With best wishes,

James Ogden

P.S. I was interested in O.P. Govil's comments on Vanashree Tripathi's style, p. 99. "wife baiting" is not the same thing as "wife-bashing". (a) These words are not coinages, though they may be debased currency. But in general Mr. Govil's attack on obscurity is much to be applauded. What a lot of obscure nonsense we find in academic work nowadays.

Dated: 18 August 2004

Dear Professor Ansari,

You should by now have received a package containing my index to the *ACM* and a covering note. You should have no difficulty in adding references to 14.2.

In the covering note I said I would try to contribute to 14.2. You will I hope be glad to hear that I have decided to send you my "Recollections of F.R. Leavis". But these will not make much above half-a-dozen pages, and I am soliciting material about Leavis from friends who knew him better than I did. There will be some delay but I hope to send the article before the end of September.

I hope you are keeping reasonably well. I appreciate that the state of your health and eyesight must make supervision of the printing of *ACM* difficult, but must beg you to give this job to some competent person or persons. Printing mistakes in the index could greatly reduce its value. And I hope there will be no bad mistakes in the Leavis article, assuming you will want to print it as well. Leavis himself hated being misprinted, misquoted, or otherwise misrepresented, and if friends provide material I will want to show the article to them. I am thinking mainly of Leavis, my friends, and the reputation of the *ACM*.

I hope you will not think I am making excessive fuss over typographical errors. I have not previously mentioned that there were about a dozen bad mistakes in my "Notes on Shakespeare's Comedies", sometimes making nonsense of what I had written, with the result that I felt unable to photocopy it for friends.

My friend David Crane is publishing my *Poetical Works*. I sent my typescript some months ago. He typed it into his computer and sent me a print-out, which I corrected. He then typed my corrections into this computer and changed the typeface, and sent another printout, which I have also corrected. He will type these further corrections into his computer and then, I believe, provide the printers with camera-ready copy. The process with *ACM* may be similar but should not require more than one set of corrections. I do not know how bad mistakes arise, but it should be possible to stop most of them.

In case you have had difficulty in seeing the *Writers & Artists' Yearbook* I will just mention that the addresses of the publishers I mentioned are:

> Rachel Lynch, Literary Editor, Ashgate Publishing Ltd, Gower House, Croft Road, Aldershot, Hants GU11 3HR
>
> Literary Editor, Cambridge University Press, The Edinburgh Building, Shaftesbury Road, Cambridge CB2 2RU
>
> John Betts, Academic Director, Gerald Duckworth & Co. Ltd, 61 Frith Street, London WIV 5TA

But I would try and see the *Yearbook*, as there may well be more publishers who would be interested. I unfortunately do not have much influence with anybody, and am not yet certain that my own book, *Milton's Dislodgement,* will find a publisher.

You will recognize that the title of my book is a quotation from Leavis. If my friends do not provide material for my Leavis article I will probably complete it with a short account of my reasons for agreeing with him that Milton has been "dislodged", and for not wholly agreeing with his criticisms of Milton in *Revaluation.*

Best wishes,

Yours sincerely,

James Ogden

Dated: 28 September 2004

Dear Professor Ansari,

Many thanks for your letter of 9 September

I enclose "Impressions of F.R. Leavis" for your *Miscellany.*

I mentioned the misprints in my last article mainly because I was concerned that there should not be any in the index, and partly because it would be sad if Leavis was misrepresented. That reminds me, I hope the index arrived safely?

Leavis's lecture on the "Two Cultures" was reprinted in his book *Nor Shall My Sword.*

I have not heard from the English Association recently, and will write again, about the Fellowships. To be fair, I believe the Association's small staff is overworked.

Best wishes,

James Ogden

Dated: 8 November 2004

Dear Professor Ansari,

Thanks for your letter of 13 October.

I was glad to hear that you liked my article on F.R. Leavis, and that it would appear in the next Miscellany.

I had the mistaken impression that you had met Leavis in Cambridge. In a way a long letter from him is preferable however, as he always strove for sincerity and so in his letters gave real insights into his thinking. I look forward to seeing it, and of course your own reflections, in the *Miscellany*.

I read some of C.P. Snow's novels with interest, because they gave some idea of what went on in the "corridors of power" from which people like me were completely excluded. However, I thought his distinction between science and the humanities was superficial, and I was glad Leavis attacked it, though I thought the attack was unduly negative.

I am sending this booklet of Poetical Works, which I hope will be of some interest to you, Mrs Talat Asloob, Roshan and Iffat Ara. Perhaps my genealogical note at the end should have mentioned that I married Vena Theaker, and that our daughter is called Rachel. They join me in sending love and salaams to you all.

Sincerely,

James Ogden

Dated: 01 July 2005

Dear Professor Ansari,

Many thanks for *The Aligarh Critical Miscellany* vol. 14 no. 2, which reached me here yesterday. I was very glad to see it, and to note that it had been posted as recently as 20 June; I hope I am right in deducing that you remain in reasonably good health and spirits. I hope there has been no further deterioration in your eyesight.

This latest issue of the *Miscellany* seems a good one. You may rightly be proud of your daughter's interesting contributions. In a discussion, I might have tried to persuade Iffat Ara to take a more indulgent view of Autolycus. – the mercurial character whose cheerful if obscure songs are the first hint of a turn for the better in the hitherto grim events of the play. He has an element of the divine mystery of which Roshan writes in her essay on Wittgenstein. I have not done much more than read these two contributions, as at present I tire easily; I have not fully recovered from the eye operation I had last May, and of which I told you in my last letter I think. I look forward to reading all the other essays especially of course your own on the sex symbolism in Blake's prophetic books. I do not think I had fully appreciated before that Blake advocated the reciprocity of sexual relations of which you write on p. 200. I have myself thought that idea important ever since I read Simone de Beauvoir as a student.

I notice that you have not printed the index, and on the inside of the front cover you seem to imply that the *Miscellany* is to continue. Perhaps I misunderstood your intentions, and other members of the editorial board will take the work forward? I hope to hear more about your health and prospects eventually. My friend Anne Gardiner was asking how you were recently, and I had to say I had heard nothing since January, when you wrote mainly about my *Poetical Works*.

Glad to see my "Recollections of Leavis" in print. Since writing it I have written another, on "Priestly and Leavis", for the *Journal* of the J.B. Priestly Society. Doing some background reading for that, I realized that at least some of Leavis's notorious quarrels were attributable to his wife, who was more inclined to cherish resentments than he was. However, their low view of Priestly himself was purely literary, not personal, though harshly expressed. Times have changed, and I am older, perhaps wiser, and disinclined to take sides in these ancient arguments.

Best wishes,

James Ogden

Dated: 14 February, 2006

Dear Professor Ansari,

I hope you and your family are keeping well, and in particular that your eyesight has not deteriorated further.

Last time we exchanged letters you were still feeling tempted to bring out another volume of your *Miscellany*. If you are doing so, and want to include my essay on "J.B. Priestly and F.R. Leavis", please let me know, and I will send a revised version. It has just been published in the *Journal* of the J.B. Priestly Society, but I think it needs some adaptation for a very different readership. I do not suppose there is much interest in Priestley in India, so it may hardly be suitable at all. Leavis said he had no time for Priestley at all, but perhaps spoke hastily, as their ideas converged somewhat as they grew older. One of Priestley's most impressive books is *Literature and Western Man,* a study of European and American literature from the Renaissance to the Modernists.

Well, we live at a time of great tension between the Islamic and the Christian worlds. Much of the trouble arises from our horror at the Holocaust, support for Israel, and antagonism of the Arabs. But President Bush is a Christian extremist, and Prime Minister Blair is not much better. There might have been something to be said for intervention against the genocidal dictator Saddam Hussain, but I fear they did not act for the best motives, and anyway they did not know what to do once he had been removed from power, and only encouraged terrorist atrocities. What a mess. Where will it all end? And yet worse problems loom ahead. If China, India, and other great developing countries are to imitate the bad examples of Europe and America, there will be atmospheric pollution and waste of resources on a still greater scale. Already Beijing has replaced bicycles with cars. I am glad to say we are at least thinking, here, of replacing cars with bicycles, but I believe that if human life on earth is to be sustained, we will all have to think about simpler modes of life. *II faut cultivar notre jardin.*

Best wishes,

As ever,

James Ogden

Dated: 06 May 2006

Dear Professor Ansari,

Thanks for your recent letter. Sorry, but not surprised, that your *Miscellany* has ceased publication. I suppose that, like me, you are not getting any younger, and need to preserve your eyesight and general health. I hope you and your family are all well.

Regret to say that there is no immediate prospect of my Milton book being published, but I have not given up hope. Meanwhile here is a photocopy of my essay on "J.B. Priestley and F.R. Leavis", *Journal of the J.B. Priestley Society,* vol. 6, October 2005, pp. 26-38.

Recently John Tasker, the editor of Leavis's *Letters in Criticism,* wrote and asked for a copy of my "Recollections of F.R. Leavis" published in your journal, and I have sent him one. I hope some interesting correspondence may result.

Priestley on Blake: "Those who believe that the society we have created during the last hundred and fifty years is essentially sound and healthy will continue to believe, if they ever think about him, that Blake was insane. But there is more profit for mind and soul in believing our society to be increasingly insane, and Blake to be sound and healthy. And as doubt about our mechanical progress has grown, as has Blake's stature both as a poet and thinker, and it has not stopped growing yet … one of his strongest pieces, *The Marriage of Heaven and Hell,* not only anticipates the discoveries of depth psychology but also reveals how close his thought came to the profoundest Oriental philosophy, then unknown." – *Literature and Western Man* (1960) pp. 140-1.

Please keep in touch

Best wishes,

Your sincerely,

James Ogden

Dated: 14 June 2008

Dear Professor Ansari,

Many thanks for inviting me to write a foreword to *Shakespeare the Existentialist*, and for sending the compact disc.

I immediately telephoned the Edwin Mellen Press, and they told me that they expected the foreword to be about two pages.

I do not have a computer here, but I have been able to find out what is on the disc, and a friend of mine will print out those essays of which I do not already have copies – I have most of *AJES* vo1. 8 to 18, and an almost complete set of *ACM*. I haven't seen *AJES* for some years, and hope it is still being published.

The opening paragraph of my fore word will probably read as follows, but please let me know if there are mistakes of fact or emphasis:

My good friend Asloob Ahmad Ansari has made the study of literature his life's work. His mother-tongue is Urdu, and at an early age he was inspired by the Indian, Persian and Arabic poets and mystics. With this background it is not surprising that his first love in English literature was the visionary poetry of William Blake. His book *Arrows of Intellect* (1965) and an essay on "*Blake and the Kabbalah*" made his name well known among the international community of Black scholars and enthusiasts. Soon afterwards he became Head of English at Aligarh Muslim University, where he launched the *Aligarh Journal of English Studies*, while in retirement he edited the *Aligarh Critical Miscellany*. Over a period of some thirty years these biennial journals published work by established and aspiring scholars and critics on a wide range of literary topics. They include Professor Ansari's further studies of Blake and his many essays on Shakespeare; the former resulted in the recent publication of *Blake's Minor Prophecies* (Edwin Mellen, 2001) and the latter form the basis of the present book.

Professor Ansari's approach to Shakespeare originates in his direct response to the plays and what he has called the "philosophical-symbolical-imagistic" criticism of Wilson Knight, L.C. Knights and Derek Traversi. He rightly believes that this approach is not invalidated by the more fashionable tendency to treat the plays as stage works rather than dramatic poems. This belief is supported by insights derived from existentialism or, to be precise, analogies discerned between the implicit ideas of Shakespeare and the explicit philosophy of Karl Jaspers. Professor

Ansari's daughter Roshan Ara's book, *Existenz and Boundary Situations* (Aligarh, 2002), offers an introduction to Jaspers's philosophy, but it may suffice for readers of *Shakespeare the Existentialist* to be familiar with his leading ideas: Existenz is the potential within human life for growth and transcendence, "boundary situations" are experienced when people are severely tested by guilt, misery, and the approach of death. In Shakespeare's comedies and tragedies there are many examples of characters who develop that self-awareness to which we all should.

There will then be a paragraph going into rather more detail, in which I would hope to mention Iffat Ara's book on *Concepts of Nature and Art*. However, I need to read or re-read your essays before I can write that. I would conclude:

It is often said that we live in a global village, and if that metaphor has validity we must accept that many of our quarrels are trivial. Writers and critics sometimes participate in them, but they should be peacemakers. Here an English dramatist of a remote time, a German philosopher of the early twentieth century, and an Indian scholar happily still with us, combine to explore the foundations of human understanding. I am honoured by the invitation to write a foreword for this book.

Best wishes,

Yours sincerely,

James Ogden

Dated: 25 July 2008

Dear Professor Ansari,

Many thanks for your recent letter about the "Foreword" to *Shakespeare the Existentialist*, and for sending *Iqbal the Visionary*.

I was glad to hear that, in a general way, you approved of my foreword, and that I had got nothing positively wrong. I had sent it to the Edwin Mellen Press before I received your letter, but I suppose it could be altered should any changes be thought absolutely necessary. I had better say plainly that I can't see the necessity. Firstly, I think being Head of a Department at a University is an academic honour; nobody made me head of anything. In any case, it would seem odd not to mention your term of office at Aligarh. Secondly, I don't think my wording suggests that your recent book on Blake and the present one on Shakespeare are mere collections of essays. No doubt the work already published in the journals has been revised and augmented. And anyway there is no shame in proceeding in the way you have done; after all, Dr. Leavis did the same for *Revaluation* and *The Great Tradition*.

I am sensible of the honour of being given a complimentary copy of *Iqbal the Visionary*. I have read parts of it, but it may be some time before I can make an intelligent response to the whole, the subject being so unfamiliar. You will perhaps be interested to hear that a friend of mine, a Lay Reader in the Church of England, surprised me recently by declaring that "God is energy", which is not exactly orthodox Christian doctrine. I was able to tell him that Blake said "energy is eternal delight". And that I had sometimes been reminded of this saying when watching children at play. I was not surprised to find your statement, derived from Iqbal, that God is "a rationally directed creative force or energy" (p. 4). And yet it seems that Iqbal, like Blake and apparently Milton, admired a form of energy they associated ultimately with Satan (p. 96), so it seems the emphasis should fall on reason and creativity. Energy as such, as in the scientific formula E = MC2, appears neutral, and it must be admitted that the energy of children is often destructive.

I look forward to reading more of your book.

I will keep in touch with the Edwin Mellen Press and try to persuade them to go ahead quickly with publication of Shakespeare the Existentialist.

Best wishes,

As ever,

James Ogden

Dated: 19 January 2009
(Martin Luther King Day)

Dear Professor Ansari,

Many thanks for your letter of 12 January. This afternoon I phoned Mrs Williams at the Edwin Mellen Press in Lampeter, and asked about the delay over *Shakespeare the Existentialist*. She says a colleague has written to you, and you should have a reply probably before you receive this letter. There are problems with formatting, which has to be exactly right, otherwise they cannot proceed. You overcame such problems with *William Blake's Minor Prophecies,* and I feel sure you will overcome them with the present book, but I do sympathise with your frustration.

I was rather surprised to hear that you have another book of *Shakespearean and other Essays* ready for publication, and contemplate publishing it with Edwin Mellen. I think you must decide for yourself whether the game is worth the candle. You will again need a preface and sponsors, and you will again have formatting problems. On the other hand, your local publishers and printers made a nice job of that collection of *Essays on Shakespeare in Honour of A.A. Ansari.* I do not know all the ins and outs of it, but I think I would be inclined to approach an Indian publisher if I were you.

Another surprise was the forthcoming publication of *Letters from Abroad,* including some from me.

You will be interested to hear that after writing the preface or foreword to your book I found myself in renewed contact with Edwin Mellen, and decided to let them publish my book on *The Milton Tradition,* which will include my essays on Milton's sonnets and on Walter Raleigh as a Milton critic, both of which were originally commissioned by you; you have previously said that I could publish them again in my book. I hoped to publish with Associated University Presses, who brought out *Lear from Study to Stage*, but they turned it down on what seemed to me debatable grounds, but of course there was no point in arguing. At least with Mellen you get a contract pretty quickly, and as it were appoint your own readers. I did have some difficulty in finding three people with sufficient knowledge of Milton and interest in me, and did think of approaching you, but in the end was happy with my former colleague Raymond Stephens, Professor Tom Craik, and Professor Anne Gardiner. I have resolved the formatting problem by approaching the computer Unit at Aberystwyth University, who agreed to do it because I am a retired member of staff. So I expect *The Milton Tradition* will be published this year or next. My experience with this book certainly helped me to understand your difficulties, and I do not think I will try to publish another in this way.

Actually I am seventy-two, and hence unlikely to write another book, except perhaps my memoirs. Looking back, I suppose my main endeavours have been directed at literary scholarship and higher education, and I am reasonably pleased with what has been achieved and what is in prospect. Of course when I look beyond, at the world's problems, I am less optimistic. The widening gap between the rich and the poor, terrorism and warfare arising from ideological differences, "global warming" and now the economic crisis: all these are depressing. When I meet, as I still do, highly intelligent and idealistic young people, I can only admire, and sometimes apologize.

I infer from your account of your activities that you are keeping well. Be guided by your wife and talented daughters. Best wishes to you all.

Yours sincerely,

James Ogden

Dated: 28 April 2009

Dear Professor Ansari,

I hope you remain in good health and spirits. And that you received my letter in reply to yours of 12.01.2009, mainly concerned with your books *Shakespeare the Existentialist, Shakespearean and Other Essays,* and *Letters from Abroad.*

As a result of deciding to publish my own book, provisionally entitled *The Milton Tradition,* through the Edwin Mellen Press, I now understand better the reasons for their delays. My book had to be typed into a computer, a slow and rather expensive process. I have recently compiled the index, and when that has been computerized we will finally be able to send the publishers the disk they require. I understand that *Shakespeare the Existentialist* has had to go through a similar process, and hope to hear that it is now nearing completion.

My own relations with the Edwin Mellen Press are not as good as they were in its early days, when its Chairman was my friend the late Professor Simon Evans, and I was introduced to its Managing Director Professor Herbert Richardson. I believe Herbert still visits Lampeter but I have not had any recent communication with him, and I have had to deal with Mrs Williams and Mrs Gibbons, who are agreeable enough but unwilling to do much more than discuss matters rather non-committaly on the phone.

I have recently re-read parts of your book *Iqbal the Visionary,* mainly with a view to ascertaining, if possible, the views of Iqbal and Blake concerning the after-life. I do not feel that I *have* ascertained their views, perhaps because they avoided definite statements on what is, after all, not to be known with any certainty. However, that feeling has not prevented the world's religions from making such statements and from disputing about them.

At Easter I read an article by Geza Vermes, the distinguished Jewish biblical scholar, about "The Resurrection". His argument is that the idea of the after-life, either as spiritual survival or as rising from the dead, gained prominence in Jewish thought in the years 200-100 BC (or 200-100 BCE if you prefer that). The principal innovators were the Pharisees, who promoted the doctrine of resurrection. It was not, according to Vermes, a central tenet of Jesus Christ's teaching; he was more inclined to the idea of spiritual survival. His announcements of his own death and resurrection are not authentic, but were added to the gospels by his followers. They knew that after entombment his body had disappeared, but based their idea of his resurrection mainly on his appearances to them from Easter onwards. His survival seemed bodily rather than spiritual. It is certainly true that their lives were transformed at Pentecost, when as Vermes would say Jesus rose in their hearts. The doctrine of bodily resurrection is associated chiefly with St Paul, and has of course become a dogma of the Christian church. Indeed one Christian friend of mine, to whom I put Vermes's arguments, was quite scandalized.

I suppose that what really interests me is not whether one doctrine or another is the more plausible, but why people of all religious persuasions hold such doctrines so tenaciously. One does not have to be an out-and-out materialist, to resist dogmatism in spiritual matters.

Salaams and best wishes,

James Ogden

Dated: 22 October 2009

Dear Professor Ansari,

I hope you are well, and making progress with your literary projects, particularly *Shakespeare the Existentialist,* over which you ran into difficulties with Edwin Mellen over formatting.

As I think I told you in my reply to your last letter, I decided to publish my book on Milton with Mellen. I too ran into difficulties about formatting, which I think have at last been resolved. To my surprise, I have found the publishers difficult to deal with, especially Mrs Gibbons, who has now left the firm. The delays have left me ill-tempered. I hope you have taken my advice and have found another publisher for your *Shakespearean and Other Essays.*

My other work has proceeded reasonably well, and I was heartened recently by the news that my edition of *She Stoops to Conquer* for the "New Mermaid" series is to be reprinted. I must say the publisher, A. & C. Black, are considerably more efficient and courteous than Mellen; unfortunately they do not publish academic monographs like my Milton book.

I am in fairly regular correspondence with John Tasker, who edited F.R. Leavis's *Letters in Criticism* a good many years ago. He is now collecting and editing the personal correspondence of F.R. and Q.D. Leavis, with a view to publishing selections. He has recently attended a conference about the work of the Leavises at Downing College, Cambridge.

John Tasker tells me that Professor Singh has died, which is sad though not unexpected news, as he has been ill for some considerable time. He will be remembered for his book on Leavis and probably for other work less familiar to me.

I hope to hear good news of you and your family.

Yours sincerely,

James Ogden

Dated: 02 December 1996

Dear Professor Ansari,

Thank you for your letter about the late Professor Kenneth Muir. I enclosed a photocopy of *The Times obituary.* It says almost all that needs to be said, except perhaps that he was made a Fellow of the British Academy in 1974. Of course it does not mention all his books, but probably only the best known. There is a fairly complete list in his *Who's Who* entry – I assume Aligarh Muslim University has a recent issue. I myself found his book on *Shakespeare's Sources* useful, though the truth is he was transferred into writing too much. I did not know Professor Muir very well. I heard his lecture several times and I believe his lectures were always well-informed, comprehensive and regularly delivered, but rather impersonal. I was not surprised to read that "he left little space for small talk" Perhaps I will eventually track down obituaries in *The Guardian* and *the Independent*, and there will be others in *Transactions of the British Academy* eventually. Glad to hear you are going to write about Professor Muir in *the Miscellany*, and look forward to reading your obituary and his letters.

Best wishes,

James Ogden

Dated: 07 March 1997

Dear Professor Ansari,

Many thanks for sending your daughter's book *The Concepts of Nature and Art in the Last Plays of Shakespeare,* which reached me this week. It looks attractive and I hope to read it quite soon. If all goes well I may have written a review for *ACM* as promised before the end of A.H. 1417.

At present I am busy with the page proofs and index of *Lear from Study to Stage*, which will be published not later than A.H. 1418. You may remember my co-editor *Arthurs Scoutre* died (about two years ago). And I am having to do all the work myself but it is nearly finished now.

Best wishes,

James Ogden

Fachbereich Neuere
Feremdsprachen Und Literaturen
Aktenzeichen

Dated: 14 May 1974

Dear Professor Ansari

It means a great pleasure to receive vol. 3, no. 2 of The Aligarh Journal (together with 10 off-prints of my article) these days. Thank you for all your endeavours on my behalf.

Your thorough analysis of *Troilus and Cressida* in the same number is very remarkable. Your basic idea is quite convincing that Troilus is in search of his identify and has to outgrow the sphere of idealistic love. This is a major article and extends the matter in a new dimension.

With, again, many thanks and all best wishes

Yours sincerely,

Horst Oppel

Dated: 04 October 1977

Dear Professor Ansari

Thank you very much for your kind letter. I feel myself honoured to be invited to contribute to your splendid periodical. At the moment I have no paper ready which might prove to be adequate to this purpose, but I hope to come back to your kind invitation at a later time.

I heartily welcome your instructive articles on 'The Ambivalence of Caliban' and on 'Fools of Time'. You give a well learned and deeply interesting account of problems which are outstanding in recent Shakespeare criticism. I am always fascinated by the various aspects of the Caliban-figure. You back this aspect with clarity and wide-ranging understanding.

My best congratulations.

I confess to be an ardent reader of *The Aligarh Journal of English Studies* and am ready to welcome every new number.

With best wishes and kind regards,

Yours sincerely,

Horst Oppel

Dated: 14 May 1977

Dear Professor Ansari

Thank you very much for your great kindness to make the first two numbers of The *Aligarh Journal of English* Studies available. I congratulate you on the editorial task of this fine and highly interesting review. I am deeply impressed by your article on 'The Ambivalence of Caliban, covering a wide field and stressing new aspects. I am seeing forward to the following numbers and can only state that I am very grateful that you have drawn my attention in this direction.

With kind regards

Yours Sincerely,

Horst Oppel

Date 31 October 1978

Dear Professor Ansari,

Some time ago you have kindly asked me to contribute to your excellent periodical (favoured by many of my students) *The Aligarh Journal of English Studies*. I have pleasure in enclosing an article on *King Lear* and would regard it as an honour if you were able to accept it.

In the meantime, I have thoroughly studied your excellent paper 'The Ambivalence of Caliban' and estimate it as an outstanding contribution to *Tempest*-Studies. In a forthcoming study on Caliban as depicted in the fine arts I had the opportunity to draw the attention of European scholars to your salient article.

Looking forward to hearing from you and getting an affirmative reply,

With best wishes,

Yours sincerely,

Horst Oppel

Englisches Seminar
Der Philips-Univrsitat
355 Marburg/LAH,
Krummbogen 28 D.

Dated: 9 September 1979

Dear Professor Ansari,

Thank you very much for the Special Andrew Marvell Number of *The Aligarh Journal.* Congratulations on the valuable contribution to Marwell Studies. Your excellent article on "The Body-Soul Dialectic" is thorough-going and convincing in the analysis. The comparison with the late years should be extorted in a future study. I am impressed, as ever before, by the high standard of you in journal and feel honored to have had the opportunity to publish my article on *King Lear* under your direction.

With kind greetings and all good wishes,

Yours sincerely,

Horst Oppel

David Ormerod

Dated: 24 July 1994

Dear Professor Ansari,

Many thanks for your letters of 18th April and 25th May, and my apologies for the long silence that has intervened. The reason is that I sent you the article on emblems in the A-Text of *Doctor Faustus* immediately prior to my departure for London on three months study leave. Sent it, in fact, virtually on the way to the airport! I returned from my trip a couple of days ago, to find your letters awaiting me. Unfortunately, there was no one here to forward my mail.

It is obviously too late now, as you have gone to press. Had I been here, I could have expanded the article in the form in which I originally intended it, viz., it was to have contained reproductions of the emblems. I assume that in view of the expense of manual typesetting these days, your journal is produced photographically, and the illustrations could hence easily have been incorporated in the text, or on separate leaves. Pressure of time prevented me from doing this, and I decided—ill-advisedly, I now realise—that the article was perfectly intelligible, if less interesting, without the illustrations. I could not, I'm afraid, expand the article with additional letterpress without a lot more thought on the matter. Although, of course, additional examples could be included, but at the risk of repetitiveness.

I can only reiterate how sorry I am about all this. Please accept my apologies for all the inconvenience I've caused you. If you think the article, with illustrations and extra examples, would be suitable for a future issue of your journal, I would be only too happy to comply. If you can't find room for it, I will perfectly understand, and will try to rework it at some future date for *Emblematica*.

Yours sincerely,

David Ormerod

University of California
Dept. of English
Berkeley, California 94720

Dated: 27 January 1971

Dear Professor Ansari,

Thank you for your kind remarks on my review article. I am surprised that you have not yet received *Energy and the Imagination*. I had asked the Clarendon Press to send you a review copy in April 1970. I will write to them again, but as you probably know there is a postal strike on in England and therefore, no mail for England is being accepted here, so this may take a little while.

I hope the *Blake Newsletter* is reaching you satisfactorily. We now have a new publishing arrangement with the University of New Mexico. Should there be any problems, the person in charge of mailing is my new co-editor: Professor Morris Eaves, Dept. of English, University of New Mexico, USA, and all the printing, mailing and record-keeping is done there. I understand that the Autumn issue was sent out – rather late, as usual – at the end of last month.

Cordially,

Morton D. Paley
Associate Professor of English

M.D. Paley
Flat 34
29 Abereon Place
London, N.W., 8

Dated: 01 October 1979

Dear Professor Ansari,

Thank you for your letter of July 17, which reached me in London only last week; I don't know why forwarding took so long. I am here doing further research for my books on *Jerusalem*, which I hope to finish before I return to teaching at Berkeley a year from now.

It is kind of you to invite me to contribute to the *Aligarh Journal of English Studies* (which I appreciate your sending to me). As I'm fully committed to the book at present, I can't undertake any new articles; but I do appreciate your asking me, and I hope I may be able to do a short piece for you at some future time. It occurs to me that there is an essay to be written about Blake's use of Indian materials from such sources as Welkin's *Gita*, Jones's *Oriental Researches* and *Moore's Hindu Panthon*, But, as I say, I regret that I cannot do any such thing in the immediate future.

With best wishes,

Yours sincerely,

Morton D. Paley

Dated: 1 April 1985

Dear Professor Ansari,

Thank you very much for your kind invitation to contribute an article to the *Aligarh Journal of English Studies*.

I have been thinking about what I could give you by the end of June 1985. My problem is that I am completing a book that according to contract must be delivered to the publisher by this June, and so I am not free to undertake a new project before then.

However, I do have an article that is scheduled for publication in *BLAKE: AN ILLUSTRATED QUARTERLY*, and that I could withdraw and give you to publish instead. It is entitled "*Milton* and the Form of History", and is especially concerned with the roles of Whitefield and Wesley, and to a lesser extent Swedenborg, in Blake's poem.

The article has already been copy-edited at *BLAKE*, but it has not been set up; so if you would like to include it in your journal, I will withdraw it from *BLAKE* and send it to you. Perhaps you could let me know what you think of this idea.

With best wishes,

Yours sincerely,

Morton D. Paley

Dated: 11 July 1985

Dear Professor Ansari,

Thanks for your letter of June 19, which I received only yesterday upon returning from a trip to England.

Unfortunately, I have no copy of my article here in Sweden, and the quotation in your letter doesn't give me enough to reconstruct the sentence. All I can suggest is that if you could send me a copy of the whole paragraph – the best thing would be a Xerox of the two pages – I would then reconstruct the passage in question and sent it to you by return air mail.

In Sweden mail will reach me more quickly if sent to the address on the reverse of this aerogram.

Might I ask you to send the proofs of the article when ready to my Berkeley address? I expect to be there from August 15 on (and here in Sweden until that date).

With best wishes,

Yours sincerely,

Morton D. Paley

Dated: 05 June 1990

Dear Professor Ansari,

I have just returned from a semester in Europe and found two letters from you. For some reason they had gone to UCLA in Los Angeles and then been sent here, where they should have been forwarded but weren't. I am very sorry for the delay.

I am also sorry I was not able to contribute to the Blake issue, which looks fascinating. Thank you for sending it and also for your kind remarks on "the of the ancients". Regarding picture rights: these are held by the owners, who would have to give permission for reproduction.

With best wishes,

Morton D. Paley

Dated: 12 February 1993

Dear Professor Ansari,

Thanks you for your kind letter and for your much appreciated gift of the *Aligarh Critical Miscellany*.

I would very much like to contribute to your journal – I have an article on the *Songs* in mind – but right now I am over-committed. I'll keep it in mind, and I'll write to you again once I get clear of a couple of pressing obligations.

I'm having a copy of the new *Blake Quarterly* sent to you under separate cover.

With best wishes,

Yours sincerely,

Morton D. Paley

Dated: 21 April 1993

Dear Professor Ansari,

Thanks for your letter. I am sorry the *BLAKE* didn't reach you; I'm having another sent from Rochester.

I haven't forgotten about the article but must wait until the end of term before I can do any additional revision.

The two most likely sources of research support for your Blake project, I think, are the Fulbright Commission and the Henry E. Huntington Library. For information about fellowships at the Huntington, you should write to:

> Director of Research
> The Huntington Library
> San Marino, California 91108

I don't have the Fulbright address at hand, but I'll look it up tomorrow and append it below. Unfortunately, I can't think of no sources in the Berkeley – San Fransisco area. However, if you were able to do research in the U.S., I am sure we could find a way of getting together to discuss Blake. It would, needless to say, be a great pleasure to meet you.

With best wishes,

Yours sincerely,

Morton D. Paley
Professor

Dated: 10 September 1996

Dear Professor Ansari,

Thanks for your letter of late August and for your kind remarks about my Coleridge article. I am flattered that you wish to reprint the article, but I am afraid permission does not lie with me to grant; Oxford University Press doesn't want me to republish any of my "later poetry" material as they have now published my book on the subject. However, I will think of something else for your journal after I've met my current outstanding commitments.

Meanwhile, I'll send some copies of *Blake* by Air Mail/Printed Matter (so they may arrive a few days after this). If you'd like more just let me know which issues you wish to have.

With best wishes,

Yours sincerely,

Morton D. Paley

Dated: 07 October 1999

Dear Professor Ansari,

Thanks for your recent letter. I am delighted to know that your book on Blake is about to be published. If you could send me details of publication, including the

ISBN no., I'll have our library order it. Pease send the copy for review in *Blake* to Nelson Hilton, and he will find a reviewer for it. His address is: Dept. of English, University of Georgia, Athens GA 20602

I'll be delighted to contribute an article to your journal when I have one, but that may not be for some time. The last couple of years have been spent in finishing *Portraits of Coleridge and Apocalypse and Millennium*, and consequently there has been little time for anything else.

Professor Bentley's address is 246, Macpherson Avenue, Toronto, Ontario M4V 1A2.

Yours sincerely,

Morton D. Paley

Morton D. Paley
Berkeley, California 94720-1030
Department of English
322 Wheeler Hall # 1030

Dated: 06 August 1999

Dear Professor Ansari,

Thank you very much for sending me Vol. X no. 1 of the *Critical miscellany*. I look forward very much to reading your article on *America* as well as some of the other essays.

I enclose, with compliments, the most recent *Blake Quarterly*.

With best wishes,

Yours sincerely,

Morton D. Paley

Department of English
The University of Florida
Gainesville, Fl 32611
(904) 392-0777, 392-0794

Dated: 23 November 1982

Dear Professor Ansari,

I am pleased that you like my essay on *Richard III*. I will not object to dropping the opening paragraph, but then the opening sentence of what is now paragraph 3 needs to be revised. I suggested: "Like the characters whom I discuss in an earlier essay in this journal", etc. Then footnote I and footnote 3 can be combined. I want to refer to the earlier essay because of the exposition of Harvey which it contains. If you have a different idea, I will be happy to consider it.

I look forward to seeing my essay in your pages. When do you think it will appear.

Sincerely,

Bernard Paris

P.S. *Richard III* at the end of paragraph 3 should be italicized.

Dated: 27 April 1983

Dear Professor Ansari,

The enclosed essay is a version of my piece on *Richard III* which I prepared for the Shakespeare Association of America meeting this month. If you prefer it to the version which I sent you, please feel free to use to. It is shorter and it contains and exposition of Harvey's theory. When you have an idea of where my piece will be published, I would appreciate having the information.

Sincerely,

Bernard Paris

Dated: 05 March 1984

Dear Professor Ansari,

I shall be pleased to contribute an essay on Shakespeare to the Commemorative Volume. It will be something from my book-in-progress (as was the piece on *Richard III* which you published); I trust that there will be no objection to my republishing it in that context when the book in finished. I have not decided yet what to send you, but I'll make that decision within a few months.

It is an honour to be included in the Volume, and I congratulate you upon the distinction of which such an occasion is the measure.

Yours sincerely,

Bernard Paris

Dated: 19 June, 1984

Dear Professor Ansari,

Thank you very much for the *King Lear* number of *The Aligarh Journal,* I read your piece and Kenneth Muir's with particular interest. I enclose a draft of my chapter on *Lear*, which also tries to describe, as you will see, the "vision" of the play. The chapter needs cutting, I know. I'd be happy to receive any other suggestions you might have for revision. The book is proceeding apace. I hope to have it finished by August, 1985.

With best regards,

Bernard Paris

Dated: 17 December 1985

Dear Professor Ansari,

Enclosed is a copy of my curriculum vitae from which you can take what information you like. I am pleased that the Commemorative volume will soon appear; I look forward to seeing it. It will be of help to me to have the bibliographical information for my essay (title of volume, place and date of publication, publisher, and page numbers) before the beginning of March so that I can include the essay among my publications for the 1985-86 academic year.

Thank you for sending me the *Aligarh Journal.* I have read your essay on Brutus with interest, since I, too, see him as having a divided self. I enclose my chapter on *Julius Caesar*- you need not return it. My book on Shakespeare is nearing completion, and I am trying to decide what publisher to approach. I would like a publisher that reached the English – speaking world. Oxford does, I know. Do you see much of Methuen in India? They have published A.D. Nuttall's *A New Mimesis,* which is highly compatible with my own approach.

Again, I look forward to seeing the volume in your honour.

With sincere regards,

Bernard Paris

Kathleen Raine
47 Paulton's Square
London SW3 5DT
0171-3524643

Dated: 16 August 1998

Dear Professor Ansari,

I was so glad to hear from you, and remember my visit to Aligarh with much warmth. Please remember me to Mrs. Ansari and the members of your family I met down to the grandson who chanted the poem so beautifully. I am so glad you enjoyed the Temenos Academy Review and especially Corbin, who is to my mind a great writer on the holy Wisdom.

I would be honoured to write a foreword to your forthcoming book '*Blake's Minor Prophecies*'. But can you please let me have some more information about its contents and any other relevant information? Perhaps the press could let me have a copy of the material? Whatever you think best.

Piloo did nor come to England this year, I have missed her. I had a wonderful ninetieth birthday party and I am still carrying on with the Review until my successor Professor Grevel Lindop of Manchester University takes early retirement in the year 2000. I hope, I can carry on until them, but if I don't I am sure the Academic Board will manage somehow. If the world lasts too long.

With warm regards,

Kathleen Raine

Dated: 11 May 1999

Dear Professor Ansari,

I have much enjoyed reading of the manuscript of your book on Blake's early Prophetic books, and I hope the preface I have written will do. I also showed your chapter on Kabbalah to Jewish Kabbalist friend. Shimon ben Halevi, author of many books on Kabbalah, who thought it very good. I am glad you dedicated the book to Desiree whose *Hidden Riches* is one of the best Blake books.

I have recently had a letter from Piloo who is coming (she hopes) at the end of this month, but maybe delayed by a public launch of her long-awaited book on the Zend Avesta, which our recent dear Ambassador Dr. L.M. Singhvi is arranging for her, and Prof. Lokesh Chandra had promised to review, will be published later this month. Our first issues included a paper by Prince Charles on relation with Islam and also a paper on Rumi by Prof. Anne-Marie Schimmel, and in this issue we have a paper on Henry Corbin and his work by Dr. S.H. Nasr who also gave our second L.M. Singhvi lecture a few weeks ago. It was held at Nehru Centre and the audience was the largest they have ever had-people had to be turned away when there was no more room on the floor or the staircase. So we do, I think, keep Islam well in view, we have had some lovely seminars on Nizami by Dr. Gomshel from Tehran.

I have most happy memory of my visit to your house and of meeting your wife, daughters and sons-in-laws and the grandson who chanted so beautifully I don't recall what poetry or Scripture. I hope you are well and all your family. I also much enjoyed my visit to the University of Aligarh.

I will return the manuscript if you want me to do so but I imagine you have other copies. I noticed a few misprints as on p.14 there is no *Natural* religion (line 12) but no doubt you have picked these up. I wish the book the success it deserves.

I am now in my ninety-first year and am no longer likely to revisit India, of which I have so many wonderful and happy memories.

With warm regards,

Kathleen Raine

Professor Ansari has been known as one of the leading Blake scholars of his time. This important contribution to the understanding of Blake's early 'Prophetic Books' confronts issues which scholars have tended to avoid. Blake is of course known as 'a mystic', but it is a misapprehension to suppose that, as such, he was indifferent to, or unaware of the dramatic public events being played out in his time. His concern was, on the contrary, to relate 'the politics of time' to 'the politics of eternity'. The difficulties presented by the combination of a purely personal mythological structure and terminology with a precise and detailed knowledge of current affairs scholars have been unable or reluctant to confront; Professor Ansari has undertaken the laborious but rewarding task of making an intensive study of the current of events, especially in France and America, in the years between 1790 and 1795. His work on the 'Lambeth' books is an invaluable contribution to our knowledge and understanding of Blake's importance in the context of history.

Blake was born in the year 1757, the year in which, according to the prophesies of Swedenborg, a new spiritual era was to begin. Swedenborg's 'Church of the New Jerusalem' was to supersede the two thousand years of the Apostolic Church, whose organization would continue to exist outwardly, but no longer as an expression of the Spirit. Blake saw the revolutions in France and America as manifestations of the new spirit which was sweeping through the world, and felt himself to be the heir of this 'new age' who must give voice and expression to the new vision. His last and longest poem, *Jerusalem,* bears the Swedenborgian title of the holy city 'coming down from God out of heaven', and proclaims the 'Divine Humanity', a term Blake adopted from Swedenborg. From the outset, therefore, Blake participated in the events of his time with a prophetic ardour proper to an actor of history rather than to a spectator. His friends included Thomas Paine, the revolutionary and author of *The Rights of Man,* and Mary Wollstonecraft, and himself came into conflict with the law at one time on account of his radical political views. Yet Blake's politics were at no time those of a political activists; he took upon himself, from the outset, the role of a prophet- and as it was later to prove of England's one national Prophet- and Professor Ansari has brought insight, detailed and exact knowledge, and understanding to Blake the Prophet in his formative years. One of the most valuable books on Blake to have been written, and one whose value will not diminish with time, since it is grounded in accurate scholarship – a work for which scholars will be grateful.

Kathleen Raine

Kaith Raine
Temenos

Dated: 17 February 1992

Dear professor Ansari,

I have been reading the *Aligarh Critical Miscellany* Vo1 4 1991 with great gratitude for your most generous and authoritative review of my last Blake book. That I should receive such a review from you is an honour indeed and your understanding of Blake – to whom I have tried to be faithful – contrasts with the Occidental *critics* who have little understanding of the view of a sacred universe in which Blake's thought is rooted. Blake would have been happy that his vision should form a link with Oriental spiritual traditions. I have also been reading your own contribution on the *Book of Urizen*. Unfortunately in Urizen's kingdom (Western materialism) he still reigns, though not unchallenged anymore! That reign I believe is now doomed, and Temenos is not now alone in calling in question, not the conclusions, but the premises of materialism. Northrop Frye made a fine contribution to Blake scholarship but I can't feel the same about Harold Bloom who has his own 'isms' although as a Jew he might, in the light of the Jewish mystical tradition, have understood him.

What a very interesting Review you produce, and I am honoured to have been a contributor.

I am sorry that I did not have the opportunity of coming to know you on my visits to India or of visiting Aligarh. I hear news of you from Piloo Nannavutty (Jungalwalla) on her annual visits to England. I have now given up travel, at eighty-three and with an unreliable heart. Also my task at present lies here, for we are at present establishing the Temenos Academy of Integral studies- with the intention of teaching all subjects relating to meaning and values from the stand point of the Perennial Wisdom- Blake's 'Everlasting Gospel' – in Blake's belief that 'All religions are one'. Naturally there is great resistance, but now we have the support of our remarkable Prince Charles, who has established his own Institute of Architecture with a similar intent and has invited us to operate from a base in his building. I hope this represents a turning of the tide, at first scarcely discernible. If not the world has little hope. But there are other signs.

I am posting separately a copy of Temenos 12, and the thirteenth issue will be our last. But the Academy, I hope, will develop our ideas in a different form. I hope the critical miscellany will continue to give voice to your vision.

With grateful regards,

Kaith Raine

Jacqueline Raleigh

Dated: 4th October 1988

Dear Professor Ansari,

Quite by chance I discovered your "Essays on Sir Walter Raleigh" in Oxford last week. We were looking for some of his books to send to our son in Australia, Sir Walter was my husband's Grandfather. He didn't know him as he died the year my husband was born but his widow Lady Raleigh only died just after the war so she was well known to me as well.

Unfortunately when Lady Raleigh died we were not in England and so much was sold so we are now trying to collect together some of Sir Walter's books for our two sons.

You have obviously done a tremendous amount of research on Sir Walter, you must feel that you almost knew him we should very much like to meet you one day.

I should very much like to buy another copy of your book "Essays on Sir Walter Raleigh" so that both our sons can have copies. Could you let me know if there is anywhere in England it can be purchased. I should be very grateful or alternatively if I sent the money to India have you possibly got a copy you could sell me?

I look forward to hearing from you.

Yours sincerely,

Jacqueline Raleigh (Mrs)

---

22 Marywood Square
Strathbungo
GLASGOW
G41N 2BJ
UK

Dated: 21 January 2000

Dear Professor Ansari,

A few years ago I wrote a book-length study of Byron which included the piece on *Manfred* that you so kindly published in the *Aligarh Critical Miscellany.* Since about 1996 this study has sat in a box waiting for me to find a publisher for it. I've now done this and write to ask if you would mind me including the *Manfred* piece in the published version of the book-length study. I would also include, of course, a prominent acknowledgement of the fact that the piece first appeared in the *Aligarh Critical Miscellany.*

Does this meet with your approval? I would be most grateful if you could let me know as soon as possible- things this end are rather rushed and I must send a final manuscript to the publisher within the next two/three weeks. I am sorry to rush you and hope will understand and forgive me.

Yours sincerely,

Dr. Alan Rawes

R.T.H. Redpath
Trinity College
Cambridge

Dated: 7 January 1981

Dear professor Ansari,

I apologize for not replying earlier to your letter. We have had a good deal of illness in the family, and my correspondence has got behind.

I most certainly remember meeting you at the Shakespeare Conference at Stratford last August, and I hope to have the pleasure of doing so again.

With regard to your kind invitation to me to contribute an article on *Hamlet* to your journal, I feel I must most regretfully decline. I have, indeed, the intention of completing some work on *Hamlet* at some time during the next year or so; but at present I am working on quite different things, and cannot switch my attention from them. I am, moreover, going abroad as a Visiting Professor for a good deal of this year, and expect to be fully engaged on yet other work during that period.

I am, however, grateful to you for the invitation, which I wish I could have accepted.

With kind regards,

Yours sincerely,

R.T.H. Redpath

W.W. Robson
15 Cobden Crescent
Edinburgh
EH9 2G, Scotland

Dated: 31 December 1985

Dear Professor Ansari,

Thank you very much for your letter. I have only just received it: it was sent on to Oxford, where I was a visiting Fellow at New College, and then re-forwarded here, during the disruptions caused by the Christmas-New Year interlude, hence the considerable delays.

I am most honoured by your kind invitation to contribute an article to *The Aligarh Journal of English Studies*. (I received a copy of Vol. 10, No. 1., just before leaving Oxford, which I read with great interest.) Nothing would have pleased me more than to say yes, if I had had something publishable on Lawrence, but unfortunately I have not. I am unable to contribute any new material, having turned away from Lawrence to other studies.

All I can do is to express my sincere gratitude for the invitation (and for the copy of the journal) and my best wishes for the success of the Lawrence number.

Your sincerely,

W.W. Robson

Department of English,
Brown University
209, Angell Street,
Providence, Rhode
Island – 02912

Dated: 18 April 1966

Dear Professor Ansari,

To honor S. Foster Damon on his seventy-fifth birthday, I am preparing to edit a collection of original Blake essays, these to be presented to Professor Damon as a *Festschrift* volume sometime around January or February of 1968. As it is presently conceived, the volume will serve two large ends, both honorary and scholarly. Although Professor Damon is still busy at work on a variety of projects, he has behind him a record of scholarship that is highly impressive generally and, in Blake studies specifically, illustrious. His important *Blake Dictionary* is only one year old and there are more Blake things to come, but it is already fitting to honor him, and his seventy-fifth birthday is being chosen as the occasion to do so. In addition to the honorary function of the volume, however, it is hoped that the proposed collection of essays will stand as an important contribution to Blake studies in its own right. Accordingly, the leading Blakeans of America and abroad are being invited to contribute essays.

I very much hope that you will wish to contribute to the volume. Only previously unpublished essays can be considered, but otherwise no restrictions as to the type or range of essay will be made. Contributions both scholarly and critical in Blake studies at large will be welcome.

The Brown University Press, which has previously published two of Professor Damon's Blake books, will also publish the *Festschrift*. Since the nature of the publication demands a deadline, contributions should be submitted any time between receipt of this letter and the Christmas period of 1966.

I shall be honored by your participation in this venture and will appreciate any communication indicative of your interest even before submission of manuscripts. The latter will, of course, be acknowledged upon receipt.

Sincerely yours,

Alvin Rosenfeld

Dated: 18 April 1966

Dear Professor Ansari,

Professor Damon has told me something about your recent letter to him and also about your interest in Blake. I know that you are the author of a book on Blake, and so I thought you might be interested to learn about a collection of original Blake essays that I am currently preparing to edit. The enclosed letter will tell you more. Should you have an essay that you would like to contribute, I would be happy to reserve a place for you in the volume.

Perhaps you would be kind enough to help me with another matter. In January I wrote to Mrs. P.A. Jungalwalla (Piloo Nanavutty), another Blake scholar in India. Unfortunately my letter was returned to me just this week. It seems that the address I have for her is not correct. I wrote her care of 3 Ronaldshay Road/Alipore/Calcutta 27/India. Should you know another address for her, I would be most grateful if you would let me have it. Thank you for this kindness.

Cordially,

Alvin Rosenfeld

Dated: 2 May 1966

Dear Professor Ansari,

Thank you for your quick reply to my letter of 18 April about the proposed Damon *Festchrift*. I appreciate your interest in the volume and am delighted that you will be contributing an essay. It is not necessary that you tell me the specific topic you will be handling right now, so do not feel pressed on that matter. Anytime at your convenience will do. I might mention now that you should think in terms of a typescript of 20-25 pp. at maximum. There are so many good contributors for the volume that I am forced to make certain limits as to the length of the essays. I hope you do not find that that limits you too much.

I also thank you for giving me the address of Mrs. Jaungalwalla. I will get off a letter to her tonight also.

That's all this time. Please do not hesitate to write me again should you have any questions or special problems.

Sincerely yours,

Alvin Rosenfeld

Bar-Han University
Ramat-Gan, Israel
Department of English
Murray Roston
51 Katznelson
St.Kiryat One,
Israel

Dated: 10th December 1975

Dear Professor Ansari,

I have just received the copy of *Essays on John Donne* which you sent me, and should like to congratulate you on its publication.

On a visit I paid to India a few years ago, to attend a Fulbright Seminar, I remember being deeply impressed by the standard of English and American studies among the Indian professors and lecturers who participated, and I find that this collection of essays maintains that high standard. It is also encouraging to know that there is such a strong interest in Donne among the staff at your university.

It was gratifying to know that you found my own book of interest. For me it was a labour of love, as I have long been an admirer of Donne, and it was good to see from your own fine article in the collection that you share that interest.

I hope it will be possible for us to meet one day and to share some of our thoughts on him.

With many thanks, and best wishes,

Sincerely yours,

Murray Roston

Dated: 31st October 1982

Dear Professor Ansari,

I have just returned from spending a sabbatical year teaching at the University of Virginia, and found awaiting me here the copy of the *Aligarh Journal of English Studies* with the lengthy review of my Milton book. As I have been receiving the journal from you so regularly, and have enjoyed reading its contents, I thought it a good opportunity to thank you both for sending it to me and for having always reviewed my books as they appear.

The review by Mr. Hasan was generous indeed, and it is always a pleasure to read one which reveals a real understanding of the theme. As regards his observation that I did not deal with Milton's other works, in fact the only one I do regard as belonging within the baroque is Samson Agonistes, and I promised in my book that I would deal with that later. In December of this year a lengthy article on that theme is due to appear in the Milton Quarterly. I would be grateful if you could mention that to him.

It is hard to realize that it is twelve years since I visited India on the Fulbright seminar. I have often thought of your country, and have been following with interest the developments there. I do hope that before long I shall be able to visit it once again and to renew friendships made there.

I mentioned to Macmillan who have just published a new book of mine *Sixteenth Century English Literature*, that they should send a review copy to your journal. Actually, it is aimed at a more general audience, and may not be appropriate for review in your journal, but at all events I thought it a good way of ensuring that you receive a copy...

I would be interested in hearing what you are working upon at the moment.

With kind regards,

Sincerely yours,

Murray Roston

Dated: 21st August, 1976

Dear Professor Ansari,

I have just returned from a visit to England to find your letter of June 16 awaiting me together with the copy of the *Aligarh Journal of English Studies* which you kindly sent me.

First let me congratulate you on the appearance of the first number and wish you every success in the future. I found this, like the collection of Donne essays, excellently produced and it is a journal of which you can feel justly proud. Thank you also for the generous review of my book which it contained. It is always encouraging to read a review which shows that the book has been deeply understood, and I can honestly say that yours showed that without a doubt. In a way that is even more important than whether the review is favourable or not, and it was an added bonus for me to know that you liked it.

Your invitation to submit an article for a future number has caught me at an unfortunate moment. I am just engaged in rechecking the Donne book in preparation for a reprinting and at the same time and more deeply engaged in a full length book on Milton. With the best will in the world, therefore, I cannot see any possibility of being able to offer you anything for some considerable time.

I hope, however, we will remain in contact.

With best wishes,

Sincerely yours,

Murray Roston

Keith Sagar
MANCHESTER, M13 9PL
ENLGLND
TELEPHONE 061-273333

Dated: 10 June 1986

Dear Professor Ansari

Thank you for the copy of the *Aligarh Journal* and the invitation to contribute. I'm afraid I don't have any unpublished material on Lawrence so soon after the publication of *Life into Art*. An article which would have served your purpose, 'D.H. Lawrence: The Man and the Artist' is to be published shortly in a memorial volume for Harry T. Moore. I have had to make resolution this year that I will undertake no new work until I have finished editing my volume of Lawrence letters for the Cambridge edition, a very time-consuming project on which I am already years behind.

Why not invite Professor Sharma to write a review of *Life into Art* for your Lawrence special number?

Best wishes

Yours sincerely,

Keith Sagar

"LE BALCON DE LA REINE"
Cengle de Negrel
13790 Chateauneuf-le-Rouge
France

Dated: 24 September

Dear Professor Ansari,

I am back home; I thought much of you, of your European grand Tour, and I expect you are back too, by now. First of all, a surprising and pleasant piece of news: the other *Essay on Shakespeare,* at long last, reached me at the Faculty! Needless to tell you, I did what you kindly suggested – offered it as gift from you to Maria, who was delighted. I had some time to pursue some of contributions, and I liked most of them very much particularly those of K. Muir, Salingar and M. Mahood. I also appreciated the one by Paris, in fact (between you and me) more than I had expected. My feeling is that *The Essays* are a very fine book since their substance perfectly agreed with the fine painting we spoke of in Stratford!

A sadder piece of news now: perhaps you have heard of the forest fires in the South of France. Well, they destroyed most of our trees (about 200 pine trees) the very day I came back from England (24 August). I hope all is well with and you will write soon.

Best wishes,

Pierre Sahel

Dear Professor Ansari,

Thank you very much for your tactful gift. Pierre told me that the second sample of your Commemorative volume was for me. I see you are still the kindly gentleman I met with pleasure in Stratford six years ago! Sorry I could not come with Pierre this summer.

Sincere yours,

Maria

Dated: 26 September

Dear Professor Ansari,

Here is my contribution to Commemorative Volume in your honour. I am pleased I could finish it in due time, as I am just back from England. I spent a nice week in Stratford and though you had let me know you would not be there, I kept hoping you might have changed your mind. My paper, though it is somewhat odd on my part to say so, was a success. The Chairman who introduced me of course mentioned my contribution to *AJES*.

More than before I hope you will appreciate my present study.

Yours sincerely,

Pierre Sahel

I would naturally be immensely pleased if you could kindly send me a copy of the volume when it appears.

Dated: 20th October 1980

Dear Professor Ansari,

Thank you for your letter and for the copy of your *AJES.* I read with pleasure your article on *The Winter's Tale.* Apropos your view that "artifice and nature were even poised against each other", it has always seemed to me that in that play, Shakespeare was playing with and on the art and nature debate and telling us: "which, of art or nature comes first? It is like the problem of the egg and the hen".

I wish you had invited me to write on the history plays. It would have been very easy and pleasant to me since I am rather a specialist of politics in Shakespeare and the history plays. On the other hand, I recently wrote a paper called "The Cease of Majesty in *Hamlet*". Yet there are quite a few ideas on *Hamlet* which I should still like to couch in article form. So I am ready to accept your offer. Please let me know when you expect to publish this *Hamlet* issue? I hope it will be soon enough.

I remember that at the Stratford Conference, you wished to meet Jan Kott. I am sorry the post-paper whirl and rush made that meeting impossible. But there has been some recent correspondence (mainly on *As You Like It*) between Jan Kott and me. So if you want to give him a message through me or if you would like to have his address, it will not be difficult.

My wife and I send you our best regards.

I hope to hear of you soon.

Yours faithfully

Pierre Sahel

Dated: 23 June

Dear Professor Ansari,

I received a sample of the *Hamlet* issue of the *AJES* and the off prints of my own "War in *Hamlet*". What a brilliant number! I read all the studies and appreciated them very much-thank you.

I made enquires about a possible article on Virginia Woolf. But apparently everyone is afraid of her about here: I had no success!

A last word about Stratford: Eventually, we are not going there either.

Faithfully Yours

Pierre Sahel

Dated: 30 November

Dear Professor Ansari,

Thank you so much for your kind suggestion. I immediately wrote my brother – who accepted with pleasure to contribute an article on guide. I hope you will like it since you said you are extremely fond of guide. I am personally very happy that you appreciate our literature so much.

Time passes but, dear Professor Ansari we often speak of you with Maria, and of the day when we had the pleasure of meeting you in Stratford (sometimes it seems so long ago!)

Please let us know your literary (and other) plans.

Best wishes,

Yours,

Pierre Sahel

Dated: 10 April 19

Dear Professor Ansari,

I did all I could to send you my contribution to the April issue of *AJES* in due time. I have just given my typist the article which I could complete only recently. It is called "The Coup d' Etat of Shakespeare's *Richard III:* Politics and Dramatics". Sorry I am so late! I will send it by separate mail, and you will soon have it: it is a matter of 2 or 3 days. When you have received it, will you please write to say if it reached you in time?

Thank you,

With best wishes

Pierre Sahel

Dated: 7th October

Dear Professor Ansari,

I am only replying now to your kind word because I have been expecting until today my brother's answer about his possible article on Sartre's *Flies*. I am sorry to say this answer is negative: he writes he could not possibly contribute a very *original* paper on Sartre; of course he would be delighted to help should he be asked to write something on his specialties (Camus, Gide, Northern and Western African literatures…) Please forgive me for this rather long (and eventually useless) delay.

Thank you for the *AJES* issue which I have just received at my faculty address.

Best wishes from my wife Maria and from.

Pierre Sahel

Dated: 06 December

Dear Professor Ansari,

I am late this time in answering your letter (dated 12 November). The reason for my delay is perhaps that I have been reconsidering Hamlet's procrastination for the past few weeks! I can now tell you that I shall be able to send you in due time a short but original article on *Hamlet*. Before that, i.e. as you wished, by the end of this year, you will have received the study of Shakespeare's histories which you kindly offered to publish in the March issue of your Journal and which I am writing at the moment.

Yours faithfully

Pierre Sahel

Dated: 19 December 1980

Dear Professor Ansari,

Here is my article on the history plays which I have written for your *Journal*. I hope you will like it and it will appear in March issue. Could I please have some off prints of it? With reference to your recent study of *The Winter's Tale*, I also enclose my review of the play as it was performed during the last Avignon Festival (I hope you understand French). I am not forgetting *Hamlet*, and I have been working hard on it recently!

Please receive my and Maria my wife's best wishes for the approaching new year.

Yours sincerely,

Pierre Sahel

Dated: 27 January 1981

Dear Professor Ansari,

Thank you very much for your letter dated 10.01.1981, I am pleased you like my article on Shakespeare's histories. I hope you will also appreciate my study on *Hamlet* which, as I had promised, is short and original. I worked very hard on it and I find it rather dense. You will please tell me your impressions of it. If contributors to your journal usually get off prints, I shall receive some with pleasure.

Yours sincerely,

Pierre Sahel

Dated: 07 September 1981

Dear Professor Ansari,

Thank you for sending me the new issue of *AJES* and off prints of my article on Shakespeare's Histories: I have just received them. Our little boy, aged 6, who knows quite a few things on Shakespeare, was more interested, however, in the wrapping paper which was covered with unknown characters! I ventured to tell him that the script was Devanagari … I hope I was not wrong!

I wonder whether you attended this year's Stratford Conference. My wife and I did not.

Best wishes for the forthcoming issues of your Journal (when will the *Hamlet* issue appear?)

My wife sends kindest regards,

Faithfully yours,

Pierre Sahel

Dated: 19th April 1982

Dear Professor Ansari,

I have not received any news from you for some time, and I hope no letter from you got astray of its way to France. Was the October issue of *AJES* (The *Hamlet* one) brought out safely? I look forward to reading it if it did appear. Maria and I plan to go to Stratford next summer. If we attend the conference, we shall not have the pleasure to see you again, but if you have any message, we shall deliver it for you.

With all good wishes,

Yours sincerely,

Pierre Sahel

Dated: 04 September 1982

Dear Professor Ansari,

Please forgive me for replying so late to your letter.

Of course I know Sartre and *Les Monches* well enough, but I do not feel competent to write an original article on the subject. I think my brother, Andre Sahel, who holds a Doctorate thesis and is a specialist in modern literature (particularly Gide, Camus, on the one hand, and third world *franco phone* literatures on the other hand) might have interesting points to make on Sartre. I have not yet asked him whether he was willing to propose an article for your Review because I wanted to know your opinion first: Do you think I should ask him? Secondly, when must the article reach you? Lastly, can the quotations be given in French?

With all good wishes

Yours faithfully,

Pierre Sahel

Dated: 21 April 1983

Dear Professor Ansari,

I am sorry about the postal inconvenience which you mentioned in your letter of 4 April. We are also sorry we did not receive your Christmas card. Thank you for your suggestion of writing an article on *King Lear*. I have been working on some ideas which may be of interest, but this work could hardly be completed before the beginning of June: so please let me know if this may be too late.

Please receive Maria's and my good wishes.

Yours sincerely,

Pierre Sahel

PS: I hope you have by now received my brother's article.

Dated: 21 November 1983

Dear Professor Ansari,

Thank you very much for sending me the *AJES* issue. I shall very soon attend the meeting of the French branch of the Shakespeare Association in Paris where I am to give a paper on myth and history. I shall also bring there all the *AJES* issues you kindly sent me and put them on an exhibition table. As for the Stratford conference, yes, I think I shall go. It may be I shall be asked to give a short paper.

Best regards from Maria and Pierre Sahel

Dated: 03 March 1984

Dear Professor Ansari,

I shall be proud and happy to contribute an article on Shakespeare to be published in the volume which is to appear in your honour. May I offer you my sincere congratulations for this commemorative work? I also wish to thank you for the very kind words in your letter: I shall do my best hoping that my study will testify to the high esteem I feel for your person and career.

I realize I did not answer your kind suggestion to send the paper I gave to the French Shakespeare Association. The organizers wish to publish it in the proceedings of the meeting held in December in Paris. I shall, of course, send you an off print.

I do not know whether my "War of the Theatres in *KL*" appeared. Could you let me know? I have just written to the Shakespeare Institute that I shall attend the next Stratford Conference. Perhaps Maria and I shall have the pleasure of meeting you again: I should be delighted to discuss your scholarly plans for the future.

Please note our new address: we are now no longer in AIX, my university town, but in the countryside, at the foot of a lovely mountain (Montagne Sainteen Victoria), made famous by the French artist Cezane in his paintings of Southern France.

With best wishes,

Yours sincerely,

Pierre Sahel

Dated: 25 July 1984

Dear Professor Ansari,

I did receive a copy of the *Lear* number of *AJES* and later, several off prints of my article. Thank you. I think these special numbers (I am thinking of the *Hamlet* issue as well) are important critical landmarks. Do you know if *Lear* number was reviewed by another journal? I liked your contribution very much, probably because the statements you make perfectly agree with my own views of the play and also because I found it was admirably written. As for my contribution to the commemorative volume, I think I will respect the dead-line you had mentioned. I do not have a long way to go to complete it. In fact, it may well have been finished by now, but since I am to give a paper during the Stratford conference, I am also working on it. It seems reasonable to expect that my contribution will be ready in October. Its title will be: "History in Shakespeare's Tragedies, Tragedy in Shakespeare's Histories".

Best regards from my wife Maria.

Yours sincerely,

Pierre Sahel

Dated: 30 October 1984

Dear Professor Anasari,

Many thanks for sending me the April 84 issues of *AJES*. I read your long article with much interest. As you may well suppose, I did not agree with all your points. I am pleased you liked the article I contributed for the commemorative volume though you must have disagreed with some of my point! Do you know when the volume will appear? I shall try to write something for the April 85 issues, but, owing to pressure of time, I cannot promise.

Best wishes from

Pierre Sahel

Dated: 29 November 1985

Dear Professor Ansari,

Thank you very much for your kind letter. I have indeed received the April issue of *AJES* and off prints of my article, but they reached me only one day before your letter. Thank you for these too. I am very pleased that the printing of your commemorative volume is under way. It is very kind of you to tell me that you will send me a copy as soon as possible. I enclosed a few words for "Note on Contributors".

Have you retired indeed? You seem to be still extremely busy!?

Please receive my best wishes and my wife's regards.

Yours sincerely,

Pierre Sahel

Dated: 10 May

Dear Professor Ansari,

I have just received *AJES* (2, 1986) and I presume you dispatched it; thank you so much. I have not yet read it, but I will with great pleasure. I suppose – you told me so in Stratford-that you will go on editing the Journal and I send you my best wishes. I have not written to you for a rather long time. Since then I have gone through a number of problems, e.g. I was once taken to hospital where I was operated on, the pine forest surrounding our house was destroyed by a fire-the house itself was *hardly* licked by the flames etc.. The list of my recent misfortunes could go on, but *c'est lavic* this is life!

I hope things are well with you. Maria sends her best regards.

Yours truly,

Pierre Sahel

Andre' P. Sahel
CPR
Tanges (Morocco)

Dear Professor Ansari

My brother, Piere Sahel, of the University of Aix, France, wrote to me about a contribution that I could offer on Andre' Cide.

I am delighted to know that, as he said, you have a keen interest in my favourite French author. My contribution deals with Andre' Gide's journey to North Africa, and I hope you will like it. I shall be extremely pleased to see it published in your Journal. Please forgive me for sending it rather late (I have been unwell for some time).

Looking forward to reading a letter from you.

Faithfully yours,

Andrie P. Sahel

Trinity College
Cambridge
CB2 ITQ

Dated: 30 November 1980

Dear Professor Ansari,

Thank you for your letter, and for your copies of *The Aligarh Journal of English Studies*. I have read some of the articles with a great deal of interest-particularly your own, which deals in a very balanced way with a "topic (the relations between Art and Nature, I mean) that seems to me of prime importance with regard to Shakespeare's last plays. I have been struck by your comparisons with Blake and Hopkins and Keats.

I think the main point of any novelty that I have to make about *Hamlet* (the significance of Hamlet's alteration between speech and 'Silence') was included in the lecture I gave at Stratford. The only other question on which I think I could have anything to say—apart from a brief linguistic note on a point I have been discussing with Professor Edwards- is the question of the function of the players in *Hamlet* and of the reference to play-acting and the theatre. By now, that is probably a rather hackneyed subject. But if you think some reflections about that would be of any use for your purpose, I shall be writing to see what I can do. When would you want an article if I should write on?

With best regards,

Yours sincerely,

Leo Salingar

Dated: 29 June 1981

Dear Professor Ansari,

A brief note about the *Hamlet* article I am writing for the *Aligarh Journal*: unfortunately I was not able to begin work on it until recently. However, I am now in the middle of the article, and expect to finish it in a day or two. I will post it to you at once, so I trust it will reach you shortly after this letter. I hope that will still be in time for your editorial arrangements.

Yours sincerely,

Leo Salingar

Dated: 02 July 1981

Dear Professor Ansari,

Here is the article on *Hamlet* that I promised. I am sorry it comes rather late, but as I mentioned in the note I sent you a couple of days ago, I was not able to settle down to it until late – I was away on holiday (taking advantage of a spell of leave) for several weeks, and had several minor but urgent things to do afterwards. This also has meant that I have not been able to do as much fresh reading for the article as I could have wished, and perhaps that will be evident to you; I am really not sure whether the points I have made are fresh or not, though I have not seen some of them in print myself. Anyway, I hope the article will be acceptable.

I will be in Stratford early next month. Perhaps we shall meet again there – or at next year's conference.

Yours sincerely,

Leo Salingar

Dated: 04 January 1984

Dear Professor Ansari,

I have just received your latest letter (dated December 21st). Please forgive me for not replying earlier to the previous letter. It so happens that I have recently published an article on *Lear* elsewhere- in *Anglo-American Studies*, which is published in Spain – and have been working on a subject quite unconnected with Shakespeare's tragedies. So I have been trying to think whether I could possibly have any fresh topic connected with *Lear* to write about, in response to your kind invitation. Unfortunately, I cannot see any such topic at present; so I am afraid that

I must send you a negative answer. Thank you, just the same, for inviting me to contribute to AJES.

With best wishes,

Yours sincerely,

Leo Salingar

Dated: 26 January 1984

Dear Professor Ansari,

Thank you for your letter inviting me to send you my article on "*King Lear,* Montaigne and Harsnett" for publication, or re-publication, in your journal. In principle, I have no objection – provided that you have the consent of the editors of *Anglo-American Studies*. However, I should mention that it may be rather long for your purposes (about 30 large printed pages), and also that as yet I have no offprint to send you.

Perhaps the quickest way to deal with this matter is for you to write, if you have no objection, and ask the editors for a copy of an offprint, with permission to reprint; from a letter I have received today from Spain, I gather that although I have received an advance copy (which contains a few misprints, incidentally), the other copies of the journal containing my article are still being printed, and the offprints will then follow. Maybe a copy of the November 1983 issue could reach you sooner than a separate offprint.

The editor who has been in touch with me is: Professor Ramon Lopez Ortega, Universidad de Extremadura, Facultad de Filosofiay Letras, Caceres, Spain. If you care to write to him and mention that I am willing to let you publish the same article in Aligarh (of course, with suitable acknowledgment of its prior appearance in *Anglo-American Studies* – and not otherwise), then I imagine you would have a favourable response. I trust you will understand why I ask you to go to that trouble.

Yours sincerely,

Leo Salingar

Dated: 09 April, 1984

Dear Professor Ansari,

Clearly, I owe a reply to your two letters about your *festschrift* – the second of which, dated 2 April, arrived today. I am afraid I did not know quite in what terms to reply at first. On one side, I would be glad to oblige if possible; on the other, I have no fresh Shakespearean topic in mind and will have little or no time to think out a fresh article over the coming months, because I am already behindhand with other pieces of work. I hesitate to offer a promise that I might not be able to keep, and which might only be an embarrassment.

There is only one possibility that I can see: within the next couple of months, I have to revise an old (unpublished) lecture for a conference at Warwick. This lecture deals with the word 'art' in Shakespeare, with some references to Italian Renaissance conceptions of art. As it will be delivered at a conference, it may be published afterwards by Warwick; but, even if it is, they may have no objections ('they' being Prof. J. R. Mulryne) to my sending you the same article for your Commemorative Volume as well. I will ask Professor Mulryne and, if he has no objections. will send you a copy during the summer. I can see no chance of writing anything entirely new, so I hope that this article will suit you – assuming there are no objections from Warwick.

I am pleased to see that *Anglo-American Studies* have sent you a copy of my piece on *Lear.*

With best regards,

Yours Sincerely,

Leo Salingar

Dated: 20 May 1984

Dear Professor Ansari,

Here is the article I promised you on "Shakespeare and the Italian concept of 'Art". I delivered it yesterday as a paper to a conference at Warwick University. Possibly Professor Mulryne may reproduce it for a series of occasional publications he edits connected with this conference. But that need not interfere with your using it. I ought also to mention that I would like to include it in a collection of essays of mine, if I get that collection published; but that should be no interference with your book, either.

With best wishes for the success of your book.

Yours sincerely,

Leo Salingar

Dated: 27 November 1985

Dear Professor Ansari,

Thank you for your letter of the 20th. And thank you for the latest *AJES*, which I have received but have not yet had time to read.

You ask for my biodata: will this do?

> Leo Salingar, Fellow of Trinity College, Cambridge; formerly Staff Tutor in English of the Board of Extra-mural Studies and Lecturer in English, Cambridge. Contributor to the *Pelican Guide to English Studies* and to *Dramturgie et Societe* (CNRS, Paris 1968); author of *Shakespeare and the Traditions of Comedy* (Cambridge 1974) and of articles on Elizabethan drama in *Scrutiny, Shakespeare Quarterly, AJES* and other journals; (a selection to be published shortly at Cambridge under the title, *Dramatic Form in Shakespeare and the Jacobeans).*

If the above note is too long for your purpose, please feel free to cut and edit it.

I look forward to seeing the Commemorative Volume in your honour. I feel sure that you must have contributed vigorously and substantially to the study of English literature in India, which to my mind is something very important. My best wishes for the success of your Commemorative Volume.

Yours sincerely,

Leo Salingar

Dated: 08 July, 1986

Dear Professor Ansari,

You asked me to let you know when the copy of your *festschrift* that you have kindly sent me had arrived. This is to let you know that it has now reached me safely, and that I am very grateful for the gift. So far I have only had time to glance through the list of contents and dip in here and there. But it looks to me a handsome volume, with interesting contents, which I look forward to reading bit by bit, and which I shall be glad to have for reference on my shelves. I am sure you must feel gratified by this tribute to the work you have done for English studies, especially Shakespeare studies, in India; and perhaps I may add, without inclining towards cultural imperialism, that the keeping up of higher English studies in India seems to me a very important task indeed.

I did not know, by the way, that Sir Walter Raleigh had been one of your predecessors at Aligarh. A distinguished lineage.

May I hope that the appearance of this book augurs every good fortune for you in the years to come?

Yours sincerely,

Leo Salingar

Dated: 22 July 1987

Dear Professor Ansari,

Thank you for your letter of invitation, but I am afraid I cannot help you over the Sir Walter Raleigh Work. I am sure you will find another contributor. It occurs to me that you might like to approach an ex-colleague of mine, Dr. John Leonard, who is making a name for himself as a Milton Scholar. He is now a Lecturer at a Canadian university, but this summer he is back in Cambridge, and if you wished to write, you could reach him at Trinity College.

Yours sincerely,

Leo Salingar

Dated: 21st October 1992

Dear Professor Ansari,

Please forgive me for not replying sooner to your letter of July, asking me for a Shakespeare article. For some time I was not sure whether I would have anything possibly suitable to send you or not.

However, I have now finished writing the text of a lecture on *The Tempest*, which I am sending you. If you do not want it, or if it comes too late to be of use to you, please let me know.

If you do publish it, please add a footnote saying: "This is the text of a lecture delivered at the University of Graz, Austria in October 1992".

Also, if you do publish it, please note that I may possibly wish to publish the article a second time, somewhere else – with due acknowledgement of the priority of your journal. I should be grateful if you would confirm that you would have no objection to this.

With greetings,

Yours sincerely,

Leo Salingar

Dated: 29 July 1993

Dear Professor Ansari

Thank you for your letter. Yes, I have received my copy of the *Critical Miscellany*, which looks very interesting. And thank you also for inviting me to contribute on Marlowe. In view of some other commitments I have, I do not feel confident that I can prepare an article for you in time for December, but I will think about it carefully, and will send you an article if I can. I will write again if it looks as if I shall have an article for you.

With best regards,

Leo Salinger

Dated: 29 March 1994

Dear Professor Ansari,

Thank you for your letter, and the recent copy of your *Critical Miscellany.* But I am afraid I do not have a Marlowe article to send you. I think I said in my last letter to you that it was very unlikely that I would be able to write an article of Marlowe at present; and so it has proved: I have had a couple of other commitments which have kept me busy, and in any case it is a long time since I did any work on Marlowe. I am sorry. Perhaps I may have something for you on another occasion, if you want an article from me. Meanwhile, my best wishes for your next *Miscellany.*

And best regards,

Yours sincerely,

Leo Salingar

Dated: 26 March 1996

Dear Professor Ansari,

You wrote to me some time ago, asking for an article. Please forgive my long delay in replying. For a long time, I was uncertain whether I could think of anything to send you, but did not want to refuse. Then it occurred to me that perhaps I could put together some ideas about Richard II. I have not had time to look up recent scholarship about the play, but I have at least (and at last) written an article, which is almost finished. I am going away for a few days, but I expect to finish it quickly as soon as I get back, and I expect to put it in the post for you in about a week's time. I hope you will find it interesting and I sincerely hope it will reach you in time to be of some use.

I hope also that all goes well with you.

Meanwhile, my best regards,

Yours sincerely,

Leo Salingar

Dated: 08 August 1996

Dear Professor Ansari,

Did you receive the copy of my article about Richard II that I sent you some months ago? In case it failed to reach you for some reason I am sending you another copy. Please let me know if you intend to publish it or not.

Perhaps we may meet at the Shakespeare Conference in Stratford later this month.

Best regards,

Your sincerely,

Leo Salingar

Dated: 22 October 1999

Dear Professor Ansari,

Many thanks for your letter of September 5 and for the latest copy of the *Critical Miscellany,* which I have received with pleasure.

I am sorry not to have replied earlier, because I have been preoccupied with illness at home. But I think I can let you have an article about *Measure for Measure* within the next month. However, I should explain that I have been planning or hoping to plan – a longer study of the play, (perhaps two or three articles), and the material I intend posting to you will form part of that. I should be sent, therefore, your assurance that I may use the material of my article to you (possibly in the same from) within the longer study. Of course, if I do that, I shall acknowledge prior publication in your *Miscellany* (that is, if you accept the material I send you, eventually). I should be grateful for a note giving me your permission on same terms.

With apologies for troubling you, and for my delay.

Best regards,

Yours sincerely,

Leo Salingar

Dated: 16 December 1999

Dear Professor Ansari,

By now I trust you will have received my article on *Measure for Measure* - with my apologies for lateness.

Looking through my copy again, I have noticed four misprints, which I had not seen previously. If you are going to publish my article, as I hope you will, will you please make the necessary corrections? Here are the mistakes:

1. P. 6, last Line: 'She rebukes Claudio' should read 'She rebukes Lucio'.
2. P. 8, Line 11: 'Fortune hath conveyed to ray understanding' should read '... my understanding'.
3. P. 18, First Line: *Mariana (unveiling)* should be printed *Mariana (unveiling)*.
4. P. 19, Line 5: 'Oh, my dear lard' should, of course, read 'Oh,... lord'.

I am sorry to trouble you with these details – not too late, I hope.

With best wishes for the "*Miscellany*" and to you personally for the coming year,

Yours sincerely,

Leo Salingar

The University of Michigan
Dearborn
College of Arts, Science and Letters
Humanities Department
Dearborn

Dated: 16 February 1988

Dear Dr. Ansari

Thank you for your kind letter requesting my submission of an article to *THE ALIGARH JOURNAL OF ENGLISH STUDIES*.

I am enclosing an essay titled "Capability and Negative Capability in *Chaucer's Clerk's Tale*, "which I hope you will find useful to the journal. Although I realize that your journal specializes in Shakespeare studies, I know that you also feature fine pieces representing other eras in literary history. I look forward to your reply.

In addition, I have mentioned your interesting journal to my colleagues at the University of Michigan; you should be receiving a submission shortly from Professor Jacqueline Lawson of the University of Michigan-Dearborn English faculty as well.

I do hope our work can enhance the diversity and international flavour of your journal. We support your efforts and look forward with interest to reading future issues.

Sincerely yours,

Melita Schaum
1300 Prescott Avenue
Ann Arbor, Michigan 48103
U.S.A.

UNIVERSITY OF CALIFDSORNIA

Dated: 9 December 1965

Mr. Asloob Ahmad Ansari
7—Zain ul Abedin Road
Aligarh

Dear Mr. Ansari

It was most thoughtful of you to send me your book, *Arrows of Intellect* which, alas, if you had not sent it to me, I might never have seen at all. Had that happened, I would have suffered a great loss, for I have read your book with great pleasure and profit. I think that you touch upon all of Blake's interesting themes and examine closely those of the greatest importance. I especially enjoyed your chapters on "Fancy and Imagination" and "The Apocalyptic Imagination." Here one comes into the heart of the matter, and what a difficult and complicated heart it is, for all its Innocence!

Gratefully yours,

Mark Schorer

The University of Southern Mississippi

Dated: 11 November 1993

The Aligarh Critical Miscellany
Asloob Ahmad Ansary, Ed.
Gufishan Civil Lines
Aligarh, 202 011
India,

Dear Asloob Ahmad Ansary:

I would like to submit the present essay "Infatuation-Devaluation in Shakespeare's Sonnets 141-145" for publication. I am a young scholar and poet, and although Shakespeare is not my main focus, I have developed some deep interest in the poetry of John Donne and Shakespeare. I hope that you will enjoy reading my essay, I would greatly appreciate any comments that you could make. Thank you for considering my submission. I am looking forward to hearing from you.

Sincerely,

Jean-Marc Sens

Bio: I was born in France and educated in Paris; I have been living in Mississippi, Hattiesburg, for the past five years. I published translations into French of Hart Crane's *Key West* and "Voyages". I published a few poems in small publications Prenez parti, Product 7 and 8 *Exquisite Corpse*, *Saturday Afternoon*, *Tampa Bay Review*, the *Black River Review*, and more recently in *Cape Rock*, *International Poetry Review*, *Nexus*, and *Faultline*. I have poems forthcoming in *Context South*, *Pegasus*, *Portland Review*, *Nexus*, *The Crucible*, *Cimarron Review*, and *Xavier Review*. I am a Ph.D. candidate at the University of Southern Mississippi, Hattiesburg.

Humanities Research Centre
The Australian National University
Box-4, Post Office Canberra, A.C.T.

Dated: 17 May 1977

Dear Professor Ansari,

I have at last been able to produce a slightly revised version of my paper on *Four Quartets* which you were kind enough to solicit for the *Aligarh Journal of English Studies*. Unfortunately the typist has introduced one or two slips and I have had to correct these with the pen though I think the corrections are clear. I have also added a title and a few pertinent footnotes.

I may stop in India when I return to London at the beginning of September. But plans are still uncertain and it may be I shall have to visit Damascus or another of the Arab capitals in connection with an educational project.

With kindest wishes to you and your colleagues.

Your sincerely,

Roger Sharrock

Dated: 24 February 1977

Dear Professor Ansari,

Thank you for your very kind letter. I remember with pleasure my visit to Aligarh and only wish it had been longer (and more punctual). I will certainly, as I said, send you a copy of the Eliot paper for the *Aligarh Journal of English Studies*. But if you could be patient with me, I should like to keep it a little longer to make a few revisions and smooth it out a bit for the transition from the spoken to the written word. As I think I mentioned, the paper will probably be published also in London before the end of the year, in A.E. Dyson's magazine *Christian*, but I think you said you had no objection.

It has been extremely hot in Canberra but now the heat has broken with two days of heavy rain. Australia seems to have minor monsoons!

With all good wishes.

Your sincerely,

Roger Sharrock

Dated: 29 August 1978

Dear Professor Ansari,

I too remember with great pleasure my only too short visit to Aligarh a year ago last January. I do hope that, possibly with the assistance of the British Council, I may be able to make another visit to India and see you all again. It was a pleasant reminder of you when one of your colleagues called to see me in King's a few months ago.

I have read with great interest the issues you have sent me of *The Aligarh Journal of English Studies*. I felt honoured to see my article cheek by jowl with that of the late Dr. Leavis on Eliot.

I should like very much to send you my essay on Marvell but there is a difficulty. I delivered part of it as a paper at Appleton House in Yorkshire last November as one of the tercentenary lectures arranged by the University of York. But in its written form the essay was so long that it far exceeded the due limits for the volume of papers APPROACHES TO MARVELL in which the lectures were to be collected. Therefore I am publishing it in the periodical *English;* the editor Martin Dodsworth is having a double number in November and is prepared to give me the space.

The copy of *Journal* with your letter only arrived a week ago which explains the lateness of this reply.

All good wishes,

Your sincerely,

Roger Sharrock

Dated: 4 April 1979

Dear Professor Ansari,

I am so sorry that I shall not be able to provide you with anything for your Marvell special number. I had hoped to make something up out of a part of my very long article in *English* but there are copyright difficulties which make it impossible. I do hope the Marvell issue will be a success and look forward to seeing it.

As for your second query about recent books on Marvell I think the best account is to be found in the Oxford bibliographical guide, *English Poetry*, edited by A.E. Dyson. The Marvell Chapter there is by D.I.B. Smith and gives a good list of modern works with comments.

With kindest regards,

Your sincerely,

Roger Sharrock

Dated: 15 June 1988

Dear Professor Ansari,

I remember with great pleasure my visit to Aligarh nearly ten years ago and what a good host you were to me!

I should dearly like to contribute something again to the excellent *Aligarh Journal of English Studies*. But this year is the 300th anniversary of John Bunyan and I am under much pressure for articles and lectures on him. However, I will try to write a short piece on *The Waste Land*. You may say that this letter is encouraging but certainly not positive. What is you deadline.

Yours sincerely,

Roger Sharrock

Dated: 20 October 1988

Dear Professor Ansari,

Thank you for your letter. I am glad that you received the article on *The Waste Land* safely and that you like it. I don't think this question of the relation of poetry to the novel in the twentieth century has been much looked into and I hope if we consider it more insight might be obtained on the effect on particular writers of each medium's awareness of the other (Larkin, for instance, must have thought much about contemporary novelists' ways of searching for truth).

I shall look forward to seeing the article and the others in your special Eliot number. I liked much in the issue of *The Aligarh Critical Miscellany* which you sent me.

Yes, Dr. Usmani has sent me a copy of his book of essays and a few other things and I have been having a look at them. I shall try to express my reaction in a separate paragraph in a form which could be put before the Interview Committee.

Z.A. Usmani is clearly a mature scholar and everything he writes carries the marks of one who has thought long and deeply about great literature. The essays in *Shakespearean and Other Essays* (Meerut, 1981) make a serious contribution to the interpretation of English poetry to the Indian academic public. Two essays stand out for their penetration and their passionate involvements: those on *Lear* and on Forster. In these essays Dr. Usmani shows that he is at his best when he moves from mere verbal analysis to handling profound philosophical and religious theme, as they are exemplified in literature. He must be an inspiring teacher.

As for your other query for Peter Ackroyd's address you should write to his publisher, Hamish Hamilton, Garden House, 57-9 Long Acre, London WC2E 9JZ. I can't help you over Leon Edel: he used to teach at the University of Hawaii, but has probably retired by now.

With all good wishes,

Yours sincerely,

Roger Sharrock

Dated: 10 October 1989

Dear Professor Ansari,

Excuse my lateness in replying to your letter. I have been ill and am recovering slowly from a serious operation which was complicated by heart trouble. I can't offer you an article at present.

At another time your suggestion of an article on religious vision in Blake and Bunyan would have engaged my interest.

The copies of *Aligarh Critical Miscellany* arrived safely. Many thanks.

With kind regards,

Your sincerely,

Roger Sharrock

T.J.B. Spencer

Dated: 23 June 1976

Dear Professor Ansari,

I thank you for your kind letter of 16 June and for your sending me a copy of the first number of *The Aligarh Journal of English Studies*. We send you congratulations on its publication and hope that it will do well. I am reading it with much interest, and I was, of course, particularly pleased to see the three articles on Shakespeare.

I am grateful to you for your invitation to contribute to your journal. Like almost everyone nowadays, I have far too much on my desk. But I will do what I can, when I can.

I was glad to have news of your colleague Mr M.H. Khan. I ask you to convey to him the greetings of his many friends at the Shakespeare Institute.

With best regards,

Yours sincerely,

T.J.B. Spencer

F.W. Sternfeld
Emeritus Reader in the History of Music
University of Oxford

Dated: 25 May 1988

Dear Professor Ansari,

Thank you for your kind letter, it would give me much pleasure to contribute an article to your journal. Unfortunately, serious illness interrupted my career in 1985, I was obliged, to sell my house, car and library and move with my wife to this retirement and nursing home where I have lived since 1986. I rarely get to Oxford and am now endeavouring to hire a research assistant to look up things for me in the Bodleian Library.

The title of my book is *Music in Shakespearean Tragedy*, published by Routledge, Kegan Paul, Second edition, 1967, still in print in 1988.

With all good wishes for your journal.

Yours sincerely,

F.W. Sternfeld
Emeritus Reader in the History of Music
University of Oxford

University of Ibadan
Nigeria
Department of English
Professor D.E.S. Maxwell

Dated: 4th January 1967

Dear Mr. Ansari,

I received your unexpected and welcome gift of *Arrows of Intellect* a little while ago; I should have acknowledged it last week. I intend to settle down to study it in the next few days.

No, I do not think I was unfair to W.B. in that article, though I would amend it in some ways if I were to write it again now. A poet who makes a show of writing a poem in a certain tradition need not conform to that tradition, but he should expect to be judged by his handling of it, successful or otherwise. I am not convinced by the ingenious 'Ages of Man' theory of Damon! or other I have seen yet. In my view, *Jerusalem* is a multifaceted view of the state of man, not a narrative poem at all. B's biggest mistake was to try to cast it in a narrative mould. A sort of "ode-sequence" would have been more the kind of thing.

Best wishes for the new year,

Yours sincerely,

W.H. Stevenson

Dated: 6th January 1967

Dear Dr. Ansari,

I am sorry to have taken so long writing to you; as usual, there are too many things to do, and I wanted to answer your letters properly. I thought that your treatment of the philosophers Blake disliked so much, and your explanations of the source of his dislike, were very welcome. There has been too much general Blake criticism in the past, and too little of this kind of specific exposition.

I wonder, though, about two things. On p. 143 you say "It would be wrong to deny the presence of Christian and Gnostic elements in Blake's thinking". True: but surely Blake meant the whole basis of his later poetry to be Christian? Unorthodox in some respect, perhaps, but at any rate the main themes are these: the devastating effects of sin on human life; the despair which a sense of sin produces, which makes repentance impossible; the belief that God=Christ=Love=Forgiveness which breaks this deadlock? *Jerusalem* in particular is founded on the assumption that his readers were Biblically educated, so that they would see this trend of thought without his having to explain it from the start. It is significant that in *Jerusalem* Los, though he does what he can, is unable to put an end to evil himself; he can only keep it at bay even in his own being. Renewal has to wait for the Divine Voice, the Divine Hand, the Divine Breath. And, of course, Jerusalem herself is seen in typically biblical terms as the personified city, beloved but enslaved, in images which make sense only when they are read in the tradition of the prophets and *Revelation*. Certainly Blake rejected the tyranny of priesthoods, but he wrote within the tradition of Bunyan and Watts – the supposedly lower-class religion of the enthusiasts, not the polite religion of, say, Jane Austen.

My second point stems out of this last bit; you say somewhere that "Jerusalem is Spiritual Liberty" – my point is that she is a much less Urizenically simple concept than this. I feel quite strongly that critics ever since Yeats misled them have been in turn misleading the public by suggesting that Blake's characters can be depersonalized as simple abstract ideas. This is surely Urizen at work! To say that Urizen=Reason, for example, ignores the fact that he is *first* (in *America)* the tyrant. Blake has in his mind a complex of ideas; he hates tyrants, hates control and rigidity of mind; he sees (as you show) how the rational mind works out its natural laws through fear of the unregulated world – fear of the abyss which makes Urizen build his palace – which is the same fear as that of the tyrant who must have his whole world safe – and out of this comes the one figure Urizen. In *The Book of Urizen* he is the archetypal tyrannical mind—not Reason alone personified. And so on.

I do not know if your remarks on 205-6 that *Jerusalem* is not "a poem of bewildering chaos" is aimed at me? – If so, I think we are actually in fair agreement.

W.H. Stevenson

P.S.: My space is gone. My point is that B. certainly has these themes and himself knows what he intends. But unlike Milton he can't write an epic. Congratulations on the Book & best wishes.

W.H. Stevenson

A. G. Stock

Dated: 7th October 1976

Dear Dr. Ansari,

Thank you for sending me *The Aligarh Journal of English Studies*. It arrived two days ago, and as yet I have only had time for a very quick glance at some of the contents, so I cannot give you a considered critique. But first impressions are decidedly favourable and I wish it well, and hope it may be able to keep up its promising standard. I know it's a bad time for English studies and I admire the courage of your Department in embarking on the venture.

I am sorry I cannot, just at this moment, accept your invitation to contribute, because it happens that I am on the point of leaving for a month to Canada, where I shall not be in a position to give my mind to it. I will, however, keep it in mind, and try if possible to think up an offering for the April issue. Don't count on it. I will if I can but I cannot dash off articles in the airy way some people appear to do, and it must depend on an unpredictable amount of work.

Wishing you all success,

Your sincerely,

A.G. Stocks

The Troy State University System
PO Box 457,
Fort Rucker,
Alabama 36362

Dated: 2 March 1984

Dear Professor Ansari,

Thank you very much for your letter of 13 February 1984, in which you invite me to write an article on Shakespeare to be included in the Professor A.A. Ansari Commemorative Volume.

I would be pleased and honored to make a contribution to the volume in your honor. In fact, I already have an idea for the article and will work on it in the next few months. When I complete the article, I will forward it to you.

In addition, please accept my congratulations and best wishes as you approach your sixtieth birthday. Your academic and scholarly achievements are worthy of great praise. You should be proud of them.

Again, thank you for your kind and gracious request. I shall be in touch when I complete the article.

Sincerely,

Jack R. Sublette
Ass't. Professor of English

Dated: 8 August 1984

Dear Professor Ansari,

Enclosed please find an article entitled "The Distorted Time in *Henry IV, Part II*," which I am submitting to you to be included in the Professor A.A. Ansari Commemorative Volume.

As I have said before, thank you very much for requesting the article and congratulations on your birthday.

Please let me know when you receive the article so that I will know that it did not get lost in the mail. I look forward to hearing from you and to receiving a copy of the commemorative volume.

Sincerely,

Jack R. Sublette
Ass't. Professor of English

Dated: 26 January 1985

Dear Professor Ansari:

Thank you very much for sending me a copy of *The Aligarh Journal of English Studies*, 9, No. 1 (1984). I enjoyed reading your article, "Political Man in Shakespeare's *English History Plays*."

I still look forward to receiving a copy of the A.A. Ansari Commemorative Volume later in the spring.

Best wishes for the rest of 1985!

Sincerely,

Jack R. Sublette
Assoc. Professor of English

University of Exeter
Drama Section
School of English
Thornlae

Dated: 28 August 1984

Dear Professor Ansari,

I'll do my best to get the *Twelfth Night* essay to you as soon as possible. I have been interrupted by family matters over the summer.

Thank you for sending the *Lear* issue and for the off prints.

Yours sincerely,

P.W. Thomas

J.J.M. Tobin
1 Newport Road
Cambridge, Massachusetts 02140

Dated: 17 August 1981

Dear Professor Ansari,

Thank you for your letter of 7 July 1981 which I found upon my return from England and the Shakespeare Congress in Stratford. I am flattered by your invitation and shall be happy to respond with a piece on *Hamlet* and the origin of the sexual tension between Hamlet and Gertrude and that/or not that/between Hamlet and Ophelia. If you think such a piece would do, please let me know the date by which you would need to receive the article.

Thank you for your kind words.

Yours sincerely,

John Tobin

Dated: 15 December 1981

Dear Professor Ansari,

As of this morning I have your most recent letter requesting my promised essay on *Hamlet*. I am chagrined to learn now that you needed the piece at the end of November, for surely, I have not received here in Cambridge your earlier letter telling me the same. I am embarrassed to be holding up your schedule.

The best that I can do is to have the typist get to work now so that I can mail the manuscript to you by 21 December. If this proves not fast enough please accept my most profound apologies and feel free to dispose of the manuscript.

Again, I hope that the 21 December mailing will make amends.

Sincerely,

John Tobin

Dated: 21 December 1981

Dear Professor Ansari,

Please find enclosed the promised piece on *Hamlet*. I hope that it is satisfactory and that it arrives in time for your use. I have added a second piece on *Macbeth* if you feel that the *Hamlet* piece is not long enough you might like to link the two pieces (and then change the title to *Hamlet*, *Macbeth*, and *Christ's Tears* over *Jerusalem*) or you might care to use the second piece at a later date. At all events, please let me know of the safe arrival of these pieces and of your plans for them.

With kindest regards,

John Tobin

Dated: 19 January 1983

Dear Professor Ansari

Please find enclosed the latest of my studies of Shakespeare's use of *Nash*. I hope that you see merit in it sufficient to warrant publication in your journal. As in the other pieces which you have been good enough to publish I have used *The Reverside Shakespeare* for quotations from the play and McKerrow's great edition for quotations from Nash.

If you can use the piece, will you please inform me as I can earn credit at my university with the news of an acceptance.

Thank you for the attention.

Sincerely,

John Tobin

Dated: 6 November 1983

Dear Professor Ansari

I hope this note finds you well and happy and that your valuable work progresses nicely. I write to inform you of a change of address – I have moved from Cambridge to BELMONT (a town about four miles west of Cambridge and would like very much to receive any communication from you at this new home: 78 Long Avenue, BELMONT, Massachusetts, USA, 02178.

I am, of course, especially looking forward to your volume devoted to *King Lear* and my contribution to it (on Nash and the texture of that play), however, modest that contribution is.

Thank you for the attention.

Sincerely,

John Tobin

Dated: 30 January 1984

Dear Professor Ansari

Your letter of 22.12.83 arrived here on 26 January 1984 and I was very glad to hear from you and of your desire to teach in the United States for a year/term. I am not at all sure that I am the person who can help you, limited as my knowledge is of such matters. However, I am sending to you this year's directory of Visiting Fulbright scholars and occasional lectures which may be of help – certainly the *Council for International Exchange of Scholars at 11 DuPont Circle, Washington, DC 20036* can provide you with both information and the necessary forms. Equally certain is it that your scholarly achievement and editorial experience make you an ideal candidate for one of the many awards.

I hope that you will let me know if this letter and the catalogue (sent under separate cover) arrive safely – and that you will let me know how your dealings with Fulbright people progress.

I hope this is of some help,

With every good wishes,

John Tobin

Dated: 3 March 1984

Dear Professor Ansari

Thank you for the letter regarding the commemorative volume (arrived three days ago). I am honored by the invitation to contribute and I shall provide you with an article on Shakespeare, one which I hope will please you. You may look for its arrival *before the middle of July*. Again, let me say how pleased I am to be among those honoring you – and please convey to Professor T.R. Sharma my delight at the idea.

I want to ask now whether a letter and a catalogue of Fulbright Scholar sent by me a few weeks ago ever reached you, in response to you query about visiting this country.

I hope that all is well with you.

With best wishes,

John Tobin

Dated: 27 July 1984

Dear Professor Ansari

Please find enclosed my contribution to your *Festschrift*, "Shakespeare, Bacon, Milton, and Marvell –Thomas Nashe." I hope that you see it as I intend it: a tribute to you and your contribution to English studies.

I would be pleased to learn of the safe arrival of the enclosed manuscript – and indeed anything at all of the likely date of the appearance of the volume honoring you and of the availability of the volume for purchase by contributors.

I look forward to hearing from you.

With all good wishes,

John Tobin

Dated: 22 May 1985

Dear Professor Ansari

I hope that the enclosed is of interest to you. Accept it with my best wishes.

Has your *Festschrift* appeared? Are you pleased with it? I look forward to receiving a copy when possible. I am glad to have been a part of the tribute to you.

I hope all is well.

As ever

John Tobin

Dated: 12 August 1985

Dear Professor Ansari,

Thank you for your recent letter and the valuable issue, (vol 10, # 01) of *AJES* with its Shakespeare and Blakean riches, your own elegant essay on Brutus, divided self, not least among them.

My old friend read your request as one for biographical information. I hope that I am correct and that the following will serve [J.J.M.Tobin, associate chairman of the Department of English, University of Massachusetts-Boston, is the author of *Shakespeare's Favorite novel* (1984) and a number of articles on English Renaissance authors. He is currently editing the English poems of George Herbert.]

I look forward to the arrival, whenever it becomes available, of your Festschrift volume, one I am pleased and honored to be part of

With best wishes,

John Tobin

Dated: 29 September 1985

Dear Professor Ansari

Thank you very much for the copy of the most recent issue of *AJES*. I liked very much your own lead article on Othello and the rigorous, but fair-minded review, of the book on the Leavises.

We look forward to the publication of your *Festschrift* but you really must not write so frequently and so well, else we'll have to get you yet another volume of tribute!.

Best wishes,

John Tobin

Dated: 09 March 1986

Dear Professor Ansari,

Thank you very much for the Xerox copy of the first eight pages of your Festschrift volume. I am pleased to be among the many contributors, almost all of whom I have read or known and who by their distinction, as well as their essays which I look forward to reading, make up a splendid roster for you. I can imagine how pleased you must be, though you must if I may say so, balance your delight with the knowledge that you have earned this tribute.

I look forward to receiving the volume however long it takes to travel across the seas. It is possible for me to purchase a second volume or have it sent by air mail? I believe that I could send an international money order equivalent to the cost of book and postage if you could eventually have the volume sent. I suspect this is a minor matter and of detail beneath the dignity of the Festschrift of the recipient himself, so do not trouble yourself if there is not. Somebody to of send the matter.

I enclose off-prints (2) of three notes from *N+Q* (Oxford, site of some of your triumphs). One of which happily refers to *AJES*.

Again my thanks for the Xerox – and congratulations yet again.

With best wishes,

John Tobin

Dated: 19 May 1986

Dear Professor Ansari,

I have now read all the essays in your Festschrift – how pleased you must be with the range, variety and passing over own modest contribution, the high quality of the pieces. Many a volume designed as a tribute succeeds as a gesture only but you have both a splendid tribute and a collection of essays which make genuine contributions to our understanding of Shakespeare.

I must add how pleased I am to find a photograph of your self in the Volume, with your high intelligence shining forth from your noble head. Please accept my thanks for the trouble you took to have the two copies sent by air mail. The books arrived in Belmont on 28 April. On 13 May I sent by way of the U.S mails an International Money Order of 40$ to you at the University. Do please let me know if you have received it. I hope that it covers the cost of the extra volume and the heavy postage. If not, I shall send difference.

I hope that you are continuing your editorial work and that you might yet be receptive to some future piece of my own. I enclose a recent note in MCR by Professor Evan of Harward who takes care to cite *AJES* in a note.

Let me repeat my heartiest congratulations and express again my thanks for generosity of time and energy in sending me the books by air.

With best wishes,

Sincerely,

John Tobin

Ruthven Todd

Dated: 27 June 1968

My dear Professor Ansari,

Your totally unexpected and delightful present arrived this afternoon, and I have been going through it ever since. On the whole, I think you make your point about the "intellects" being also "States" rather than "Personalities." We know that Blake, on the only recorded meeting with Reynolds, was charming to him, and I have no doubt that his spirit is today enchanting Locke, Newton and Bacon. He was, after all, a delightful person and even when "put upon" seems to have been willing to make peace rather than to descend to "personalities." If your book should persuade the students of India into believing that he was not an "Enemy" of those whom he attacked for representing "Shades" it will achieve much in this troubled world.

I myself suggested, in my *Tracks in the Snow*, 1946, that Blake, despite his proclaimed horror of science and mechanics, owed much more to the spirit of his times than later commentators, dyed in the art for art of the 19th century, would allow, and I think that your book carries my point a good deal farther. I thank you for it.

Tracks in the Snow, under a different title with an added essay on Blake's techniques in printing, is supposed to be appearing in a paperback from Dover in New York within the next year (I don't know the title yet). I reread it before sending it back to the publishers and decided that I dare not alter it or bring it up to date. But if I was to do so, I feel I would have to mention your book.

I am at present hard at work trying to make my edition of Gilchrist not only a definitive edition of the life, with sufficient illustrations, but also, owing to the notes, a basic book for all research. I hope the new publishers will allow me to revise my Bibliographical List.

Having no book to send you in return, I offer a photograph of a portrait which I was given for my 54th birthday two weeks ago.

With very many thanks,

Yours most sincerely,

Ruthven Todd

Assoc. Dean of Arts and Sciences
Akademie der Wissenschaften der DDR
Zentralinstitut fur Literaturgeschichte

Dated: 17 September 1990

Dear Professor Ansari,

Upon my return from Stratford I find among my mail a copy of your own *Critical Miscellany*, with a very fine and thoroughly successful translation of my piece on *King Lear*. I hasten to write to you in order to thank you for your generous initiative and say how sorry I was not to have contacted you at the Shakespeare conference in August. It was only on the last but one day that I noticed your name in the programme but failed to speak to you (I would have liked to thank you for letting me have copies of the *Journal*). But then I had no idea whatsoever that you had actually made preparation for a translation and that this translation had in the meantime come out already.

Again, accept my thanks for your interest in my work. With every good personal wish.

Yours sincerely,

Robert Weimann

PS: As I peruse your cogent reading of Blake's *French Revolution,* I come across your noting "the vicissitudes of the tumultuous, contemporary scene" (p.45) and –albeit on much more modest scale – feel confronted with what happens around me…

Dated: 30 July 1993

Dear Professor Ansari,

Thank you so much for your recent letter with its kind invitation to contribute to the Marlowe issue of *ACM.* Yes, of course I do remember your splendid gesture generously to have translated one of my German essays on Shakespeare. I was so pleased (and proud) to be published in India, and it is also a great pleasure for me to acknowledge the more recent 1992 issue of the same journal which you sent me, again with matters of considerable interest to me.

This is only one more reason why I shall seriously consider to contribute to the Marlowe issue. I am somewhat reluctant quite to commit myself, because I am under a threefold pressure (deadlines of a book project plus teaching at UCI and research project in Berlin). But if it is at all possible I promise to do my very best to be able to send some thing by the first week of December this year.

Again my thanks and my expression of deep appreciation.

Your sincerely,

Robert Weimann

Dated: __________

Dear Professor Ansari,

Let me thank you for the recent issue of your *Miscellany,* together with your note and invitation to contribute, that arrived a week or two earlier. Let me hasten to assure you how much I appreciate your continuing interest in my work and that I would gladly follow your friendly suggestion. But, alas, having postponed the publication of my own project (Part II) for so many years now, I trust that you understand that for the next three years or so I am unable to follow your kind invitation.

My regards and very best wishes,

Sincerely yours,

Robert Weimann

Dated: 08 February, 1994

Dear Professor Ansari,

Do please accept my apologies for not heaving been able quite to meet the deadline you had set for contributions to the Marlowe issue. The reason is that, unexpectedly, one of my colleagues here fell seriously ill and I had to take over one of his courses.

With my teaching load significantly increased, I just could not cope.

One more reason why I am writing this to you. I hope you would not be too much disappointed when the essay in the circumstances can only be a brief one. Believe me that I have done my very best indeed, as far as time and energy allowed. After this is in the mail, I shall call you or send a FAX so as to let you have definite news and remove any further uncertainty.

My sincere thank for your kind invitation to contribute. I am sending you my warm personal regards.

Yours,

Robert Weimann

Dated: 23 April 1994

Dear Professor Ansari,

Much to my consternation your letter (dated 04.03.1994) is forwarded to my present UCI address, according to which you did not receive my contribution to the Marlowe issue that I had mailed from here on February 8, 1994.

Even there I had so tried to establish your phone number (spending about an hour to get direct information from New Delhi) to confirm completion and posting of the article. All in vain. What I can now do is, simply, to copy very previous letter and article and send it again by air mail to the address that you gave.

May I ask you kindly to confirm receipt of my second attempt to convey the MS to you.

I am so sorry about these complications and tend to apologize for what inefficiency is on this side of the Pacific.

Sincerely and respectfully yours,

Robert Weimann

Dated:___________

Dear Professor Ansari,

I am writing to thank you for kindly letting me have 2 (7/1994) of your Journals, again with interesting material on both Shakespeare and Blake. (This Card is in response to what, in your fine essay, you call 'Theme of Descent, Eternity and Finitude in 'The Book of Los)'.

Incidentally, have I by any chance missed the issue to which you had kindly invited me to contribute a piece on Marlow? Or could it be that the address you use for sending is no longer correct? In any case, if the issue is forthcoming please use no other address than the following:

R.W. Muhlenbecker Str.22
16352 Basdorf
Germany

My thanks and friendly greetings,

Robert Weimaun

Dated: 21 September 1993

Dear Professor Ansari,

I am sorry not to have thanked you for your kind invitation to write on Marlowe for your *Journal*. Unfortunately I have no current material on him but I passed your letter to Chris Wortham and David Ormerod, editors of *Doctor Faustus*, and I hope they might respond.

Yours sincerely,

R.S. White

Dated: 29 November 1993

Dear Professor Ansari,

Thank you for sending copies of the *Miscellany* which certainly has some fine articles by distinguished writers. I am sure I can write something, perhaps, entitled "Coriolanus and War" Could you please let me know what your deadline would be?

Thank you for thinking of me.

Best Wishes,

Rob White
(R.S. White)

Dated: 18 April 1994

Dear Professor Ansari,

Here, as promised, is "Coriolanus and War". If you do not think it appropriate for publication. I shall not be at all offended. If, however, you wish to print it, I can supply it on Compact disk (DOS – or ITIAC) if that would help to minimize printing errors.

Many thanks for your invitation

Best wishes,

Bob (R.S) White

The University of Western Australia
Department of English
Nedlans, Perth
Western Australia 6009

Dated: 11 August 1993

Dear Professor Ansari,

Professor Bob White has passed on to me your letter concerning the special issue of *Aligarh Critical Miscellany* on Chrsitopher Marlowe. I co-edited *Doctor Faustus* some years ago. Our edition is a set text for the Open University of Great Britain. If you like, I would be prepared to write an article for you. Please let me know.

I am sure you have already been in touch with the Marlowe Society of America. In case not, I suggest that you write to Bruce Brandt, Editor, *Marlowe Society of America Newsletter,* English Department, South Dakota State University, Brookings, SD 57007, USA.

With best wishes for the success of this special venture.

Yours sincerely,

Christopher Wortham

Associate Professor

Dated: 22 December 1993

Dear Professor Ansari,

I enclose my promised essay on Christopher Marlowe. I am sorry that this comes to you a couple of weeks after the requested date. Unfortunately this is our busiest time for public examinations in the schools as well as for the university, so for a short time everything else comes to a stop.

My printer is playing up a bit, so the page lengths are not quite right. Accordingly, I have left the MS in a continuous roll so as not to break the text. I hope this will not be too inconvenient for you. I also enclose the notes to go with the article, on a separate sheet. I would like my article to be attributed as follows: Christopher Wortham, University of Western Australia.

How did you fare with the Marlowe Society of America?

With best wishes for your forthcoming Marlowe issue.

Yours sincerely,

Christopher Wortham

Associate Professor

Embassy of the Federal
Republic of Germany
No. 6, Shantipath
Chanakyapuri
New Delhi

Dated: 19 March 1985

Dear Professor Ansari,

I take great pleasure in sending you two photographs of the plate set up at the house in Heidelberg, Ziegelhauser Landstrasse, where the great Urdu poet Iqbal lived in 1907.

The plate was formally unveiled on September 16th, 1966, by the Minister for Culture of the state of Baden-Wuerttemberg, Prof. Dr. Wilhelm Hahn, in the presence of the Ambassador of Pakistan, Abdurrahman Khan, and the Mayor of Heidelberg. All these details of the ceremony are engraved at the bottom of the plate but rather difficult to decipher.

You may, of course, reproduce the photograph in your Journal but the photographer has asked us to mention his name ("photograph by Christian Conrad"). C. Conrad, a student at Heidelberg University, is an amateur photographer and the nephew of Prof. Dr. Luett at the South Asia Institute of the University. Dr. Luett was kind enough to help us to get the photographs.

Yours sincerely,

(Dr. G. Vogel)
Cultural Counsellor
G. Vogel

Asloob Ahmad Ansari was formerly Professor of English at Aligarh Muslim University. A notable literary critic, he has extensively published in both English and Urdu. He was also the editor of the prestigious *Aligarh Critical Miscellany* and *Naqd-o-Nazar* (Urdu).

Born in Delhi, Professor Ansari was educated in Delhi, Aligarh and later graduated from the Honour School of English Language and Literature in the University of Oxford. His first publication, *Arrows of Intellect*, came out in 1965; it was subsequently reprinted in the USA in 1970; his second book, *William Blake's Minor Prophecies*, was published by the Edwin Mellen Press, Wales (UK) in 2001. Besides being an internationally recognized Shakespeare and Blake scholar, he has also published substantial critical studies of Ghalib and Iqbal. In English studies he made his mark by his significant contribution to Shakespeare scholarship and this has been recently climaxed by his *The Existential Dramaturgy of William Shakespeare*, published by the Edwin Mellen Press, Wales (UK). In Urdu he is indisputably held as the initiator of Practical (Text-based) Criticism. He participated, a number of times, in the World Shakespeare Conference in Stratford (UK). He also attended the conference on Time and Space in Islam in Chicago (USA). Abstracts of his articles on Shakespeare have been included from time to time in the *Year's Work in English* (London). He has received the Sahitya Academy Award, President of Pakistan Award, Mir Taqi Mir Award, UP Urdu Academy Award and Ghalib Award – all this is referable to his assessment of Iqbal in terms of textual criticism. He has been cited in *Shakespeare's Poetics* (Cambridge) and *Watchmen of Eternity* (London and Boston). The honorary degree of D.Lit. was conferred on him by the University of Gorakhpur in 2006.